Faces of
Latin America

Faces of
Latin America

Duncan Green

First published in the United Kingdom by
Latin America Bureau
1 Amwell Street
London EC1R 1UL
www.latinamericabureau.org

© Duncan Green 2006

Latin America Bureau is an independent research and publishing organisation. It works
to broaden public understanding of human rights and social and economic justice in
Latin America and the Caribbean.

ISBN 1 899365 70 2

First published in the United States of America by
Monthly Review Press
122 West 27th Street
New York, NY 10001
www.monthlyreview.org

Library of Congress Cataloging-in-Publication Data is available from the publisher.

ISBN 1-58367-151-X

A CIP catalogue record is available from the British Library

Editing: Jean McNeil
Cover and interior design: Andy Dark

Printed in Canada

contents

Dedication

For Catherine, Calum and Finlay

Acknowledgements

A number of people gave invaluable advice and commentary for this new edition. In particular, I would like to thank William Booth, Constantino Casasbuenas, Julian Filochowski, Jonathan Hellin, Antonio Hill, Peter Lambert, Richard Lapper, Marcela López Levy, Jean McNeil, Katia Maia, James Painter and Simon Ticehurst. Thanks also to Tito Castro, for taking the trouble to set me on the right road on the shores of Lake Titicaca back in 1981, and to Jenny Pearce for providing the initial inspiration for this book. All opinions and errors are, of course, my own.

List of tables and figures

Table 1.1
Estimated indigenous population of America at the time of European contact

Table 1.2
Major world commodities

Table 1.3
Commodity dependence, figures for 2002

Table 1.4
Industrialisation in Latin America

Figure 1.1
Total foreign debt and capital flows to and from Latin Ameirca and the Caribbean, 1975-2002

Figure 1.2
The Latin American roller-coaster: percentage increase/decrease in GDP per capita, 1982-2004

Table 3.1
Percentage of population living in urban areas, 1960-2000

Table 3.2
Population of Latin America's largest cities (incl. urban areas), 2003

Table 4.1
Date of women's suffrage in the Americas

Table 5.1
Religious demographics in Latin America

LATIN AMERICA

Peters Projection

Introduction

Carnival in Rio; Inca ruins; condors; witty Zapatista *comandantes* in Mexico; Colombian cocaine barons in plush, purpose-built prisons; sleek, best-selling novelists on TV; glue-sniffing street children; death squads and disappearances: these are snapshots of a continent that fail to add up to a sense of place and people.

Latin America has been portrayed to the outside world through stereotype and myth since El Dorado, the mirage of a golden king in a golden city, first excited the Spanish *conquistadores'* greed. Back in Europe, idealised accounts of the Inca and Mayan civilisations inspired Thomas More's *Utopia*. The West has both plundered and been dazzled by Latin America ever since. Today the new heroes are Latin American writers such as Mario Vargas Llosa, Isabel Allende and Gabriel García Márquez, who have, in the words of one critic, 'become the equivalent of the Amazon rainforest, providing oxygen for the stale literary lungs of the developed world.'

This book tries to fill in some of the missing pieces, to make sense of the jumbled images that pour from television, newspaper, novel and tourist brochure. It is about Latin Americans: not just generals and presidents, but the millions of faces of the shantytowns, small farms, mountains, rainforests, factories and plantations. It explores the processes that have shaped peoples' lives, the jobs they do, where they live, and how they see and want to change their world. Through the lives of its inhabitants, the book attempts to capture the everyday ebullience and dynamism of Latin America, a world away from the cynicism and corruption of much of its formal political life.

Far from being the passive victims of circumstance, ordinary Latin Americans possess depths of courage and creativity, enabling them to confront with humour and grace a seemingly endless array of problems: how to feed and educate their families, find a home, improve their neighbourhood. Many such attempts at self-help have in recent years been led by women, struggling to free themselves from the stifling values of *machismo*. The indigenous peoples of Latin America have also belied their reputation for passivity by fighting vigorously to defend their ways of life.

They face a dispiriting number of obstacles. Internationally, Latin America is a region in decline, still largely dependent on the export of its raw materials, with an ever diminishing slice of world trade. The last two decades of the twentieth century saw a debt crisis usher in a devastating sequence of market reforms, bequeathing a harsh world where economic growth does not create jobs, and the gulf between rich and poor grows ever wider. At home, the rural poor must struggle for a plot of land on which to feed their families in an environment devastated by deforestation, soil erosion, and unregulated mining and industrial development. Landless peasants flock to the shantytowns that encircle the region's cities, where they must improvise both a house and a means of earning a living if they are to survive.

Faces of Latin America was first published in 1991, in the run-up to the 500th anniversary of Christopher Columbus' first voyage to the Americas. Much has happened since then: civil wars have ended in Central America, an unprecedented period of elected government has held sway; neoliberal economics has steamrollered across the continent at vast human cost, and a series of centre-left presidents in South America has tried to find a more humane path to development. This third edition includes a considerable amount of new material covering developments up to 2006.

The quincentenary briefly aroused great passion on both sides of the Atlantic, as people took stock of Latin America's scarred history. Since then, the media circus has moved on. Latin America is of only marginal significance in the so-called 'War on Terror', and is insufficiently poor to attract the official donor agencies seeking to halve world poverty by 2015. In North America and Europe, Latin America still surfaces sporadically in the news, but is largely confined to the financial and sports pages. Ignored by the headlines, the forgotten shantytowns and peasant villages of the continent struggle towards an uncertain future. If this book has one principal purpose, it is to celebrate the vigour, hope and inspiration that the region offers, and to urge its readers not to turn their backs on Latin America's people.

Duncan Green, 2006

The Curse of Wealth: Economics

1

CONTENTS

History and Power

What is Latin America?

From Tijuana in the north to Cape Horn in the south, ringed by islands in the Caribbean Sea and both Pacific and Atlantic Oceans, Latin America is a region defined by shared colonial experience. Colonialism's most obvious legacy is linguistic. From Mexico southwards, Spanish, Portuguese and, in a few cases, French put the 'Latin' into Latin America (the English-speaking islands of the Caribbean and a few mainland ex-colonies such as Guyana are not included). Even the name 'America' comes from conquest, derived from that of Italian explorer Amerigo Vespucci.

Pre-Latin America

The apparent facial similarity between Andean villagers and the nomads of the Mongolian steppes is no accident. People first came to the Americas from Asia, crossing the frozen seas of the Bering Strait to Alaska and the west coast of North America. This migration probably began around forty thousand years ago, although large swathes of the 'new world' remained uninhabited until much later.

Driven by a search for food and the pressure behind them of new waves of arrivals, the Americas' first peoples moved slowly southwards, sparsely populating the entire continent as far as Tierra del Fuego. Some remained as hunter–gatherers, but others discovered agriculture, enabling them to settle in towns and develop diversified societies.

Many small urban civilisations sprang up and disappeared, either defeated by warlike neighbours or absorbed into a surrounding culture. Some early societies left vast, complex ruins like Teotihuacán in central Mexico, a series of pyramidal structures to rival those of Egypt; others left almost nothing.

The Maya were a nation of astronomers and architects, already in decline before the Spaniards came. They were brilliant mathematicians, developing the concept of zero long before any other civilisation, and making astronomical calculations of astonishing accuracy. Their ornate temples are still being rescued from the jungles of Central America, and it is not yet clear what caused the Mayan empire to go into a sudden decline around 1000 AD.

In the mid-13th century, an itinerant warlike people known as the Mexica settled in the area now called the Valley of Mexico. Over the next two hundred years, through conquest, tribute and cultural domination, the Aztec empire was created around the great capital of Tenochtitlan. This city was built in the middle of Lake Texcoco, accessible only by long causeways from friendly territory or allied city-states. From this stronghold, the Aztecs were able to subdue their rivals; by 1500, they ruled virtually all of central Mexico as well as parts of Guatemala. The empire was fuelled by a tribute system which required conquered societies and allies to send goods and slaves to the metropolis. Human sacrifice was a key element of the political and religious system, and by the late fifteenth century the Aztecs began to make war with their neighbours with the sole objective of capturing future victims.

At the same time, the Incas were forging a huge empire in South America, and by 1400 had emerged as the dominant culture of the Andes. Less brutal and more practical than the Aztecs, the Inca political philosophy was more pragmatic than spiritual. Defeated enemies were conscripted rather than sacrificed, and conquered cultures were integrated into the social hierarchy. The Incas introduced a vast road network throughout the Andes, along which relay runners took messages as swiftly as modern buses. The cultural and political system established by the Incas brought unity to a huge, disparate region; unlike that of the Aztecs, the Inca legacy was looked upon favourably and inspired several popular uprisings against the colonial authorities after both civilizations had been overwhelmed by the conquistadors of Spain.

Despite their greatness and the differences between their political systems, both Aztecs and Incas rapidly succumbed to a handful of European adventurers in the decades following the landfall of Columbus in 1492. In one of history's most extraordinary collapses, hundreds of thousands of armed indigenous warriors were overwhelmed by Spanish muskets, cannon, horses and old-world diseases to which the indigenous peoples had no immunity.

Conquest and Colonisation

The late 15th century was a period of expansion and conquest for the dominant Spanish kingdom of Castile. Ferdinand and Isabella had pushed the muslim Moors back to the Mediterranean in what became known as the 'Reconquest', and the exuberant king and queen saw no need to limit their belligerent Christianising mission to the Iberian peninsula. The Genoese explorer Cristóbal Colón (Christopher Columbus) – better known in exploring circles for his bluster and greed than for his seafaring talents – received the monarchs' blessing to seek a westward trading route to the Indies. Colón first sighted what he believed to be the Indies in October 1492 – they were, in fact, the Bahamas, part of the Antilles island chain that also includes Hispaniola and Cuba, discovered soon after. These lands were claimed for Spain with the approval of the Pope (although Portugal submitted a successful counter-claim for most of Brazil, where they landed in 1500 and charted and settled over the next hundred years). Over the next three decades, many expeditionary forces crossed the Atlantic to the Caribbean, aiming to settle and Christianise the newly-charted territory in the name of the Spanish throne.

When the first Europeans arrived, the Aztecs and the Incas were the two great city-dwelling civilisations in the region. Initial contact, however, was limited to the small, relatively primitive tribes of the Antilles islands in the Caribbean, where little resistance was encountered either to the extraction of surface gold or to the enslavement of the indigenous population. The limited potential of these islands for the production of precious metals soon pushed adventurers towards the continental mainland.

Hernán Cortés led the conquest of Mexico. His strategy depended on alliances with local enemies of the Aztecs, and, by playing off the indigenous factions against one another, he was eventually able to capture Tenochtitlan. Francisco Pizarro, against incredible odds and with only a few dozen men, brought the Inca empire to its knees. Like Cortés, he made use of spies and gathered accurate intelligence; both were also aided by the devastating effects of European viruses that ravaged the local

Table 1.1:
Estimated indigenous population of America at the time of European contact

	estimated population (million)	% of total
North America	4.4	7.7
Mexico	21.4	37.3
Central America	5.65	9.9
Caribbean	5.85	10.2
Andes	11.5	20.1
Lowland South America	8.5	14.8
Total	**57.3**	**100.0**

Source: William M. Denevan (ed), *The Native Population of the Americas in 1492*, Madison: University of Wisconsin Press, 1976.

population. Pizarro ably exploited divisions in his enemies' ranks – his invasion coincided with a war of succession between two Inca princes. In 1532 at Cajamarca, Peru, Pizarro captured the emperor Atahualpa and, without losing a single man, defeated an Inca army of many thousands. The initial unfamiliarity of gunpowder and horses, along with prophecies of the providential return of white-skinned gods, may have led the inhabitants of the new world to see Cortés and Pizarro and his lieutenants as supernatural, although this theory is contested. Even without fear of godlike powers, native weaponry was no match for metal armour or shot.

History is written by the victors, and partisan chroniclers frequently romanticised the subjugation of Mexico and Peru, usually on the grounds that the Aztec and Inca civilisations were unusually cruel and barbaric. The conquests were portrayed as Christian civilising missions, and there is little doubt that the conquistadors – and the missionaries who accompanied them – put a great deal of effort into the conversion of the local population. Yet some of the invaders subsequently experienced remorse. The conquistador Mansio Serra de Laguizamón recalled: 'We found these realms in such order that there was not a thief, nor a vicious man, nor an adulteress ... we have destroyed by our evil behaviour such a government as was enjoyed by these natives.'

Whatever their religious motives, the conquerors were utterly rapacious in their pursuit of wealth, and the extraction of the abundant indigenous riches. Bernal Díaz, a chronicler among the conquistadors, recalled the obsession with treasure and bounty: 'Moctezuma's treasure chamber did not contain many jewels or golden ornaments, because all the best had been extracted to form the magnificent offering that we had sent to his majesty.'

The attentions of the colonial bureaucracy soon became focused upon the silver-rich regions of New Spain (Mexico) and Peru (which also included modern-day Bolivia). In both areas, silver ore could be mined by an abundant supply of indigenous slave labour, providing a steady source of income to the Spanish crown.

By about 1600, the boundaries of Spanish America were drawn, while the mapping of Brazil followed soon after. British, French and Dutch colonies were founded in the previously unexplored area east of Venezuela, though later attempts by these countries to expand their influence and territory were largely unsuccessful. Having been among the less wealthy and successful European powers, Spain and Portugal now began to benefit from the labour and products of their resource-rich colonies. Thanks to the alliance between the white colonial elite and the locally born creoles, Spain and Portugal were able to maintain vast empires with relatively little manpower. The general population, a mixture of indigenous and mixed-race (*mestizo* and *mulatto*) peasants, was taxed and policed.

What the Spaniards Found

On the Aztecs
And when we saw all those cities and villages built in the water and other great towns on dry land, and that straight and level causeway leading to Mexico, we were astounded. Those great towns and buildings rising from the water, all made of stone, seemed like an enchanted vision from the tale of Amadis ...

On the Incas
I say again that I stood looking at it, and thought that no land like it would ever be discovered in the whole world, because at that time Peru was neither known nor thought of. But today all that I then saw is overthrown and destroyed; nothing is left standing.

Bernal Díaz, *The True History of the Conquest of New Spain* (trans. J.M. Cohen), Harmondsworth, Penguin, 1963

Once the centre had been removed, the Spanish viceroys replaced the emperors as the supreme authority and the former empires fell into their hands. Where indigenous groups were less advanced and centralised, the Spanish encountered much greater difficulties. In southern Chile and Argentina the native Mapuche peoples successfully resisted the colonial forces well into the 19th century, finally losing their fight to the new Chilean and Argentine armies following Latin America's independence from Spain. Argentine schoolchildren now learn the names of the heroes of the 'War of the South', a 19th-century campaign to exterminate indigenous people, during which soldiers were paid a reward for each pair of testicles they brought in to their commanders. The extermination of the indigenous people opened up the south of Argentina for sheep and cattle ranching.

An enduring legacy of the conquest was the misnomer 'Indian', dating from Columbus' first landfall in the Americas, when, thanks to a miscalculation of the circumference of the globe, he was convinced he had reached Asia. In the furore surrounding the Columbus quincentenary in 1992, many indigenous Latin Americans rejected the term 'Indian', which in Spanish carries distinctly derogatory overtones. This book instead opts for the rather clumsy alternative, 'indigenous people'.

For the indigenous peoples everywhere in the continent, the conquerors' military victory was only the beginning of the process of extermination. Within a century of the conquest, as much as 90 per cent of Latin America's indigenous population were wiped out in what became known as 'the Great Dying'. In the Caribbean, the Arawak peoples who first greeted Columbus with delight soon rued the day they had paddled their canoes out to his ships, bearing gifts for the exhausted sailors. Enslaved to the Spanish lust for gold, those who survived smallpox, influenza, measles and other new diseases committed mass suicide by poisoning and hanging. Mothers even slaughtered their new-born babies

Indians having their hands chopped off for failing to meet the gold dust quota. From a book by Bartolomé de las Casas entitled *Spanish Cruelties* published in 1609.

to prevent them being enslaved by the Spanish. Within 25 years of Columbus' arrival, only 3,000 Arawaks remained of an original population of 600,000, and by the mid-16th century they were extinct. Five centuries later, the youth of Brazil's Kaiowa people met the same threat in the same way. In 1990 alone, 20 boys and girls from the threatened tribe, all aged between 13 and 18, killed themselves by hanging or poisoning. Thirty others tried but were saved. On February 3, 1991, 15-year-old Maura Ramírez hung herself from a tree. Her mother said, 'she was sad. She dreamt Helena was calling her.' Helena, Maura's elder sister, had committed suicide three months earlier. Psychologists blamed the deaths on the dislocation caused by leaving home to work on the sugar plantations.

Although more indigenous people fell victim to the diseases introduced by the Spanish and Portuguese than died in the mines, plantations or battlefields, the level of economic exploitation and misery inflicted by the Europeans was at least partially responsible for making them so vulnerable to illness. Millions were literally worked to death. The colonial authorities adopted various systems for exacting tribute and labour from their indigenous 'vassals'. During the initial period the *encomienda* (forced agricultural labour) system rewarded Spanish officers and favourites with whole indigenous communities. In return for supposedly bringing their allocated vassals to Christianity, the *encomenderos* were authorised to demand tribute and unpaid labour. In the densely populated regions of Mexico and the Andes, this left Indian villages more or less intact. In more sparsely peopled regions, the *encomienda* system degenerated into raiding parties to abduct slaves. European writers and theologians put forward a variety of ideological justifications to show that the natural inferiority of the indigenous people made their enslavement both necessary and an act of mercy.

As the centuries passed, racial boundaries became blurred. Since men far outnumbered women in the European colonial communities, indigenous women were frequently obliged by their owners to have sex with them, and the subsequent intermingling of blood created a growing mixed-race population, known as mestizos. Other indigenous people abandoned their traditional dress and learned Spanish, often moving to the cities. Over time, cultural criteria, rather than physical characteristics, became the means of identifying ethnic background. An 'Indian' wore non-European dress and spoke little or no Spanish, whereas a 'mestizo' adopted both the white language and western dress. In the coastal regions of Latin America, indigenous groups were swiftly wiped out on the plantations and were replaced with African slaves, who added a further ingredient to the continent's racial mix. By the time independence came in 1825, 12 per cent of Latin Americans were black, 28 per cent were mestizo, and only 42 per cent were indigenous. The remaining 18 per cent were white.

This racial mix continues to characterize the region. Statistics are even more unreliable than in the case of indigenous groups, but by one calculation, the black and mulatto population of Latin America (i.e. excluding the English-speaking Caribbean, US and Canada) is around 150 million, significantly exceeding the indigenous population. The largest black population by far is in Brazil, where almost half of the country's 180 million inhabitants are directly descended from slaves, followed by Colombia, Haiti and Cuba. Racial integration has not brought social equality. Although slavery was abolished in 1888, Afro-Brazilians remain at the bottom of social pyramid, often living in shantytowns, with minimal power or representation in national political life.

The Curse of Wealth: The Commodity Trade

> **'The Indians have suffered, and continue to suffer, the curse of their own wealth. That is the drama of all Latin America.'**
>
> Eduardo Galeano, *Open Veins of Latin America* (trans. Cedric Belfrage), London: LAB, 2000

Fourteen thousand feet up on the Bolivian plateau, Cerro Rico ('Rich Hill') looms high over the bleak mining town of Potosí. A giant rust-red spoil heap, it tells the story of Bolivia's cruel past and impoverished present. For two centuries after the Spanish *conquistadores* marched into the Andes and defeated the Inca empire, a stream of silver ore flowed down the slopes of Cerro Rico, through the furnaces and mints of Potosí and over the sea to Spain. Hundreds of thousands of press-ganged indigenous labourers died bringing out the ore.

The silver rush made 17th-century Potosí into the largest city in the Hispanic world and earned Cerro Rico a place on the Bolivian national flag, but today only some fine colonial churches recall the days when the streets were literally paved with silver. For the Corpus Christi procession of 1658 the authorities ordered that the cobbles in the centre of the city be removed and replaced with solid silver bars.

Boomtown Potosí was a chaotic, brawling city of 160,000 people, including, according to a census in 1601, 800 professional gamblers and 120 prostitutes. Today, some Latin Americans still describe immense wealth with the phrase 'worth a Potosí', first coined by Cervantes in *Don Quixote*. But behind the splendour of the churches and the antics of the Spaniards lay the grim reality of the *mita*, the Spanish-imposed system by which each

---

The Mita

'Without Indians there can be no mines, because there is no one else to work them and their shortage has caused more damage than war or plague.'

Bernal Díaz, *The True History of the Conquest of New Spain* (trans. J.M. Cohen), Harmondsworth, Penguin, 1963

'The day of departure is very sad. These victims of obedience line up before the priest who awaits them in his robes at the door of the church, with a cross held high. He sprinkles them with holy water and says the usual prayer and a mass which they pay for, to implore the All Powerful for a successful return. Then they go to the square with their parents, relatives and friends. Embracing each other with many tears and sobs, they say goodbye and, followed by their women and children, take the path out of the village crushed with sorrow. This mournful scene is accentuated by the sound of their drums, and the bells which are beginning to ring for prayers.'

Gabriel René Moreno, 19th-century Bolivian historian

indigenous community had to send a portion of its able-bodied men to work in the mines, working shifts of up to 36 hours, only to be swindled of what little wages they were due.

Cerro Rico is now an anthill of 5,000 tunnels, where self-employed miners scratch a perilous living from what the Spanish left behind. 'In the old days the veins were a yard thick. Now they're half an inch', says Marco Mamani, a young indigenous miner. 'It's like a tree – the Spaniards took the trunk and left us the twigs'. For many years, Potosí has been the poorest region of the poorest country in South America.

Potosí's path from poverty to riches and back to even greater poverty is an extreme example of the process which has dominated Latin American development – the commodity trade. Although the exact definition varies, commodities are the raw materials which drive the world's economy. They include natural resources, such as oil and copper, and agricultural products like wheat or coffee. Europe's insatiable appetite for commodities was the driving force behind the centuries of colonial expansion, which left the largest part of what is now called the Third World under the rule of competing European powers.

Ever since the conquest, Latin America has produced commodities for export – coffee, tin, oil, sugar – and used the proceeds to import manufactured products from industrialised nations in Europe, and later from the US and Japan. The richer nations used their power to keep commodity prices low, playing one desperate producer country off against another and when necessary using their military and technological might to reinforce their supremacy. In human terms the unequal struggle

Table 1.2: Major world commodities		
commodity	Latin America and Caribbean's share of world production (%, 2004)	value of annual world trade (2003)
Oil	14	$338bn
Cocaine (2003)	100	$27.5bn
Copper (1995)	34.0	$16.1bn
Soybeans	35	$15.6bn
Cotton	7	$8.1bn
Coffee	59	$7.3bn
Bananas	34	$4.8bn
Sugar	47*	$3.5bn*[1]

Sources: *FAO Production Yearbook, International Petroleum Encyclopaedia, World Metal Statistics Yearbook 1996, The Economist.*

*refers to cane sugar only   1 the total value of cane plus beet sugar trade is US$10.5 billion:

between commodity producers and industrialised powers has condemned millions of the Third World's people to lives of suffering and want. Only in the 20th century have the larger countries like Brazil and Mexico developed large-scale industry, and even then much of it has been under foreign control.

Since 2000, commodities have continued to exert a powerful grip on the region. In Bolivia, rows over the export of natural gas have produced presidential resignations; in Venezuela, high oil prices have propelled Hugo Chávez into a role as regional leader and benefactor; in Brazil, booming Chinese demand for soybeans and iron ore have propped up the PT government. Improved regional growth figures in 2004 and 2005 were put down to the global commodity boom triggered by the voracious Chinese economy.

Within Latin America commodities have enriched chiefly those engaged in exporting them abroad. Export crops such as cotton or sugar are more profitable when grown on large plantations, so the expansion of cash crops led to a concentration of land ownership and wealth in the hands of a few very powerful individuals. Mining interests were historically controlled by entrepreneurs like Simon Patiño (1868–1947), Bolivia's greatest tin baron, who rose from poverty to become one of the ten wealthiest men on earth. From the luxury of his European home, Patiño could make or break Bolivia's governments, acting as an absentee landlord towards an entire country.

The fabulous wealth of a few commodity exporters failed to 'trickle down' to the poor majority, since it was either invested abroad or used to import luxury goods. Farmers could make more money growing crops for export than by growing food to sell at home. The commodity barons felt no need to create a domestic market by redistributing wealth more evenly, since this would have meant giving up some of their privileges. The source of their wealth and power lay overseas; all they required at home was cheap, docile labour. When the workforce in their mines or plantations demanded better wages or living conditions, the commodity magnates were quite prepared to use the most extreme violence to prevent them winning. In El Salvador during the 1980s, the heads of the coffee-growing families ran the 'death squads' that killed tens of thousands of peasant activists and trade unionists.

White Gold

The European colonists pursued different commodities depending on the soil, climate, mineral deposits and accessibility of each region. On his second voyage to the Americas in 1493, Christopher Columbus brought sugar-cane to Hispaniola (now the Dominican Republic) and it flourished. Sugar subsequently fuelled Brazil's first and greatest commodity boom.

The Spaniards and Gold

'Of gold is treasure made, and with it he who has it does as he wills in the world and it even sends souls to Paradise.'

Christopher Columbus, logbook from his first voyage, 1492

'They lifted up the gold as if they were monkeys, with expressions of joy, as if it put new life into them and lit up their hearts. As if it were certainly something for which they yearn with a great thirst. Their bodies fatten on it and they hunger violently for it. They crave gold like hungry swine.'

Indigenous (Nahuatl) text from the time of the conquest

'Look what a stupid idol these savages are worshipping'
'Father it's made of gold'

Source: *América La Patria Grande*

Per acre, the 'white gold' produces four times the food energy of potatoes and ten times that of wheat, and sugar was in great demand to feed Europe's new industrial working class. Brazil's sugar boom was centred in the Northeast, around Salvador de Bahia.

Sugar is a capital-intensive crop, requiring substantial investment to part-process the cane immediately after cutting, before it can be shipped off to foreign refineries. In Brazil, the Dutch West Indies Company initially financed the sugar industry. The monotonous cane fields rapidly spread across the Northeast, squeezing out food crops such as beans and maize, so that even in the best years of the sugar boom there was chronic malnutrition.

The Dutch later expanded into the Caribbean, which was nearer to the European market. In Brazil, the soil was already losing its fertility through overuse. By the 18th century, the Caribbean had completely eclipsed northeast Brazil: Haiti's exports to Europe at that time exceeded those of all thirteen North American colonies put together. As production rose, prices fell, and Brazil's Northeast became one of the most deprived areas of the continent. Refugees fled its famine- and drought-stricken lands and headed for the next commodity boom – the gold rush in the south.

Sugar also left its mark on Brazil's racial composition. The plantations were worked by African slaves, victims of a deadly but lucrative trade dominated by British slavers. Today the people are largely a blend of black African and white European immigrant stock, with an unmistakable 'pigmentocracy'. Although the Brazilian government denies claims of racism, most black people are poor, most rich people are white.

In recent years, Brazilian sugar has had a revival as the government has struggled to overcome its dependence on imported oil by encouraging a switch to ethanol (a sugar-based alcohol). By 2005, with oil prices at record highs, ethanol was up to 55% cheaper at the pump, and major economies such as the US and China were looking to Brazil for lessons in reducing oil dependence.

Booms and Busts

Gold was discovered in the Brazilian state of Minas Gerais in the 1690s, and came on stream just as Portugal signed a trade agreement with Britain. Brazil's gold duly underwrote British industrialisation, and the accumulated gold reserves later paid for Britain's war against Napoleon.

Although Brazil's boom–bust cycles have been the most spectacular, they have occurred at regular intervals all over the continent right up to the present day. In El Salvador the indigo industry collapsed following the discovery of synthetic dyes in 19th-century Germany. In the northern deserts of Chile, the nitrate fields which had provided fertilisers for Europe's agriculture, and over which Chile had fought a war with Peru and Bolivia, became worthless overnight in 1909 when a German chemist discovered how to make artificial fertilisers. In the 1990s, the bottom fell out of the coffee market as new producers such as Vietnam flooded the market and coffee processors developed new techniques for producing high-quality coffee from low-quality beans.

Some commodities have produced better long term results than others. Demand for temperate-climate products such as meat and grain is steadier than that for tropical products such as coffee and sugar, whose prices therefore swing more wildly. In Argentina, the cattle and grain trades laid the basis for significant economic development, which made Argentina perhaps the tenth-largest world power in 1914. In Brazil, the coffee boom which gave the country 50–70 per cent of the world market between 1850 and 1950 made São Paulo into the economic powerhouse of the strongest nation in Latin America.

The commodity trade has shaped both European and Latin American history. The flow of gold and silver through Spain and Portugal to the

Britain and Latin America

'Take his whole equipment – examine everything about him – and what is there not of raw hide that is not British? If his wife has a gown, ten to one it is made in Manchester; the camp-kettle in which he cooks his food, the earthenware he eats from, the knife, his poncho, spurs, bit, are all imported from England.'

Description of pampas *gaucho* (cowboy) by British consul in La Plata. Sir Woodbine Parish, *Buenos Ayres and the Provinces of the Rio de la Plata*, London: J. Murray, 1839

'In all of Brazil's *haciendas* the master and his slaves dress in the products of free labour, and nine-tenths of them are British. Britain supplies all the capital needed for the internal improvements in Brazil and manufactures all the utensils in common use, from the spade on up, and nearly all the luxury and practical items from the pin to the costliest clothing.... Great Britain supplies Brazil with its steam and sailing ships, and paves and repairs its streets, lights its cities with gas, builds its railways, exploits its mines, is its banker, puts up its telegraph wires, carries its mail, builds its furniture, motors, wagons ...'

James Watson Webb, US Ambassador in Rio de Janeiro, c. 1865

manufacturing nations of Holland, France and Britain financed the early stages of their development as world industrial powers. After most Latin American nations won their independence in the early 19th century, Britain rapidly became the dominant economic influence. In 1824 the British Foreign Minister George Canning wrote to a friend, 'the deed is done, the nail is driven, Spanish America is free; and if we do not mismanage our affairs sadly, she is English.'

The first 50 years after independence were a time of political and economic chaos, but from the 1870s onwards, a new commodity boom took off, lasting until the great depression of the 1930s. Beef and grain from the Argentine pampas; Chilean copper, Brazilian coffee, Central American bananas, Peruvian silver and Cuban sugar led the way in a continental export boom which made many fortunes, many of them British. British investment in Latin America, concentrated in railways and telecommunications, went up nine-fold between 1870 and 1913, by which time it represented two-thirds of all foreign investment in the region.

When necessary, the British government used its political clout to give its businesses a helping hand. In 1879 when Chile embarked on the War of the Pacific against Peru and Bolivia, the then US Secretary of State, James Blaine, commented, 'one shouldn't speak of a Chilean/Peruvian war, but rather of an English war against Peru with Chile as an instrument.' Britain's reward lay in the hostile deserts which Chile seized from Peru, where British capital bought up the world's greatest deposits of nitrates, used as fertilisers in agriculture.

By the early 20th century, Britain had been overtaken by the US as the major continental power. Washington's hemispheric ambitions began with the Monroe Doctrine of 1823, which declared that 'the American continents, by the free and independent condition which they have assumed and maintained, are henceforth not to be considered as subject for colonisation by the European powers.' While ostensibly to protect these newly independent states from the designs of Old Europe, in practice the Monroe Doctrine provided a convenient cover for the US's own interests. The US steadily expanded its economic strength and political influence throughout the 19th century and came of age after its decisive defeat of Spain in the Cuban–Spanish war of 1898. The victory marked a symbolic changing of the guard, ushering in the 'American century' in Latin America.

Since the 1960s, European and Asian countries such as Japan, Germany, Spain and China have risen to become major economic influences, but they do not yet dispute US political dominance in the region.

Rise of the Multinationals

Up to the late 19th century, European and US businesses used their capital and control over transport, processing and marketing to ensure they obtained a low price from local growers of agricultural commodities. However, by the end of the century increasingly powerful US companies had decided to take over production as well in order to achieve 'vertical integration' – control over each stage of production, transport and marketing in their chosen product. The pioneers were the banana companies like United Fruit and Standard Fruit, which acquired so much power over domestic politics in countries like Honduras and Guatemala that these countries became pejoratively known as 'banana republics'. In the 1920s, one banana baron boasted of his company's control over local politicians, observing that 'in Honduras a mule costs more than a deputy', and in 1954 United Fruit played a key role in the overthrow of Guatemala's reforming president Jacobo Arbenz, an event which was to spark a brutal and long-running civil conflict in that country. Since then the multinational companies have steadily extended their grip to most key areas of Latin America's economy, including virtually all mineral extraction, the most dynamic areas of industry and many agricultural commodities.

Multinationals' heavy-handed behaviour led to a backlash in the shape of trade union mobilisation and occasional government attempts to nationalise their holdings. This prompted a rethink, and agricultural multinationals increasingly prefer to concentrate on the transport and marketing of a product, which are the most profitable areas. For example, just 10 per cent of the final retail value of a banana finds its way back to the plantation owners, and only 1.5 per cent to the plantation workers that grow them.

The Banana Man Comes

'Among those theatrical creatures, wearing riding breeches and leggings, a pith helmet and steel-rimmed glasses, with topaz eyes and the skin of a thin rooster, there arrived in Macondo one of so many Wednesdays the chubby and smiling Mr Herbert, who ate at the house....When they brought to the table the tiger-striped bunch of bananas that they were accustomed to hang in the dining room during lunch, he picked the first piece of fruit without great enthusiasm. But he kept on eating as he spoke, tasting, chewing, more with the distraction of a wise man than the delight of a good eater, and when he finished the first bunch he asked them to bring him another. Then he took a small case with optical instruments out of the toolbox that he always carried with him. With the suspicious attention of a diamond merchant he examined the banana meticulously, dissecting it with a special scalpel, weighing the pieces on a pharmacist's scale, and calculating its breadth with a gunsmith's callipers....

On the days that followed he was seen with a net and a small basket, hunting butterflies on the outskirts of town. On Wednesday a group of engineers, agronomists, hydrologists, topographers and surveyors arrived who for several weeks explored the places where Mr Herbert had hunted his butterflies. Later on Mr Jack Brown arrived in an extra coach that had been coupled to the yellow train and that was silverplated all over, with seats of episcopal velvet, and a roof of blue glass. Also arriving on the special car, fluttering around Mr Brown, were the solemn lawyers dressed in black....'

Gabriel García Márquez, *One Hundred Years of Solitude* (trans. Gregory Rabassa), London: Jonathan Cape, 1970

Since the Second World War, multinationals have steadily increased their influence, through a combination of new investment, buying up local companies and, since the late 1980s, scooping up a large number of state companies privatised in so-called 'structural adjustment programmes'. Today, multinationals dominate the region's exports (e.g. minerals and cereals), domestic production (e.g. cars) and services (telecoms, airlines, supermarkets and, increasingly, public utilities such as water).

Multinational companies such as Philip Morris and Nestlé (coffee), Chiquita and Dole (bananas) and Cargill (grain) make up an informal coalition with western banks and commodity brokers which exerts a powerful grip on the world market in each product. Their sheer size also places them in a strong bargaining position with third world governments competing for sources of jobs and investment and with producers seeking better prices.

Black Gold

Petroleum is the greatest commodity of all. As a fuel and source of plastics and chemicals, it drives world industry (along, increasingly, with natural gas). Latin America contains major world oil and gas exporters, such as

Mexico and Venezuela, and many other less fortunate countries condemned to dependence on oil imports. Over the last 70 years, control over oil has become a politically explosive issue. In 1938, Mexico became the first Latin American country to nationalise its oil industry, and in the decades that followed other countries followed suit, weakening the grip of the seven great US- and European-owned oil multinationals, known as the 'seven sisters'. Such was the importance of oil that governments were willing to incur US displeasure in the process, as when General Velasco's military government in Peru seized the installations of the International Petroleum Corporation in 1968.

In 1960 Venezuela joined Saudi Arabia and five smaller producers to found the Organisation of Petroleum Exporting Countries, OPEC, which became the king of commodity cartels. Mexico refused to join for fear of US trade sanctions, but both countries cashed in when OPEC shocked the industrialised world with large price rises in 1973/4 and 1978/9, taking oil from US$2.70 to US$40 a barrel. The oil producers paid the price for their defiance, as recession cut demand for oil and consumer countries responded to higher prices by investing in alternative sources of energy and energy conservation. In 1986 the ensuing price collapse took oil back down to US$10 a barrel.

State oil companies such as Petrobras in Brazil, Pemex in Mexico, and Venezuela's PDVSA became giants, wielding great economic power and channelling large amounts of cash back into exploration and development of new oil reserves, as well as funding the burgeoning public sector. Oil transformed Venezuela from a rural backwater to one of Latin America's wealthiest nations, although the poor did not always share in the bonanza. The price of success was pollution and debt, as Venezuela borrowed heavily on the strength of its oil reserves. In Mexico, Pemex had run up a debt of US$15 billion by the early 1980s.

State companies ensured national control over a vital resource and were able to use profits to benefit their countries. By investing in exploration, they managed to quadruple Latin America's known reserves between 1974 and 1988, as countries such as Colombia and Brazil became significant new oil producers. Yet they were also plagued by problems; a shortage of qualified managers was aggravated as governments made political appointments within the bureaucracy. Corruption and inefficiency reduced economic benefits, while nationalisation risked closing the door to the oil multinationals' modern technology.

Even during the debt crisis of the 1980s, as neoliberal reforms obliged governments to privatise state assets, they were reluctant to sell off state oil companies. Oil's enormous political significance has, over the years, prompted huge domestic opposition to the sale of national oil enterprises, leading to the downfall of presidents in Bolivia and to strikes by oil workers in countries such as Brazil and Peru; meanwhile the upturn in oil prices from the late 1990s onwards sustained the Chávez government in Venezuela and has allowed him to finance a wide range of social reforms. Yet most governments badly need injections of foreign capital and technology in the oil and gas sector. As a result, they have opted instead for slowly opening up the oil sector by granting exploration and production licenses to multinational oil companies, and in some cases going into joint ventures with them.

Oil in Venezuela

In December 1922, Venezuela struck vast reserves of oil, changing the country's destiny overnight. Oil multinationals swiftly began operations, and by 1936 export earnings from oil were nine times those of coffee, Venezuela's other main commodity export. Yet oil wealth did not bring development. As dollars poured in, Venezuela's currency became overvalued, destroying the competitiveness of its other exports. Cheap imports undercut and wiped out domestic industry. Venezuela became an oil junkie, a consumer culture that produces nothing, its fortunes tied indissolubly to the international price of oil. When prices rocketed in the 1970s, government spending and corruption rose and the government nationalised the industry in 1976. When they fell back in the 1980s, Venezuela slumped into a debt crisis, then, following a sharp rise in international prices in the 1990s, oil was once again able to prop up the state. Now Venezuela's state oil company, PDVSA, is the fifth-largest oil producer in the world and a key supplier to the US market, and is once more a strong voice in OPEC. Against the advice of the IMF, the Chávez government has earmarked increased oil revenues for a literacy campaign and other social programmes. Venezuelans appear at last to be reaping the benefits of their subsoil wealth, but any slump in oil prices is certain to wipe out such progress.

'Today, Caracas is a supersonic, deafening, air-conditioned nightmare, a centre of oil culture that might pass as the capital of Texas. Caracas chews gum and loves synthetic products and canned foods; it never walks, and poisons the clean air of the valley with the fumes of its motorisation; its fever to buy, consume, obtain, spend, use, get hold of everything leaves it no time to sleep. From the surrounding hillside hovels made of garbage, half a million forgotten people observe the sybaritic scene....

[Lake Maracaibo] is a forest of towers. Within these iron structures the endlessly bobbing pumps have for half a century pumped up all the opulence and all the poverty of Venezuela. Alongside, flames lick skyward, burning the natural gas in a carefree gift to the atmosphere. There are pumps even in houses and on street corners of towns that spouted up, like the oil, along the lakeside – towns where clothing, food and walls are stained black with oil, and where even whores are known by oil nicknames, such as "the Pipeline", "The Four Valves", "The Derrick", "The Hoist".'

Eduardo Galeano, *Open Veins of Latin America* (trans. Cedric Belfrage), London: LAB 2000

Commodities and Development

Over the 500 years since the arrival of the Spanish, the commodity trade has exacted enormous social costs. In the mines the Spanish forced indigenous labourers to work in inhuman conditions until hundreds of thousands died from the dust, poor food and disease.

In the countryside the introduction of each new export crop has led to more land coming under the control of big landowners and more peasants being expelled. The onward march of export agriculture has helped drive the tidal waves of displaced peasants that broke over the continent's cities over the last 50 years, creating the sprawling shantytowns which surround the continent's 'first world' city centres. By allowing peasant farmers, who generally grow food crops like maize and beans, to be driven out to make way for export crops, many countries have lost their self-sufficiency in food production – Mexico, where maize was first cultivated, now imports it from the US. On a national level the commodity trade has proved an unreliable basis for Latin America's development. In the long term, commodities suffer from two main problems: a long-term decline in prices and a tendency to boom-bust cycles, rather than steady growth. Prices fall over the long term because supply rises faster than demand, driven by technological improvements and new entrants. Vietnam's rapid rise as a coffee producer in the 1980s created a global glut and a price collapse which ravaged the Latin American coffee industry. Prices are also affected by dumping: when Latin American farmers compete with crops also grown in the rich countries, northern governments rig the rules by pouring subsidies into their agriculture, enabling firms to flood Latin American markets with food exported at below the cost of production. With the North American Free Trade Agreement (NAFTA), Mexican maize farmers have become one of dumping's most notorious casualties.

Overlaid on the long-term decline are the boom-bust cycles characteristic of commodities. When prices rise, farmers plant more, leading to oversupply, a glut and a subsequent price collapse. The problem is worse when there is a long lead time between planting and harvesting, as in the case of tree crops like coffee. When prices fall, farmers take land out of production, leading to a shortage; prices rise, and the cycle begins all over again. Volatility is exacerbated by changes in patterns of demand. In recent years the taste for better coffee in Europe and the US has increased demand for high-quality beans from Central America and Colombia, and reduced demand for lower-quality Brazilian beans.

Throughout Latin America's history whole commodity sectors have flourished and then disappeared, in some cases due to technological innovation such as the discovery of synthetic dyes in the 19th century, which wiped out the indigo industry. In other cases, mineral deposits

Table 1.3:
Commodity dependence, figures for 2002

Country	Main commodity exports	% of total exports	All commodities as % of total exports (Leading 10 products as % of total exports 2002)
Argentina	oilseeds/oils	15.6	50.4
Belize	cane sugar	18.8	39.9
Bolivia	metals and metal ores	–	74.9
	natural gas	19.5	
Brazil	iron ore	5.1	34.8
	coffee	–	
	soya beans	5.0	
Chile	copper	34.6	59.3
Colombia	coffee	–	60.0
	petroleum	21.7	
Costa Rica	bananas	9.7	53.6
Ecuador	crude petroleum	36.5	82.1
	bananas	–	19.2
El Salvador	coffee	8.7	39.1
Guatemala	coffee	11.8	54.9
Honduras	coffee	19.0	58.0
	bananas	11.4	
Mexico	crude petroleum	8.2	47.6[1]
Nicaragua	coffee	10.9	52.9
	cattle	12.8	
Panama	bananas	–	74.8
	fish	27.8	
Paraguay	soya	35.8	80.3
	cotton	3.8	
Peru	fish meal	10.9	65.6
	gold	19.6	
	copper	9.5	
Uruguay	meat	13.5	53.9
Venezuela	crude petroleum & petroleum products	78.7	88.2

Source: ECLAC, *Statistical Yearbook on Latin America and the Caribbean,* 2003

1 includes maquiladora goods   – indicates no data

have been exhausted, as occurred with Bolivian silver, or the soil has become impoverished, as befell the sugar plantations of north-east Brazil.

The price fluctuations common to commodities make planning extremely difficult. To make matters worse, countries are often dependent on one or two commodities, exacerbating their vulnerability to any sudden fluctuations. Even when prices rise, economies have difficulty coping with the windfall. Governments often use the money to increase public sector spending. Though this could, in theory, lay the basis for future economic development through improving health and education, sudden and unplanned public sector growth has often in practice encouraged corruption and inefficiency.

In the 1970s, in an attempt to avoid the problems of price fluctuations and trade wars between producer nations, many third world countries joined forces in setting up price stabilisation agreements. But even when they succeeded in guaranteeing more stable prices, these agreements have often merely encouraged producer nations to increase production, eventually leading to oversupply, a price war and the collapse of the agreement.

Many Latin American governments have recognised the pitfalls of commodity dependence and tried to avoid them. One obvious path was to develop local industry that would replace dependence on foreign imports.

For 50 years, from the Great Depression of the 1930s to the Debt Crisis of the 1980s, Latin American governments turned to import substitution as their new development model, while still relying on commodities to bring in most of their export earnings. Since 1982, the continent has largely returned to its historical reliance on commodities, as neoliberal reforms across the region have put industrialisation into reverse and given new emphasis to 'export-led growth' based on commodities and cheap labour. The exception has been Mexico, where the start of a Free Trade Agreement with the US (NAFTA) in 1994 led to a boom in manufactured exports of increasing sophistication. In many ways, NAFTA split Mexico off from the rest of Latin America, turning it into a cheap labour enclave of the US economy.

Further south, the emphasis has been on reviving traditional areas such as mining and agro-exports such as soybeans, cotton and sugar, while diversifying into new, luxury crops such as fresh fruit and cut flowers. Although diversification reduces the extreme vulnerability produced by relying on a single product, it does not solve the more long-term problems of the commodity trade. Successful economies produce computers, not kiwi fruit. Reliance on commodities risks confining Latin America for ever to the backwaters of the world economy, while the new products can have disastrous impacts on the environment.

Cocaine – Just Another Commodity?

'Were it not for the drug's effect abroad, coca would be lauded as an ideal export crop'

Financial Times, 1990

For centuries, the leaves of the coca bush have been chewed by the peoples of the Andes, providing a mild stimulant that also stilled hunger pangs. Over the last twenty-five years, however, coca production has surged as a new, booming market has developed for the leaves. Cocaine has provided Latin America's latest commodity boom. Although figures in this area are never more than informed guesswork, by 2003 the annual wholesale cocaine trade was estimated at US$35 billion in the US alone; it is the second most valuable commodity in the world after oil. Every gram was produced from coca leaves grown by Latin American peasants. More recently, a number of Latin American countries have moved into heroin production from opium poppies.

In the Andean countries of Peru, Bolivia and Colombia, thousands of small farmers depend on the scrubby coca bushes for their livelihoods. Many of them semi-process the leaves by treading them in pits filled with kerosene. The resulting coca paste is then smuggled to clandestine laboratories, where it is turned into refined cocaine powder before being shipped to the US, Europe and Japan. Colombia alone provides 75% of the cocaine and 65% of the heroin consumed in the US.

The cocaine boom began in the early 1980s, even though the drug had been known for over 100 years and was used in various forms by such illustrious figures as Sigmund Freud and Queen Victoria. For the peasants, coca is a dream crop – its leaves can be harvested several times a year, and it needs minimal attention; buyers come to the peasants, solving the difficulties of getting the product to market that dog other crops in the remote areas where coca is grown. Moreover, its illegality ensures that big companies will not enter the market to compete and drive prices down.

However, coca's illegality has fuelled corruption and criminality, in some cases undermining Latin America's political stability. In Colombia, right-wing paramilitary groups and left-wing guerrillas fund themselves with the proceeds from the cocaine trade; in Paraguay the general in charge of the country's anti-drug unit was gunned down while preparing to release evidence linking businessmen, military officers and the police to drugs.

Over the last ten years the drugs business has become more atomised, as high-profile barons such as Colombia's Pablo Escobar have been captured and replaced by more diffuse, shadowy networks. The trade's general influence has changed in the process, from having a direct, tangible impact on politics – Colombia is the best example – to something more subtle, integrated into society at a much more grassroots level. Drugs money has driven both the 'informalisation' of the economy and an alarming crime wave. Drug gangs and drug use are both on the increase; in Rio, local drug lords effectively run many favelas.

Internationally, the story of drugs remains one of the few about Latin America that regularly makes headlines, chiefly because of its domestic importance within the US. Since 1986, successive US presidents have made the 'war on drugs' a national priority, spending US$25 billion on the effort by 2004, including arming and training Latin American governments and security forces to eradicate crops and intercept shipments, funding alternative crop programmes in producer areas, and running international interdiction efforts. Yet all the money and publicity have achieved remarkably little: cocaine use in the US has not fallen; the street price of cocaine is at or near an all-time low, while the trade has expanded into Europe and the former Soviet bloc.

Within Latin America the impact of the 'war on drugs' has been largely negative. Most of the profits from the drug trade remain in the consuming countries of the North. Meanwhile, US-sponsored forced eradication and aerial herbicide spraying programmes have hit poor peasant farmers hardest. Involving local armies in the drugs war has both boosted their influence and corrupted many officers at a time when Washington was avowedly intent on consolidating human rights and democracy in the region. For all the high-profile eradication efforts, the number of hectares planted with coca remains remarkably resilient.

Drug policy analysts liken the drug trade to a balloon: squeezing it in one area merely causes it to expand in another. Crackdowns on producers in Peru and Bolivia have merely encouraged production in Venezuela, Panama and particularly Colombia, which has become the region's largest producer, ahead of Peru and Bolivia. The civil war in Colombia has allowed paramilitaries and guerrillas to take over and expand the production and taxation of drugs, running a narcotic economy with military efficiency. The US has reacted with 'Plan Colombia', a huge injection of US$3 billion since 2000 for a military aid and crop eradication programme that has achieved only limited results, partly because 80 per cent of the money has been used to finance military and security forces, supporting claims that it is a counter-insurgency measure disguised as an anti-drugs programme in order to make it more politically palatable in both the US and Colombia.

New drug mafias have sprung up in Mexico, Bolivia, Peru, Venezuela and Brazil. The most powerful newcomers are the Mexican cartels, which have taken maximum advantage of Mexico's 2,000 mile-long border with the US and the increased cross-border traffic resulting from the North American Free Trade Agreement (NAFTA). Money laundering operations and transhipment routes have also scattered to every corner of the continent, creating growing headaches for US drug control efforts. The drug trade's resilience has been extraordinary. The death of the infamous drug baron Pablo Escobar in a shoot-out in 1993 completed the dismantling of the Medellín cartel, which US officials in the 1980s had claimed was responsible for 80 per cent of the cocaine entering the US, yet it had no discernible impact on the supply of the drug.

Colombian or not, the drug cartels continue to thrive, developing, according to *The Economist*, 'all the acumen and professionalism of the big international tobacco companies'. In the 1980s, individual 'mules' were replaced by large-scale shipments by air and sea, but the cartels set their sights even higher: in 1997 a Miami businessman was caught trying to import a Piranha-class nuclear submarine from the Kronstadt naval base in St Petersburg, Russia for use by Colombian cartels in shipments to California and elsewhere, according to US Drug Enforcement Agency (DEA) officials.

Although US drug policy has failed, few viable alternatives are on offer. Every so often, a courageous or foolhardy official suggests broadening the debate to include legalisation of some drugs, arguing that breaking the link with criminality would end much of the drug trade's most damaging impact on society. Parallels are often drawn with the end of prohibition in the US, which deprived gangsters like Al Capone of their control of the alcohol trade. Legalisation would also allow governments to tax drugs, a tantalising prospect for any administration trying to reduce its budget deficit. Given US domestic opinion, it is hard to see how legalisation could come about, but it is worth considering what effect it would have on the cocaine trade. Coca would become a normal commodity like tobacco; big farmers could move in and take over production from the peasant producers who currently grow the bushes, and the Colombian and Mexican cartels would suddenly be faced by a trade war with major multinational companies. Although it might bring an end to violence on the streets of the US, legalisation would not necessarily benefit ordinary Latin Americans.

The other option is for the US to recognise that as long as the demand persists, in the shape of millions of would-be cocaine users in the US, the supply will surely follow. That would involve a substantial shift from supply-side to demand-side policies, focusing on public education within the US, perhaps as part of a broader programme of inner-city regeneration aimed at breaking the cycle of poverty and exclusion that creates new generations of drug users. Yet such a strategy is unlikely given the current state of US politics. Extra funding in recent years has been directed at faith-based programmes for addicts as well as stricter policing, and until a shift in the public agenda occurs, it seems unlikely that Congress will act as an open and rational forum for debate.

Silent Revolution: Market Economics

Growing Pains:
Industrialisation, the Debt Crisis and Neoliberalism

São Paulo is made of cheap concrete. Millions of tons, poured in a hurry, spewed forth to make houses, tower blocks, factories and flyovers. Within a few years rain and sun leave it stained and crumbling, but quantity matters more than quality, for dilapidated buildings can always be replaced by bigger and newer constructions, using yet more concrete. The flood of concrete that created the great megalopolis of São Paulo is part of Brazil's rush for industrialisation, a titanic effort which has turned a relatively primitive coffee-exporter into a great industrial power, the tenth-largest economy in the world. However, like the concrete, Brazil's industrial development is flawed and vulnerable. To pay for it, the national economy ran up huge debts in the 1970s, driving the country to the verge of bankruptcy during the debt crisis of the 1980s. State-led industrialisation has also failed the Brazilian people. In the main thoroughfares of São Paulo, the rush-hour is a stampede of the well-heeled, the manicured and beautiful beneficiaries of Brazil's growth. On the street corners the losers, the old and unemployed, earn a pittance working as human billboards. Standing in bored clumps all day, they wear T-shirts saying 'I buy gold', with a phone number.

For half a century after the Great Depression of the 1930s, Latin Americans saw industrialisation as the path to development. The satanic mills whose fumes now choke Caracas or Mexico City may seem unlikely saviours, but the region's planners pointed to the experience of the rich countries, like the UK, US or Japan, where the growth of industry had led to a rise in both political power and the standard of living. Industrialisation, they argued, offered Latin America a way out of its crippling dependence on commodity exports, and its humiliating reliance on foreign governments and multinational companies for aid and manufactured goods. Since the onset of the debt crisis in the early 1980s, industrialisation in many cases has gone into reverse as governments have abandoned local industries to sink or swim in the global economy, in many cases reverting to commodity exports as the path to economic growth.

Latin America's industrial quest started late. During the colonial period, the Spanish and Portuguese governments did everything they could to prevent the growth of domestic industry, which they feared would disrupt the continent's dependence on commodity exports. In 1785 a royal decree from the Portuguese crown banned all industry in its Brazilian colony, ordering all textile looms to be burnt. When independence arrived in the early 19th century, Britain's cheap manufactures soon undercut what little local industry had arisen as the colonial ties had weakened. Nevertheless, most countries managed to achieve a first stage of industrialisation; they semi-processed agricultural crops and minerals for export, and local industries produced simple goods like soap, clothing and bottled drinks. European immigrants set up many of the first local industries – in Argentina and Uruguay British immigrants built slaughterhouses, freezer plants and tanneries to serve the beef export industry, while Germans set up Peru's beer industry and controlled 90 per cent of Brazil's textile production by 1916.

Despite these primitive local industries, Latin America remained a commodity exporter, dependent on manufactured imports, until the late 1920s. By then, the cattle and grain trade had made Argentina the fifth-richest country in the world, and coffee had established São Paulo as Brazil's economic powerhouse. In 1929 the Wall Street Crash and the ensuing depression in the industrialised world rudely awoke Latin American governments to the perils of commodity dependence. Brazil's exports fell by 60 per cent between 1929 and 1932, and the country suddenly had no hard currency with which to import manufactured goods.

Latin America learned its lesson. Just like the US government under Roosevelt's 'New Deal', or the followers of John Maynard Keynes in the UK, they concluded that the state had to play a much greater role in running the economy if future crashes were to be avoided. In Latin America, as local entrepreneurs moved in to start producing simple manufactured goods to plug the gap left by the import collapse, several governments began looking at ways to encourage 'import substitution'. By the late 1930s they were taking the first steps to improve transport, electricity and water supplies for local factories. When the Second World War came, the dilemma of the Great Depression was reversed; the industrialised nations were now desperate for Latin America's exports, but had fewer manufactures to spare as factories were converted to war production. The largest Latin American economies accumulated great wealth during the war, and afterwards used it to begin import substitution in earnest.

Besides improving national infrastructure, countries such as Argentina, Brazil and Mexico set up state-owned companies in strategic industries such as iron and steel, and raised taxes on imported manufactured goods. These tariff barriers were essential to protect fledgling local industries from being undercut by cheap imports. At the same time, governments encouraged multinational companies to set up factories on Latin American soil, arguing that this would create jobs while providing the technology and capital that the region lacked. Volkswagen built its first factory in Brazil in 1949, with other car producers from the US, West Germany and Japan hot on its heels. By 1970, 80 per cent of the country's cars were assembled in Brazil itself.

The initial results of import substitution were impressive. Between 1950 and 1970 Latin America's Gross Domestic Product (GDP, a measure of all goods and services produced) tripled, and even in per capita terms it rose by two-thirds. In the mid-1950s, Latin America's economies were growing faster than those of the industrialised West. By the early 1960s, domestic industry supplied 95 per cent of Mexico's and 98 per cent of Brazil's consumer goods. By this time, however, there were already clear signs that the model was approaching exhaustion, as state-led development in Latin America began to suffer much the same fate as the state-run economies in Eastern Europe. Protected industries had no need to invest or innovate, and fell behind the rest of the world in technology and productivity; political interference encouraged corruption and incompetence, as people were appointed to run state companies on the basis of political favouritism rather than merit. The ever-growing state sector began to outspend meagre revenues (rich Latin Americans have always been adept at avoiding taxes), generating growing inflation.

In social terms, import substitution also failed. Latin America and the Caribbean have always had hugely unequal societies, and import substitution further aggravated the situation. In order to keep wage costs down in industry, governments held down food prices, penalising the peasant farmers who grew the food and creating poverty in the countryside. Millions of peasants gave up hope of earning a living from the land and drifted to the cities, where they joined the armies of job-seekers in the shantytowns that sprang up on the edges of the continent's cities. Some achieved their ambition of a steady, waged job, but most ended up as street sellers, domestic servants or doing odd jobs.

The local market for manufactured goods was limited because most people in Latin America were too poor to buy more than the most basic necessities. This prevented industry from growing and reducing costs through mass production. Even Brazil, the most populous country in the region, faced this problem, although there was at least a significant middle class to buy locally produced goods, enabling Brazilian industry to outperform its Spanish American counterparts. The problem of a small domestic market could have been solved if wealth were redistributed to allow more people to buy goods, but that option was ruled out by the wealthy elite.

Initially, governments responded to the lack of an internal market by establishing a variety of free trade agreements with other Latin American nations. Organisations such as the Latin American Free Trade Association and the Central American Common Market, both established in 1960, soon foundered, however, because the smaller countries opened their markets to the more industrialised nations in the agreement, but received little in return.

The Dance of the Millions

Many Latin American governments were forced to adopt austerity programmes to cope with the slowdown in growth. In Brazil and Argentina, military governments seized power in order to implement such unpopular policies. They used both the law and brute force to suppress trade unions and lower the living standards of the poor majority. The major economies then set off in pursuit of the elusive third stage of industrialisation, the move from import substitution to becoming an exporter of manufactured goods. This meant large-scale investments, which had to be funded by foreign capital. Latin America turned to the international loan sharks. The initial results were astonishing. In just thirteen years, from 1967 to 1980, Latin America's manufactured exports increased in value 40-fold, from US$1 billion a year to US$40 billion.

Brazil led the field in both industrialisation and the race for foreign loans. In 1958, it overtook Argentina as the region's leading industrial power. By 1961 it was self-sufficient in electric stoves, refrigerators and television sets. Vehicle production boomed from 31,000 in 1957 to 514,000 in 1971. In 1968 Brazilian industry finally outstripped agriculture as the major wealth producer in the country. By 1988 Brazil's industrial output was twice that of Mexico, and nearly five times that of Argentina, and by 1996 four of Latin America's top five companies were Brazilian. The one-time coffee producer had become the region's superpower.

As the factories multiplied, so did the foreign debt. The big borrowers were the state corporations which dominated the politically vital areas of steel, petroleum and electricity production. By the early 1980s, Mexico's petroleum corporation, Pemex, had run up a debt of US$15 billion. State and private banks also borrowed heavily abroad, in order to re-lend to local businesses.

The 'dance of the millions', as the round of frenzied foreign borrowing became known, took off after the oil price rise in 1973–74. OPEC oil producers recycled their new wealth to western banks, who in turn were anxious to find outlets for their 'petrodollars'. Latin America seemed the ideal borrower; it had decades of steady growth and industrialisation already behind it, and countries such as Mexico and Venezuela were sitting on huge oil reserves. Foreign bankers fell over themselves to lend as much as possible, as fast as possible. Since they assumed that governments could not go bankrupt, they paid little attention to where the money was actually going. In practice, it went into a number of unproductive areas, such as capital flight, where government officials and business leaders siphoned billions of dollars back out of the country into US bank accounts; prestige 'megaprojects' such as hydroelectric dams and roads; and arms, as military governments splashed out on the latest hardware for their troops.

In all, US$60 billion in foreign loans entered Latin America between

1975 and 1982. Sixty per cent of the money went to Brazil and Mexico, as they and Argentina became the Third World's top three debtors. In Mexico, the rain of dollars funded exploration and development of the oil industry; in Brazil it fuelled the country's further rise as an industrial power. Brazil was the only country to successfully make the leap to the third stage of industrialisation as an exporter of manufactured goods. Between 1970 and 1978 it doubled its proportion of the region's exports, becoming a producer of everything from computers to aircraft.

The dance of the millions ended abruptly in August 1982, when the Mexican government announced that it could no longer pay the interest due on its foreign debt. Many US and other banks suddenly realised that what had seemed a safe and lucrative loans business in Latin America could drive them into bankruptcy, if other countries followed Mexico's lead. The announcement sent a shudder through the international banking community, raising fears of a run on the banks and a possible collapse of the world financial system. The following weeks established the pattern for years to come. The banks and creditor governments worked together to find a solution – not to the problem of Mexico's excessive debt repayments, but to remove the threat to the banking system. The initial remedy was a

Table 1.4:
Industrialisation in Latin America

	A	B	C
Mexico	617.8	24.3	26
Brazil	508.9	17.7	22
Argentina	268.8	30.6	20
Venezuela	126.2	40.3	20
Colombia	82.4	27.9	20
Chile	66.5	28.9	24
Peru	53.0	25.5	14
Dominican Republic	21.3	32.9	23
Guatemala	20.5	19.3	22
Uruguay	18.7	26.8	22
Ecuador	18.0	28.4	23
Costa Rica	16.1	26.2	23
El Salvador	13.7	30.1	25
Panama	10.1	13.8	16
Bolivia	8.0	29.5	28
Paraguay	6.8	28.6	21*
Honduras	6.4	27.3	22
Nicaragua	2.6	25.0	18*

A: GDP (US$ billion) 2001
B: Industrial output as percentage of GDP, 2002
C: Percentage of the workforce employed in industry, 2003 (* = figures for 2000)

Source: ECLAC Statistics and Projections Division

hastily improvised affair whereby the financial system would reschedule debt repayments and lend Mexico new money, purely so that it could give it straight back as interest payments. This would avoid the banks having to write off Mexico's loans as bad debts, which would in turn have damaged their profits and sent their shares plunging on the stock market.

By early 1984, every Latin American nation except Venezuela, Colombia and Paraguay had been forced into similar rescheduling deals. Cuba and Nicaragua also avoided such agreements, since Washington was imposing an effective financial boycott on both left-leaning governments. In each case the creditors stuck together, but insisted on negotiating with each debtor nation separately. Rescheduling was good business for the banks, since they could exact particularly high interest rates in exchange for deferring repayments. In return for rescheduling US$49.5 billion in loans, the banks earned an extra US$1.7 billion. At the same time, they ended virtually all new lending to Latin American nations, other than that needed to enable them to keep up with interest payments on the original loans.

The immediate cause of the debt crisis was the sudden rise in US interest rates announced by newly elected President Reagan in 1981. Since Latin America's debts had been largely contracted at floating interest rates, this meant a massive increase in its interest payments. Each time the international interest rate rose by 1 per cent, it added nearly US$2 billion a year to the developing countries' bills. At the same time the austerity policies of 'Reaganomics' and the second OPEC price rise of 1979 produced a sharp recession in the industrialised nations, which cut demand for Latin America's manufactured exports and sent commodity prices tumbling. Latin America earned less hard currency for its exports, just as it needed to pay more interest on its debt.

The role of the West's debt collector went to the International Monetary Fund (IMF), a multilateral funding agency controlled by the wealthy industrialised countries. Its role in the debt crisis earned the IMF another name: the Institute for Misery and Famine. For Sir William Ryrie, a top World Bank official, the debt crisis was 'a blessing in disguise'. It forced Latin America into a constant round of debt negotiations, providing the Reagan government, along with the IMF and the other international financial institutions with all the leverage they needed to overhaul the region's economy, in alliance with northern commercial creditor banks and the region's home-grown free-marketeers. The state-led model was discredited, monetarism was in the ascendant with champions in the White House and Downing Street – Latin America was ripe for a free-market revolution.

From then on, almost all of Latin America and the Caribbean followed a similar path. In the initial stage of reform, known as 'stabilisation', the IMF and banks pressured governments both to crack down on inflation by cutting spending, and to keep up their debt repayments by cutting their imports and generating a trade surplus. At the same time, commercial banks decided Latin America had become a bad risk, and stopped lending. Throughout the 1980s, capital flowed out of Latin America, destined for the rich countries of the north. This perverse flow of wealth from the poor to the wealthy squeezed out US$218.6 billion, over US$500 for every man, woman and child in the region.

With time, reforms have moved on to a broader process known as 'structural adjustment', involving a relentless assault on the state's role in the economy, including cuts in social spending, privatisation, and deregulation of everything from trade to banking to employers' abilities to hire and fire at will. The aim of such measures is to move Latin America and the Caribbean rapidly to a dynamic market-based economy, but up to now the panorama has largely been one of recession and austerity.

Silent Revolution

Everyone smoked in the Mexican stock exchange, a beautiful new 20-storey mirror-glass building shaped like a Stanley knife, cutting into the smog of downtown Mexico City. It was 1992, and on a roundabout in the street below a grimy statue of an Aztec emperor cut a forlorn figure, marooned in the traffic. Inside, away from the glare of the sun, the disciples of the new economic order rushed to and fro: well-groomed men shouting orders to shoulder-padded peroxide-haired women. On the trading floor, green computer screens were the only colour to break the grey and silver monochrome of business suits and stainless steel fittings.

Efraín Caro was the Exchange's Director of International Affairs. He was 33, but looked younger. On the wall of his office a *Wall Street Journal* cartoon showed an executive being told by his boss, 'It has come to my attention that you're not under enough stress'. The following week, Efraín was hosting a worldwide conference for representatives from 60 stock-markets, and he had stress to spare. Chain smoking, grabbing phones, shouting orders to subordinates even younger than himself, he spared ten minutes to rattle off figures in perfect English: in 1992 the Mexican stock market was booming, pulling in a total of US$22 billion in foreign investments, 80 per cent of it raised on Wall Street. That day's papers carried vital news from the presidential campaign in the United States: 'Clinton Says Yes to NAFTA'. Efraín believed the dollars would be coming forever.

By 2005, it was clear that Efraín had mistaken a brief boom for Latin America's eternally elusive sustained prosperity. The Mexican economy crashed in 1994, requiring a massive US$54-billion bail-out from the US government and the IMF. No sooner was the region back on its feet than a series of crashes in Asia and Russia led to a crisis in Brazil, and effectively ended the era of easy access to capital. A global recession didn't help. Over the last 20 years, Latin America's growth and investment curves look like a particularly violent roller-coaster.

The slump in Latin America's economy precipitated by the debt crisis contributed to one war and several bloody anti-IMF riots. Argentina's military leaders invaded the Falklands/Malvinas islands to divert attention from a collapsing economy, while riots, protests and looting afflicted cities across the continent. Prior to the 1980s, Latin Americans were accustomed to a growing economy. In every year between 1964 and 1980, the regional economy grew by more than four per cent, making the

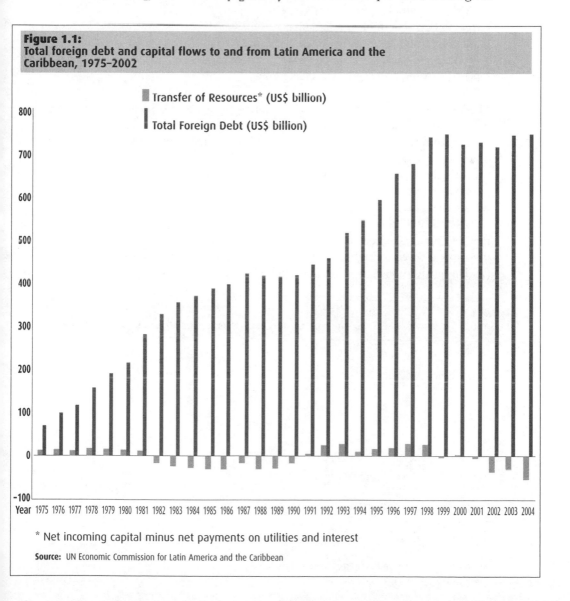

Figure 1.1:
Total foreign debt and capital flows to and from Latin America and the Caribbean, 1975–2002

Transfer of Resources* (US$ billion)

Total Foreign Debt (US$ billion)

* Net incoming capital minus net payments on utilities and interest

Source: UN Economic Commission for Latin America and the Caribbean

recession that hit in 1982 all the more painful. In 1982 Latin America's economy shrank in real terms for the first time since the Second World War. Chile was the worst hit, with per capita GDP falling by 14.5 per cent in a single year. The despair of Chile's unemployed workforce was captured in the lyrics of one of its top rock bands in the late 1980s, Los Prisioneros

> They're idle, waiting for the hands
> that decide to make them run again
> The mist surrounds and rusts them....
> I drag myself along the damp cement,
> remembering a thousand laments.
> Of when the misery came, when they said
> don't come back, don't come back, don't come back
> The factories, all the factories have gone.

The cause of the collapse was the austerity programmes implemented under IMF pressure to keep debt repayments flowing. The extraction of wealth from the region left a large hole in the economy, in the form of an investment collapse. Governments forced to adopt IMF austerity measures found it less politically costly to cut public investment than to sack employees in the middle of a recession (although many did that as well), while the private sector was deterred from investing both by the impossibility of borrowing abroad and by the recession and high interest rates at home, as governments lifted interest rates to fight inflation. Foreign investors also took fright. Across the region, gross domestic investment (which includes both local and foreign investment) collapsed from US$213

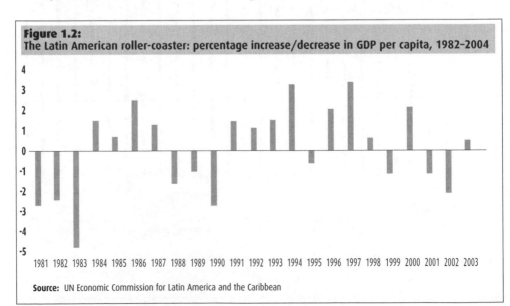

Figure 1.2:
The Latin American roller-coaster: percentage increase/decrease in GDP per capita, 1982–2004

Source: UN Economic Commission for Latin America and the Caribbean

billion in 1980 to US$136 billion in 1983. The level of investment is crucial to any economy's prospects; Latin America was mortgaging its people's future to pay its debts.

Falling investment and the domestic recession brought about by austerity programmes provoked an industrial collapse. By 1983, the degree of industrial development in Latin America had regressed to the levels of 1966. In Argentina and Peru it was back to 1960 levels, while in Chile and Uruguay it was more like 1950.

The 1980s were a period of recession and false starts, as governments desperately sought a way out of the debt crisis and continued to send billions of dollars to overseas creditors. By 1991, the capital tide had turned. Although debt repayments continued, foreign investors rediscovered the region, and started pouring money in again. They did so partly because pickings were thin elsewhere, partly because they were lured in by the latest component of Latin America's neoliberal reforms: from the late 1980s, governments had been privatising the state assets built up over 50 years of import substitution.

The pressures on governments to privatise seem irresistible. The growing fiscal crisis of the state sector, provoked by both foreign and domestic debt payments, has forced governments to increase revenue or cut expenditure; privatisation achieves both, shedding loss-making companies while raising substantial amounts of cash. In Argentina, President Carlos Menem's selling spree raised US$9.8 billion in cash, and enabled the government to lop a further US$15.6 billion off its foreign debt between 1989 and 1993 as transnational corporations bought up paper debt and swapped it for a stake in the newly privatised companies. In Mexico, the family silver raised a total of US$13.7 billion in 1990–91, during which time privatisation receipts provided just under a tenth of government revenues.

Privatisation is also part of the broader ideological shift, since neoliberals believe in cutting back the state and passing ever-larger chunks of the economy over to the private sector. Once privatised, they argue, management will be able to take decisions based on economic efficiency rather than politics, and a company's performance is bound to improve. The rhetoric employed was the same as in Margaret Thatcher's Britain, the only country to surpass the large Latin American economies in its privatising zeal. In Latin America, privatisation provided a juicy carrot with which to attract foreign investment back into the region after the capital famine of the debt crisis. Transnational corporations were expected to introduce capital and new technology into a region starved of both.

State airlines and telecommunications companies have gone on the block throughout the region, but so far only Argentina and Bolivia have allowed the rush to market to sweep away their state oil companies. Elsewhere, governments have been reluctant to hand over such strategic or highly profitable companies, preferring instead to encourage joint ventures with transnational corporations to attract technology and investment while retaining some degree of overall control. In recent years, public opinion has moved heavily against privatisation of national and natural resources, and this has been reflected in government policies. Argentina has set up a new state oil and gas company, whose remit is as yet unclear. Bolivia imposed tough new operating conditions on private companies, including a measure of renationalisation. Operating conditions for foreign investors have also been tightened in Venezuela and Ecuador.

The track record of privatisations has varied enormously. Areas which urgently required injections of capital and cutting-edge technology, such as telecommunications, have clearly benefited, but critics of the privatisation process argue that governments have missed the chance to divide up giant companies and introduce competition, and have been lax in regulating the newly privatised companies. There has often been a lack of transparency and accountability in the privatisation process, and corruption has undermined public support for privatisation even further. Privatisation programmes are, however, extremely good news for the local business class with the capital (often through joint ventures with foreign companies) to snap up the bargains. Mexico's stock of billionaires rose from two to 24 during the privatising presidency of Carlos Salinas de Gortari (1988–94), all of them with close ties to the ruling Institutional Revolutionary Party (PRI). In another echo of the British experience, Chile's pioneering privatisers in the 1970s operated a highly questionable revolving door system, moving from government posts in which they oversaw the privatisations to top jobs in the big conglomerates who cashed in on the sell-offs.

In Mexico and Argentina, the sudden inflows of dollars produced a short-lived rerun of the 'dance of the millions', as governments abandoned austerity in favour of reducing inflation by using the exchange rate. Overvalued currencies made imports artificially cheap, keeping prices down at home. Not surprisingly, imports boomed, but governments were able to use the incoming capital, as long as it lasted, to cover the resulting trade gap. It lasted until 1994, when a series of political crises, including the Zapatista uprising in Chiapas and the assassination of the PRI's anointed successor to Carlos Salinas, made foreign investors reassess Mexican risk. Capital flows to Mexico fell away, producing a run on the peso, a devaluation, and a devastating recession, costing two million jobs over the course of 1995. In the so-called 'tequila effect', foreign investors also pulled out of Argentina, which was pursuing a similar policy to that of Mexico, provoking massive recession and unemployment there during 1995. Capital inflows recovered their pre-tequila levels in 1997 only to fall away again, slowly at first and then spectacularly in the wake of the

Argentine crisis of 2001. Under pressure from global financial institutions, governments had little option but to return to the more painful 1980s style of adjustment.

By disposing of loss-making companies and pulling in one-off windfalls, the privatisation bonanza did, however, play a crucial part in curbing governments' spending deficits and getting inflation down in many Latin American countries in the early 1990s. Inflation in the region as a whole peaked at around 1,200 per cent in 1989 and 1990. After that, privatisations, further government cuts in spending and investment, and improved tax collection all helped to get fiscal deficits down. By 2000, inflation was down to single figures and the hyperinflationary nightmares of the previous decades were starting to fade.

Trade

Under a neoliberal regime, countries are encouraged to trade on the basis of their 'comparative advantage' – economic jargon for sticking to what you are good at. In the case of Latin America, this means raw materials and cheap labour. In a return to the course of development followed since the conquest, Latin America has gone back to exporting commodities, both traditional products such as minerals and oil, and a whole range of new, non-traditional exports, covering everything from cut flowers to fresh salmon. The other side of the export drive is an attempt to increase the exports of manufactured goods, usually low-tech products such as shoes or textiles, or the output of assembly plants, such as the *maquiladoras* strung along the US–Mexican border, where imported components are assembled by cheap Latin American labour. By 2000, these were employing around 1.3 million people in Mexico, and many more in factories dotted around Central America and the Caribbean. Since then, however, cheap Chinese labour has begun to encroach upon Latin America's *maquiladoras* sector, despite Mexico's proximity to the US market. It was estimated that between 2001 and 2003, one-third of Mexican *maquiladoras* relocated to China, where labour costs are often less than half as much.

Latin America's attempt to get in on the ground floor of the global economy as a purveyor of raw materials risks confining it to one of the most sluggish areas of world trade, perpetuating its traditional reliance on the fickle prices of the commodity markets. The recovery in its exports since 1982 has been matched by a flood of imports, following blanket trade liberalisation, bankrupting potentially competitive local producers and raising fears that the 'opening' has undermined the region's industrial future. Furthermore, the boom in non-traditional exports has been achieved at a high social cost, exacerbating inequality and undermining the region's food security, while both assembly plants and pesticide-intensive agriculture have damaged the environment.

Regional Integration

The region's shift away from import substitution towards the merits of 'export-led growth' also saw a renewed interest in free-trade agreements. Within Latin America dozens of bilateral and multilateral agreements have been signed since the late 1980s, the largest being the Southern Cone Common Market (Mercosur). Mercosur, which came into operation in 1995, brings together Argentina, Brazil, Uruguay and Paraguay.

The best-known free trade agreement in the region, and the only one in the world between the First and Third Worlds, is the North American Free Trade Agreement (NAFTA), between Mexico, the US and Canada, which came into force in 1994. By 2009, NAFTA is scheduled to phase out all trade tariffs and restrictions on foreign investment between the three countries. Its many critics argue that it is little more than a 'charter of corporate rights', working to the benefit of large corporations at the expense of the poor. Big companies in the US relocated to Mexico in order to cut wages, thereby increasing unemployment in the US; although some Mexicans found jobs in the new factories, far more have suffered the impact of ending tariffs on imported maize, which is produced on heavily subsidized commercial US farms at a fraction of the cost of Mexican-grown maize. Mexican business reports claim that 1.3 million jobs have been lost in the agricultural sector as a direct result of the treaty. Meanwhile, the purported benefits of NAFTA – capital inflows, factory relocation – had begun to fall off dramatically as US firms turned to China for cheap labour and high productivity.

In 2005 the Central American Free Trade Agreement (CAFTA) came into force. Trade agreements between more equal players such as the Central American republics allow members to pool know-how and achieve economies of scale unavailable to single small nations. NAFTA, an agreement between profoundly unequal players, allows Mexican consumers to enjoy the benefits of cheap food imports, the latest computer technology and even the dubious delights of an invasion of US fast food chains. But it also condemns the country to trade on its current comparative advantage (cheap labour and raw materials) rather than allowing it to upgrade its industry, as South Korea and Taiwan have done so successfully in recent decades. Such industries struggle to emerge when a regional trade agreement (RTA) forces the economy to remain open to competition from already established US companies.

Doubts over RTAs have grown in many Latin American countries, however, leading some politicians to back away from plans for a Free Trade Area of the Americas (FTAA). By 2006, a South American version of the FTAA, without the looming presence of the US, looked like a possible alternative. As domestic opposition within the US to further free-trade agreements has helped to stall progress, Brazil has stepped into the

Soft Fruit, Hard Labour

Orchards fill the Aconcagua valley north-east of Santiago in Chile. Parallel rows of peach trees stretch off to infinity, playing tricks with the eye. The monotony is punctuated by the occasional fat-trunked palm tree or weeping willow, shining with new leaf on a cold and dusty spring day.

Carlos Vidal is a union leader, president of the local *temporeros*, the temporary farm labourers who plant, pick and pack the peaches, kiwi fruit and grapes for the tables of Europe, Asia and North America. A shock of black curls streaked with grey fringe his round, gap-toothed face. A freezing wind off the nearby Andes blows across the vineyards as Carlos tells his story.

'On this land there were 48 families who got land under [former President] Allende. We grew vegetables, maize and beans together, as an *asentamiento* [farming cooperative]. There were a few fruit farms then, but we planned them. After the coup [in 1973] the land was divided up between 38 families – the others had to leave. Then it started to get difficult, we got the land but nothing else; the military auctioned off the machinery.

Then the *empresarios* [entrepreneurs] started to arrive, especially an Argentine guy called Melitón Moreno. The bank started taking people's land – foreclosing on loans – and Moreno bought it up. Three *compañeros* [comrades] committed suicide here because they lost their farms. Melitón got bank loans and bought yet more land and machinery. He planted nothing but fruit – grapes at first, then others.

My father was a leader of the *asentamiento*. The first year after the coup we were hungry, lunch was a sad time. We began to sell everything in the house, then we looked for a *patrón* to sell us seeds and plough our land for us, and we paid him with part of the harvest. Next year we got a bank loan and managed to pay it off, but the following year they sold us bad seed. We lost all the maize and the whole thing collapsed. We had to sell the land and Melitón Moreno bought it.

Of the 38 families, most are now *temporeros*. We all sold our land but kept our houses and a small garden to grow food. Trouble is, even the gardens are no good, the water's full of pesticides from the fruit. This area used to be famous for water melons and now they don't grow properly any more. They chuck fertiliser and pesticide everywhere, it doesn't matter that the earth is dead because the fruit trees live artificially. No one grows potatoes or maize any more – it's cheaper to buy the imported ones from Argentina.'

Duncan Green, *Silent Revolution: The Rise and Crisis of Market Economics in Latin America*, London: LAB, 2003

vacuum, keen to expand Mercosur into a Latin American counterweight to US economic might in the hemisphere. Mercosur has already added Chile to its ranks (after Chile was rebuffed by NAFTA) and is currently negotiating free-trade agreements with Bolivia and Venezuela.

The Lost Decade

'The Third World War has already started – a silent war, not for that reason any the less sinister. This war is tearing down Brazil, Latin America and practically all the Third World. Instead of soldiers dying there are children, instead of millions of wounded there are millions of unemployed, instead of destruction of bridges there is the tearing down of factories, schools, hospitals, and entire economies.'

Luiz Inácio Lula da Silva, Brazilian labour leader (later President) 1985

The profound economic transformation of Latin America since the 1970s has been achieved only at enormous social cost. Throughout the region, after decades in which the percentage of Latin Americans living in poverty had been falling (though not their actual number), poverty is once again on the rise. By 2002, more than 70 million new names had joined the grim roll call of the poor, leaving 44 per cent of the population – more than 220 million people – living in poverty. In rural areas, particularly in Central America, this figure rises to as much as 70 per cent. Almost half of Latin America's poor, around 97 million people, are indigent and barely exist on an income of less than a dollar a day. As the poor got poorer, the rich got richer, especially the very rich: according to *Forbes* magazine, the number of Latin American billionaires rose from six in 1987 to 42 in 1994, though it fell again to 25 in 2002, after the turbulence of the late 1990s.

The problem of rising poverty in Latin America is one of political will, not resources – there is enough money to go round. Latin American inequality is on such a scale that a comparatively minor move towards a fairer distribution of income could eradicate poverty overnight. According to the World Bank's 1990 *World Development Report*: 'Raising all the poor in the continent to just above the poverty line would cost only 0.7 per cent of regional GDP – the approximate equivalent of a 2 per cent income tax on the wealthiest fifth of the population', who in Mexico, for example, receive almost 60 per cent of income.

Neoliberal reforms have exacerbated poverty and inequality in numerous ways. According to the UN, the main cause of increasing poverty and inequality has been the 'massive decline in real wages ... the rise in unemployment and ... the number of people employed in very low-productivity jobs'. State cutbacks, recession and unemployment have all combined to suppress wages, as have adjustment policies designed to 'flexibilise' the labour market. In practice, this has meant cracking down on

Dollarisation

'In response to the economic volatility of the 1980s and 1990s, some of the smaller Latin American economies concluded that the luxury of a national currency could no longer be justified, and opted for the US dollar instead. Ecuador (2000) and El Salvador (2001) joined Panama, which had been dollarised since 1903, in abandoning their currencies. In so doing, they relinquished much of their ability to manage their economies, along with the income that governments gain from printing money, known as seigniorage. Without their own exchange rates, their interest rates are effectively determined by the US Federal Reserve, plus whatever risk premium global markets attach to the country in question, leaving only one of the three main levers of economic policy (fiscal, i.e. public finances) still available to these governments. That means that governments running into any kind of trouble have little option but to cut spending.

The argument for dollarisation is particularly strong for smaller economies, where floating exchange rates have traditionally proved more volatile and currency fluctuations have a more direct effect on inflation. Ecuador, however, also demonstrates the perils. Following dollarisation, it proved unable to get inflation down to US rates, leading to a steady loss of competitiveness. Although this was masked to an extent by new oil finds, which continued to bring in dollars, without the option of devaluation the government faced the prospect of a severe domestic recession, which would at some point get prices back in alignment.

Dollarisation is just the latest twist in an economic conundrum for Latin American governments – what to do about exchange rates? Dollarisation is also political. For many citizens, the loss of their familiar national currency is a compelling symbol of a loss of power and sovereign identity. These days the received wisdom in Latin America is that there are only two options: dollarisation or floating exchange rates. Any attempt to find a middle ground, for example, by pegging currencies temporarily to the dollar in order to ride out fluctuations, merely offers global market speculators a juicy incitement to gamble on being able to force countries to a devaluation. This was a factor in, for instance, the economic collapse in Argentina in 2001–2.'

Duncan Green, *Silent Revolution: The Rise and Crisis of Market Economics in Latin*, London: LAB, 2003

trade unions and making it easier for managers to hire and fire employees, enforce part-time work and cut costs by subcontracting work to smaller companies, often little more than sweatshops.

Women have borne the brunt of adjustment. Many of the new low-waged or part-time jobs generated by adjustment go to women, while many men lose their role as family breadwinner, as full-time waged jobs disappear, or wages fall so far that a single income becomes insufficient to feed a family. On top of this 'double day' of work and running the home, the deterioration of social services, especially in urban areas, has forced women into a third role: taking responsibility for running their

An anti-US demonstration in Caracas, Venezuela. *(Latinphoto)*

communities, fighting or substituting for inadequate state services in schools, health, drainage, water supply, or roads.

Adjustment has made all these tasks more vital to the family's survival and more exhausting: 'flexibilisation' often means lower wages, longer hours and greater insecurity, just as cuts in state subsidies have brought steep price rises in basics like food and public transport. One study of women in a shantytown in Guayaquíl, Ecuador gives a graphic picture of the impact of adjustment on women. The research found that the women were affected by adjustment in three different ways. About 30 per cent of the women were coping, juggling the competing demands of their three roles in the workplace, home and community. They were more likely to be in stable relationships with partners who had steady jobs. Another group, about 15 per cent of the women, were simply 'burnt out', no longer able to be superwomen 24 hours a day. They were most likely to be single mothers or the main breadwinners and were often older women, physically and mentally exhausted after the effort of bringing up a family against such heavy odds. They tried to hand over all household responsibilities to their oldest daughter, while their younger children frequently dropped out of school and roamed the streets. The remaining 55 per cent were described as simply 'hanging on', sacrificing their families by sending sons out to work or keeping daughters home from school to help with the housework.

If nothing is done to change the impact of adjustment policies, many of these women will also 'burn out', swelling the number of families broken by the impact of Latin America's silent revolution.

Although curbing inflation has undoubtedly improved the quality of life of the poor, adjustment policies have also exacerbated poverty by removing food subsidies and other price controls. The combined impact of changes to prices and the labour market under adjustment has shifted poverty from the rural to the urban areas.

Globalisation

Globalisation describes the process whereby individuals, groups, companies and countries become increasingly interconnected. This interconnectedness occurs in several arenas:

Foreign direct investment: the inexorable rise of giant transnational corporations (TNCs) lies at the heart of globalisation. Brand names, from Nike to Coca-Cola, have become some of the most widely recognised images on the planet. Of the world's top 200 economic players in 2001, 56 were countries and 144 were corporations. General Motors, Wal-Mart, Exxon Mobil, and Daimler Chrysler each had revenues greater than the combined economic output (GDP) of the 48 least developed countries.

Trade: Between 1994 and 2004, world trade in goods (not services) doubled to nearly US$9 trillion. Poor countries have concentrated on clothes, footwear, electronics, and food – in the UK, a trip down the aisle of the local supermarket reveals asparagus from Peru, mangoes from Brazil and wine from Chile and Argentina.

Technology: The accelerating pace of innovation in information technology (IT) is driving globalisation. The cost of a three-minute phone call from New York to London fell from US$245 in 1930, to US$3 in 1990, to about 35 cents in 1999 (1990 prices). Using 24-hour email, companies can split up their assembly lines between countries on different sides of the globe, sending designs and orders down the phone line and shifting components from one country to another to minimise costs. IT can cut costs and create a global village, but has awakened fears of a growing 'digital divide' between the haves and have-nots.

Capital flows: Capital flows, increasingly disconnected from any real trade or investment, have grown enormously since 1990. By 2005, they were running at about US$2 trillion a day (80 times more than world exports), moving around in the Alice-in-Wonderland world of derivatives, futures, and currency trading. Globalisation's supporters argue that capital flows can provide much-needed investment. However, such massive capital flows have caused severe social and economic crises in Thailand, Korea,

Indonesia, Russia and Argentina. The World Bank has found that these crises tend to hit the poor hardest, while subsequent recoveries benefit the better off, ratcheting up inequality.

Neoliberalism: the new paradigm

Latin America has so far been unable to develop an economic model that can combine the elusive goals of growth and economic equity. The last two decades have seen the consolidation of the neoliberal model foisted upon the region by the United States, the IMF, the World Bank and the World Trade Organisation, in alliance with foreign investors, the global money markets and home-grown neoliberals among the region's elites. Despite three enormous economic collapses – Mexico in 1994–5, Brazil in 1999 and Argentina in 2001-2 – the neoliberal agenda has survived relatively unscathed.

Assumptions in favour of sweeping privatisation and short-term investment mean that medium- to long-term development prospects continue to be ignored. After the unravelling of Import Substitution Industrialisation (ISI) in the 1970s and 1980s, Latin America has again decided to rely upon exports of raw materials rather than invest in the service or industrial sectors. Unlike other developing regions, especially the 'Asian Tiger' economies such as South Korea and Taiwan, Latin America has not chosen, overall, to invest in high-tech innovation. Fluctuating prices for primary exports have left the workers of Latin America hostages to fortune in the same way they were a century ago. The increasing deregulation of capital flows has left governments at the mercy of the rapid mood swings of global financial markets, adding a new, turbo-charged boom–bust cycle to the perils of commodity dependence.

While alternative ideas are regularly put forward by opposition parties and social movements, the left, once in government, has found the new agenda almost impossible to bypass. Despite the hopes of the poor – and the fears of the business community – Lula's presidency of Brazil has been characterised by extreme caution, in the shape of high interest rates and financial austerity. Only Venezuela, awash with oil revenues, can afford to buck the trend, even if it antagonises global financial institutions.

If Latin America hopes to escape from this developmental cul-de-sac, it must develop a new vision, based on a coordinated effort to free itself from the twin dependencies on commodities and foreign capital. Doing this requires not autarchy, but a deliberate attempt to shift into more dynamic parts of the global economy. This is no easy task, requiring profound social and political change. Notably, a knowledge-based, rather than natural-resource-based, economic model requires enormous investments in health and education, and an attack on the crippling inequality that has dogged the region since the conquest. Governments would have to give priority to domestic savings and investment in order to reduce reliance on foreign capital. It means giving greater emphasis to regional trade within Latin America, but avoiding the grip of a Free Trade Area of the Americas, which could kick away the ladder of development by locking Latin America into the voracious US economic system as a supplier of raw materials and cheap labour.

Cartoneros

'A stroll in downtown Buenos Aires is bound to include the fabled Avenida Corrientes, alive with lights and people 24 hours a day. In 2003 it was still possible to follow the avenue towards the river at midnight and find open bookshops to browse in after coming out of a theatre or restaurant. Locals – *porteños* – can tell that the facades are shabbier and the bookshops fewer, and they miss the crowds that used to throng here. Yet to the untrained eye, this is a city centre where all sorts of people come to enjoy themselves.

The avenue has other uses too. Late at night, when most people have gone home after their play and their meal, when only a few shops and news kiosks cast their light on the broken pavement, a fleet of coaches arrives. Out step entire families who have travelled from the city's vast reaches that spill over from the capital into the province of Buenos Aires. They are collecting anything that might be worth selling on, mostly cardboard and papers. They populate the avenue in their hundreds, filling it with their work and the voices and play of children. Several hours later they are gone, back to the jobless neighbourhoods. They are known as *cartoneros*, and are the embodiment of the poverty that has overtaken millions of Argentinians. Most *cartoneros* had jobs until a few years ago. The older ones are skilled workers, but the very young have never known regular employment – there may be as many as 40,000 working the streets of Buenos Aires alone. Their haunting presence is at odds with the uniformed waste collectors who also clean the city daily. They work from new trucks provided by the private companies contracted by the state – cleaning up the capital is worth some US$160 million a year.

Argentina in the 21st century appears to exist in different dimensions: in the "official" world, there are formal institutions to deal with public services from rubbish to education or health. Yet there is a growing dimension where the links between the state and people's everyday lives have been severed and a great proportion of the population has been cast adrift. In less than a generation, the country has gone from boasting the largest middle class in Latin America to having over half of the population – some 16 million people – below the poverty line.

Until recently, the families who today find no safety net had access to education and health insurance and owned home and businesses. In just a few decades, Argentina has changed from being a land of immigration and promise to being one of net emigration, with nearly half the economically active population underemployed or entirely excluded from the job market.'

Marcela López Levy, *We are Millions: Neo-liberalism and New Forms of Political Action in Argentina*, London: LAB, 2003

The Argentine Crash

The roots of the crisis that hit one of the most most 'middle-class' countries in Latin America in the final days of 2001 lay in a disastrous combination of economic policies, bad advice from the IMF and World Bank, and external pressures beyond the government's control.

In 1991, the government successfully ended inflation by pegging the peso to the dollar. This step, which effectively prevented devaluation, meant that the government could issue pesos only if they were backed by dollar reserves. In the event of a fiscal deficit, the government's only option was to borrow dollars to cover the gap, thereby adding to its debt.

And fiscal deficit there was, but the cause was not so much government profligacy or corruption as pension privatisation. Urged on by the World Bank and IMF, Argentina moved rapidly from a state to a private pension system. The problem was the transition period, during which the government no longer received pension contributions, but still had to pay out pensions guaranteed under the old system.

In addition, bungled and corrupt privatisations led to a high-cost economy, with tariffs for phones and electricity raised to ten times international rates. This, together with an overvalued currency and trade liberalisation, led to a surge of imports that destroyed the country's industry and inflated the trade deficit.

The vulnerability of the economy was finally exposed by the slump in international capital flows after the Asia crisis of 1997–98. The government staggered on, raising interest rates in a vain effort to pull in the dollars needed to service its escalating debt, but collapse was inevitable and, when it arrived, spectacular. A cascade of protests, falling presidents (three in a week – one of them declared the biggest sovereign default in history, on public-sector debt of US$80 billion) and bank closures prompted Latin America's greatest ever peacetime economic slump, before the government of Néstor Kirchner inaugurated a promising although still nascent economic recovery.

Ballots and Bullets: The State, the Military and Politics

2

CONTENTS

The State and the Military

In August 2004, the President of Venezuela, Hugo Chávez, overcame a recall referendum on his government, resoundingly defeating a powerful home-grown US-influenced opposition who were prepared to use every means to get him out of office. Six million Venzuelans, representing 58 per cent of the votes cast, voted for Chávez to remain in office; the 70 per cent turnout was a record for an election in Venezuela.

When Chávez was elected for the first time in 1998, he was the exception in a region ruled by conservative leaders: the dictator Hugo Banzer in Bolivia, the free marketeer Carlos Menem in Argentina; the 'perfect dictatorship' of the Partido Revolucionario Institucional (PRI) in Mexico; even Brazil's Fernando Henrique Cardoso, a progressive sociologist, had embraced the free-market model.

Chávez, meanwhile, promised his electorate a 'peaceful, democratic' revolution, inspired by his hero, Simon Bolívar. No one knew quite what to make of Chávez; four years later, during an attempted coup against him, not much had changed: some said Chávez was a breath of fresh air, a genuinely popular politician. Others related a darker story: Chávez's democratic posturing and promise of a new constitution was a ploy – he was a dark authoritarian, ruling by personal charisma and for personal prestige alone, a perfect example of the Latin American *caudillo*, or strong man.

The controversy surrounding Hugo Chávez is the latest stitch in an old pattern. The twin threads of democracy and authoritarianism run through Latin America's history since independence, sometimes alternating between periods of democratic or dictatorial rule, at other times combining to produce hybrid forms of authoritarian democracy.

The authoritarian tradition stems from the conquest. The Spain from which Columbus set sail in 1492 was a militarised, crusading society, emerging victorious from a seven-century battle with Islam and greedy for new conquests. Power lay with the Catholic monarchs, whose authority came directly from God, as they ruled by 'divine right', in alliance with the Pope. As late as the 1970s, the Spanish dictator General Franco claimed to rule 'by the grace of God'. In their new colonies, the Spanish implanted a hierarchical system, enslaving the indigenous people. Ironically, the empires they replaced in Mexico and the Andes were if anything even more authoritarian and centralised than the Spanish. Absolute power resided in the Aztec or Inca emperor (at the time of the Spaniards' arrival, Moctezuma II in Mexico and Atahualpa in Peru), allowing the Spaniards to defeat far more numerous rivals by first seizing the emperors, then replacing them at the top of the social pyramid.

In Brazil, Portuguese rule was rather more lax. No gold or silver was discovered for the first two centuries, and Portugal concentrated on its other, more profitable ventures in the East Indies. Rather than develop an all-encompassing bureaucracy, it left the Brazilian colonists more to themselves, contenting itself with taxing Brazil's exports.

The colonies were fairly stable until the mid-18th century, and continued to provide vast amounts of precious metals and luxury goods to Spain and Portugal. Both France and the Netherlands attempted to gain footholds in Brazil, but were repelled by the Portuguese. However, following tax reforms in the 1760s, rebellions began to break out throughout Spanish South America. Protests by frustrated *criollos* (natives of European ancestry), taxed without representation, were manageable, as the colonial bureaucracy could count on their support in the final analysis. More dangerous were the lengthy rebellion of Atahualpa II in Bolivia (1742–52) and the occupation of Peruvian and Bolivian cities by Tupac Amaru II in 1780–82. These indigenous rebellions aimed to re-establish the Inca empire, and posed serious threats to the material hierarchy of the colonies. For the three decades following the defeat of Tupac Amaru II, the colonial authorities were supported by the creole elite, now terrified of a potential peasant uprising.

The feared peasant outbreak did take place in the hitherto stable colony of New Spain, led by two priests, Hidalgo and Morelos. Huge armies of indigenous and *mestizo* (of mixed European and indigenous parentage) peasants defeated the colonial army, then lost the support of sympathetic *criollos* by carrying out vengeful atrocities on the inhabitants of occupied cities. The Mexican rebellion, as well as the earlier outbreaks of violence in Peru, went some way to determining the course of independence. These incidents frightened the creole elite, who recognised the dangers of a temporary alliance with the masses. When opportunities to break free of the imperial state did occur, the wealthy were determined to create independent nations controlled by a strict hierarchy. While republicanism was the dominant political ideology, democracy was not a priority, and *criollos* tended to put their faith in strong, authoritarian governments.

Independence came suddenly to Spanish America, and almost by accident. In 1808 Napoleon invaded Spain and installed his brother on the throne. *Criollos*, already restive at Spanish rule and Spain's insistence on monopolising foreign trade, seized the moment to declare independence. The monarch was now the enemy, and the American and French revolutions were still recent memories, so republicanism appeared the obvious alternative to many of the rebels (although some still supported an independent monarchy). As would come to be the case throughout the modern period, Latin Americans imported the latest political fashion from outside and attempted, unsuccessfully, to graft it on to their own traditions.

The greatest of Latin America's freedom fighters, Simón Bolívar (1783–1830), epitomised the process. His beliefs were a complex and often contradictory mixture of authoritarianism and Enlightenment-inspired republicanism. Shortly before his death, disillusioned by his compatriots' lack of experience in government and the chaos unleashed by the independence wars, he wrote the Bolivian constitution. In it, Bolívar created a president-for-life, able to choose his own successor, thereby avoiding 'the changing administration caused by party government and the excitement which too frequent elections produce.'

Bolívar's dream of a United States of Latin America soon foundered on the rivalries and geographical and cultural differences which helped to divide the region into today's republics. In the year of Bolívar's death, 'Great Colombia' disintegrated into Venezuela, Colombia and Ecuador; the former 'kingdom of Guatemala' splintered into the numerous feuding Central American republics. Each act of division took Latin America further from the path to prosperity and power that had been followed by the United States to the north.

Republic after republic approved high-sounding democratic constitutions that had little connection with political and social reality. The wars against Spanish rule were won on the battlefield, and in the aftermath of independence, the economic elite of large landowners opted out and retired to their remote haciendas, leaving politics to the former military leaders, who became the feuding local strongmen, or *caudillos*, who have been a feature of Latin American political life ever since.

The caudillos were often charismatic, paternalist figures who became the real authority in many rural areas. As one Venezuelan caudillo wrote to Bolívar, 'the people bring me all their problems – how to build a house, whom to marry, how to settle a family dispute, and what seeds to plant'. In Latin America's rigidly stratified society, the military offered one of the few vehicles for ambition and social mobility, and caudillos and their personal retinues fought endless wars. In *One Hundred Years of Solitude*, Gabriel García Márquez portrays the fictional life of a classic caudillo, Colonel Aureliano Buendía:

Colonel Aureliano Buendía organised 32 armed uprisings and he lost them all. He had 17 male children by 17 different women and they were exterminated one after the other on a single night before the oldest one had reached the age of 35. He survived 14 attempts on his life, 73 ambushes, and a firing squad. He lived through a dose of strychnine in his coffee that was enough to kill a horse. He refused the Order of Merit which the President of the Republic awarded him. He rose to be Commander-in-Chief of the revolutionary forces ...

Some of the strongmen managed to take over a whole country, such as Argentina's Juan Manuel de Rosas, or Mexico's Antonio López de Santa Anna, while others ruled over regional enclaves.

Brazil, meanwhile, followed a different path. When Napoleon invaded, the British fleet shipped the Portuguese court *en masse* to exile in Rio de Janeiro. Portuguese rule had been less restrictive than that of the Spanish, producing less anti-royalist feeling, and in 1822, without violence or economic destruction, Brazil became an independent monarchy under Emperor Dom Pedro I. Although Dom Pedro I faced a difficult few years, marked by political division, rebellions and the loss of what became Uruguay after a war with Argentina, his son, Dom Pedro II, succeeded in uniting the nation, ruling for nearly 50 years and fending off the division, chaos and economic decline that afflicted the Spanish American colonies after independence. The Brazilian monarchy survived until 1889.

By the 1850s the caudillo period was coming to an end, as the economic elites emerged from relative seclusion to reimpose order. Modern nations started to emerge from the wreckage as British capital and technology flooded in, building railways, ports, and telegraph networks. Caudillos gave way to administrators, commercial agriculture expanded (often displacing indigenous communities) and exports began to rise. By the 1880s, Latin America had become integrated into the world economy, setting the scene for half a century of economic boom based on agro-exports.

Politics at this point was a preserve of the rich. This was the heyday of landowner rule, either running the government themselves, as in Argentina or Chile, or via the imposition of dictators, as in Mexico, Venezuela and Peru. Unlike the squabbling caudillos of the first half of the century, this new brand of dictator, exemplified by Mexico's Porfirio Díaz, were modernisers, intent on building up their nations through foreign investment and economic growth.

The key political issues of the time were reflected in the endless battles between Liberals and Conservatives. Although the ideological distinctions between them were frequently less important than the personal ambitions of their leaders, Conservatives tended to be pro-Church and supported a centralised system of government which favoured the big cities, while

Liberals tended to be anti-clerical and federalist. As often as not, they conducted their discussion on the battlefield; 19th-century Colombia witnessed eight national civil wars, 14 regional civil wars and countless local disputes between the two parties.

Although many countries had universal male suffrage by the mid-19th century, the elite proved adept at preventing this from posing a threat to their rule. Using everything from ballot-box stuffing to free beer they managed to stifle political alternatives to elite rule. In the Andean countries the white elite, ever-fearful of indigenous rebellion, made sure the vote went only to the literate, thereby excluding the indigenous majority from a say in government (in Peru, illiterates did not get the vote until 1979). Since voting appeared unlikely to change anything, electoral turnout across Latin America actually fell as the 19th century wore on. In Mexico and Argentina, despite universal male suffrage, only about 5 per cent of the adult male population bothered to vote. The landowners were quite happy to keep it that way.

Bringing out the vote became the speciality of a quintessential Latin American figure, the cacique. Originally the name for an indigenous chief, the term came to mean a rural boss, an authoritative figure in traditional rural society who proved adept at drumming up support for his patrón's chosen party.

Let Them Eat Meat: Vote-buying in Colombia

'The problem was how to find something to eat. We were talking this over when Oscar arrived with the news that over at Don Tiberio's they were giving out roast suckling pig because there were elections on Sunday. We rushed over, and it was true. They were handing out meat and beer on a piece of land at the edge of the village decorated with photos of the candidates and Conservative Party flags. Everyone was very friendly. Most of the people there were relatives, plus a few drunks and others filling their bellies as if they'd never eaten before. We tucked in and promised to vote for the Conservatives.

Half drunk, we were wandering off when someone told us that, on the other side of the village, the Liberals were giving out *aguardiente* (cane liquor), so off we went. There was a great party going on, red flags, rockets and booze coming out of our ears! So once again we promised our vote, this time to the great Liberal Party.

The comrades of the Patriotic Union also had their stall to hunt votes, but all they gave people were soft drinks and lots of speeches. We left with our heads full of ideology, ready to vote for the new party.

We ate twice in each political café and in the end we each voted for whoever we liked. Everyone thought we had voted for their party.'

Alfredo Molano, *Aguas Arriba*, Bogotá: El Áncora Editores, 1990 (author's translation)

As long as Latin America remained a largely rural society, the caciques and other 'alchemists' (as vote-riggers are known in Mexico) could ensure that politics stayed in the hands of the elite. But economic growth precipitated the destruction of the cosy, if exclusive, 19th-century political arrangement. Convinced by their own racism and the need for skilled labour that European blood was needed if their countries were to develop, governments in countries such as Argentina, Brazil and Chile encouraged mass immigration, predominantly from southern Europe. With the immigrants came new and radical political influences, such as the anarchist trade unionists from Italy who founded the Argentine labour movement.

After decades of authoritarian rule, the Mexican elite moved to implement a limited liberal democracy in 1910 and in so doing unleashed a momentous revolution. Seven years before the Bolshevik uprising in Russia, Mexicans overthrew their own dictator, though, without an overall leader or fundamental ideology, the rebels soon lost their way. The dictator Díaz had been ousted by a coalition of wealthy liberals and disgruntled peasants, but once in power, the alliance broke down. The peasants, inspired by Emiliano Zapata, occupied lands belonging to local ranchers, only to face renewed constraints imposed by the new government. It was not until the nationwide land reform of the 1930s that the conflict between peasants and landowners began to abate.

Immigration, urbanisation and growth produced an urban working class that proved both more articulate and far harder to control than the peasantry. Society was becoming more complex. The abyss separating the holders of political power from these new social forces grew ever wider. Something had to give, and in the end, as with independence, it took an event thousands of miles away to provide the catalyst for change. The Wall Street crash of 1929 and ensuing depression in the industrialised nations proved a major turning-point in Latin American history.

The Great Depression of the 1930s destroyed the world market for Latin America's commodity exports, bringing to an end the era of unquestioned dominance by the agro-exporting elite. The initial effect was a rash of military takeovers and a change in economic direction towards building up industry. In the longer run, the new drive to industrialise created growing working and middle classes, laying the basis for a new kind of politics – populism. A new generation of political leaders came to the fore, bringing together workers and industrialists in an alliance that tried to bridge class barriers, often in opposition to the old guard of conservative landowners. Politics left the hacienda forever, to find its new home in the bustling world of the city and the slum.

The Rise and Fall of Populism

Populism was both popular and authoritarian. In the 1930s many of its leaders were military or ex-military men who drew inspiration from Hitler's or Mussolini's rise to power. It was also fiercely nationalistic, condemning Latin America's traditional dependence on outside powers and often nationalising key foreign-owned industries, such as Mexican oil (1938) or the hugely popular purchase of the Argentine railways from Britain (1948). By bringing together both industrialists and workers in the same alliance, it was bound in the end to generate internal conflicts, although initially these were masked by the personal charisma of its leaders.

The great populists included Mexico's Lázaro Cárdenas, Getúlio Vargas in Brazil and Carlos Ibáñez in Chile, but the greatest of them all was Juan Domingo Perón, Argentina's beloved father-figure. Perón was elected in 1946, and Peronism has dominated Argentine politics ever since, despite Perón's death in 1974. Together with his wife Eva ('Evita'), he forged a personality cult, portraying himself as the heroic defender of the nation's *descamisados* (shirtless ones), a man of the people who oversaw the growth of industry, redistribution of income, and the development of a welfare state. Evita's star quality allowed Perón to woo another new political constituency – women, who won the right to vote in 1947.

Thirty years after his death, saint-like portraits of Juan and Evita adorn walls in the shantytowns of Buenos Aires. In one of them, Ciudad Oculta, where cooking smells mix with the tang of eucalyptus leaves trampled with the rubbish into the muddy street, a mural of blonde beautiful Evita looks out at the dark-skinned Paraguayan immigrant families. As one hard-bitten local activist, Juan Cymes, recalls: 'Evita was a goddess for me when I was a kid. I wrote to ask her to help some poor neighbours and she wrote back to me within a week!' Bearing the slogan 'Social Justice will be achieved inexorably, whatever the cost, whoever falls', the freshly painted mural looks like publicity for this year's presidential candidate. Evita died of cancer in 1952, but her cult lived on. When the pop star Madonna went to Buenos Aires in 1996 to film the musical of Evita's life, outraged Argentines plastered the walls of the city with graffiti saying 'long live Evita, Madonna go home!'.

Perón expounded the doctrine of *justicialismo* (social justice), which he saw as a third way between capitalism and communism in a world gripped by the deepening Cold War. The state replaced the caudillo as the all-powerful provider; it mediated in any dispute between different sectors of society, cared for the sick and elderly, and took a commanding role in the economy via a burgeoning network of state-run industries. Perón's support rested on a highly organised and devoutly Peronist trade union movement, which became virtually an arm of government.

In 1955 Perón's conflicts with the military and the Church led to his overthrow and exile in Madrid. He returned only for a brief and chaotic period as president in 1973–74. Nonetheless, despite his exile and death, and years of military prohibition and persecution, Peronism continues to dominate Argentine politics.

Populism was more prominent in the larger countries, where industrialisation could take root. In the smaller, weaker economies of Central America and the Caribbean, a cruder solution emerged to the problems of economic collapse. In Nicaragua, El Salvador, Cuba and the Dominican Republic, military dictators took over in the 1930s. Men such as General Maximiliano Hernández in El Salvador or Nicaragua's Anastasio Somoza were willing to go to extreme lengths to stamp out unrest. After massacring 30,000 rebellious peasants in the *matanza* (massacre) of 1932, virtually wiping out El Salvador's indigenous population, General Hernández explained in a radio broadcast, 'It is a greater crime to kill an ant than a man, because a man who dies is reincarnated, while an ant dies forever'. The Central American and Caribbean dictators remained in power for decades, stifling political modernisation and sowing the seeds for future upheaval, including revolutions in Cuba (1959) and Nicaragua (1979) and a bloody guerrilla war in El Salvador in the 1980s. In the Dominican Republic, a US military intervention in 1965 helped prevent upheaval, installing another quintessential caudillo, Joaquín Balaguer, who proceeded to dominate the country's politics well into the 1990s.

Populist governments saw the state as the means to achieve development, by kick-starting the industrialisation of the economy. From the 1930s onwards, governments created hundreds of semi-independent agencies covering everything from state steel or oil companies to agencies for agrarian reform or water supply. The state came to dominate the economy, employing a large part of the middle class and owning much of industry.

In the larger countries, notably Brazil, Argentina and Mexico, populism went hand in hand with corporatism – ruling parties set up and then controlled labour unions and other mass organisations, such as those of peasants and state employees. In return for the government improving wages and working conditions, these organisations had to sacrifice any pretence of independence. The unequal dialogue between state and mass organisation played the main role in controlling and channelling the demands of the new social groups, and legitimising the government in the eyes of the public. Elections were often marred by fraud or the huge inequality between the state/party machine and any opposition. Mass organisations worked to turn out the vote for the ruling party. Any individual or organisation that rebelled against this system could expect to be excluded from the state's bounty, to be hounded by the legal system, and was likely to face physical intimidation.

The strategy worked at first, as state intervention propelled economies into industrial growth. Booming economies and taxes on exports allowed governments to keep everybody happy, and when those were insufficient, governments overspent to buy off opposition at the expense of inflation.

With the exception of Argentina and Mexico, populism's star rose and fell with that of its economic brainchild, import substitution. After notching up huge successes after the Second World War, import substitution started to run out of steam. By the 1960s, Latin American economies were slipping into crisis, and the improbable alliance of industrialist and worker came apart in spectacular fashion. Moreover, economic growth and the rise of the middle class had further increased the number of social groups clamouring for a voice in running the country. When radical elements, such as the student movement, were inspired by the Cuban revolution of 1959 to seek power through armed struggle, the generals decided that enough was enough. Military coups in Brazil (1964) and Argentina (1966) brought to power governments supported by a business sector determined to stamp out political opposition, crush the unions, reduce wages and give state-led development a new lease of life. They achieved it in Brazil, which underwent an 'economic miracle' in the form of a period of record growth from 1968 to 1975.

The switch from civilian (if authoritarian) rule to military dictatorship was also helped by the international climate. After the Cuban revolution, the US and the Latin American military were determined to prevent revolution from spreading, and Washington was happy to support almost any military government that promised to crack down on leftism. There was also widespread support for military rule within Latin America, especially from the middle classes. Latin America's interwoven traditions of authoritarianism and democracy mean that many people do not see elections as the only legitimate route to power, and may well support a military government if they think it can impose order or improve their economic situation.

In Mexico, the exceptionally adroit and chameleon-like Institutionalised Revolutionary Party (PRI) bucked the regional trend to cling, limpet-like, to power for an astonishing 71 years. It did so through a process of endless transformation, moving from being the party of the Mexican Revolution to midwife of the North American Free Trade Agreement with the US and Canada. When all else failed, the PRI was also adept at electoral fraud, sending out teams of ballot-box stuffers known as 'alchemists', and coopting promising opposition leaders. In 2000, however, it finally succumbed to political mortality, losing power to the PAN, a right-wing pro-business party led by the ineffectual former Coca Cola executive, Vicente Fox.

When the military fell in Argentina, the Peronists returned from the political wilderness in a baffling range of guises, turning themselves first into a free-market party under Carlos Menem, and then back into a statist party under Néstor Kirchner, following the catastrophic economic crisis in 2001.

Men at Arms: The Generals

General Albano Harguindeguy sat on the sofa in his Buenos Aires flat. Now a retired Latin American patriarch, his genial back-slapping style must once have made him popular with his men. Over a glass of whisky he reflected on his period in office as Argentina's Minister of the Interior, priding himself on his grasp of world events. While his wife served pizza, he mused over what he would have done differently if he had the chance to be in government all over again. 'Not so many disappeared people – we should have used the law instead', he concluded.

The bluff general in his cardigan and slippers was in charge of internal security during the worst years of the military junta that seized power in 1976. During the 'dirty war', Harguindeguy's men took thousands of young men and women from their homes, often at night, and drove them away in the sinister unmarked Ford Falcons favoured by the security forces. Their relatives and friends never heard from them again, amidst rumours of torture cells, concentration camps and mass graves. After the military regime fell, the rumours proved to be true. The official number of documented disappearances is just under 12,000, but the real number could be twice as many.

Argentina's dark hours of fear and doubt have been repeated up and down Latin America. Aída de Suárez remembers how her son disappeared:

On 2 December 1977 at four o'clock in the morning, twenty armed men broke into our house with rifles and pistols pointed at us. They were nervous. They opened and closed the cupboards, the fridge. They were looking for things, guns apparently. They took everything of any value they could carry, the few things of value that a working-class family has in their home, sentimental things. But that wasn't important to me. They could have taken everything, but my son, no. He was sitting on the bed, trying to get dressed. One man shouted, 'There's one in here!' and then two huge men with guns in their hands told me not to move. They asked only if he was Hugo Héctor Suárez and that he had to go with them.

'Who are you?' I screamed. 'We are the security forces.' They were in civilian suits but underneath they were wearing army fatigues and boots, and green bullet-proof vests, the colour of the army. So it was the army. I said, 'Why? My son has done nothing, he's not a criminal. Why have you come in like this, frightening the children with guns pointed at everyone?' – twenty armed men for a child of 21, an old woman like me, and two young children. 'We've come to take him away for questioning.' 'Why?' I asked and they pushed me and threw me against the wall. They took my son. That was the last time I saw him.

JO FISHER, *Mothers of the Disappeared*, London: Zed Books, 1987

By the end of 1976 two-thirds of people on the Latin American mainland lived under dictatorial rule. Among the major countries, only Mexico, Venezuela, Colombia and Costa Rica had no general in the presidential palace. Pinochet, Stroessner, Videla: the continent became synonymous with vicious military dictators in sunglasses and the midnight knock on the door. As the 1980s passed, the generals began to return to the barracks, some in defeat and humiliation, others managing to retain a significant voice in politics. In March 1990, Chile's General Augusto Pinochet became the last of the great Latin American dictators to leave power when he reluctantly handed over the presidency to the elected Christian Democrat leader Patricio Aylwin. In many Latin American countries the military retained considerable influence, and during the 1990s, military rumblings occurred in Haiti, Paraguay, Venezuela, Brazil and Chile, among others, but by early 2005, the 'failed state' of Haiti and Fidel Castro's Cuban regime remained the last unelected governments in the western hemisphere. The 'old' military found itself with few remaining friends, prey to budget cuts, public contempt and a profound identity crisis over its role in the post-Cold War world. Furthermore, a rash of prosecutions and overturned amnesties meant that justice could finally be pursued, Generals Pinochet and Harguindeguy found themselves under arrest (albeit the comfortable 'house arrest' variety) and facing prosecution for their parts in the murder of thousands of political opponents.

Military History

Unlike the UK or US, where civilian political control over the armed forces has long been taken for granted, the military in Latin America has always been an independent political force. The nature of the Spanish conquest, led by soldiers who defeated the Aztec and Inca empires and were rewarded with land, slaves and booty, was in marked contrast to the methods and lifestyle of the civilian settlers who emigrated to start a new life in the US and Canada. When Spanish power collapsed, Latin America won its independence through the exploits of military heroes like Simón Bolívar (1783–1830) and José de San Martín (1778–1852). Today, the streets of every Latin American capital are littered with statues of heroic military figures on horseback, swords raised, and schoolchildren diligently learn the names of the military fathers of the nation.

Between 1808 and 1826, independence wars raged throughout Spanish

America. Armed uprisings turned into liberation armies which marched across the continent in two great arcs: in the south, General José San Martín's Army of the Andes crossed the pampas from Buenos Aires, marched over the Andes into Chile and then moved up towards Peru. In the north, Simón Bolívar's followers marched from Venezuela into Colombia and down to liberate Ecuador. The two armies converged on Peru, where they decisively defeated the remaining Spanish forces at the Battle of Ayacucho in 1824. In Mexico, violent social rebellion followed a course of its own. By 1826 Spain had lost everything except Cuba and Puerto Rico. Brazil declared its independence from Portugal in 1822, but in contrast to the republics of Spanish America, the new nation emerged with little violence, ruled by members of the Portuguese royal family.

The independence armies were led by the small *criollo* class fighting to seize power from Spain, but otherwise intent on maintaining Latin America's social structures largely unchanged. 'Liberation' brought few benefits for the indigenous population. Black slaves were, however, promised their freedom in exchange for fighting, and formed much of San Martín's Army of the Andes. Indigenous people were press-ganged to fight by both sides. White leaders, whether royalist or republican, feared revolt by the blacks and indigenous people more than they feared each other – when the Spanish viceroy decided to abandon Lima in 1821, the terrified and hitherto royalist citizens asked San Martín for protection against a feared black uprising.

In the first decades after independence, the military often consisted of little more than armed members of the peasantry. Then, from the mid-19th century onwards, a process of professionalisation took place, transforming the military from an irregular army in the hands of local chieftains into a sophisticated institution, while never erasing its taste for occupying the presidential palace.

Professionalisation has involved building a national army with a proper career structure and a separate value system, encouraging its self-image as a caste apart from, and often superior to, the rest of society. Military schools and staff colleges were set up to forge young boys into tomorrow's generals. The schools take boys in their early teens and impose military discipline and values. A high percentage of the intake are sons of officers, which only increases the sense of separation from society. Once the boy has entered the military structure, he will often stay isolated from civilian society until he is a high-ranking officer – his life will revolve around the school and the barracks.

The isolation of the [Argentine] armed forces intensified over the course of the 20th century. Beginning in the 1920s, special neighbourhoods and clubs were constructed for officers and their families. These new institutions included free country clubs or '*círculos*' used for recreation, business functions and weddings of officers and their children. Paid for out of the military budget, these clubs – like the special apartment complexes erected near major military installations – accentuated the officers' ignorance of civilian values and aspirations. Usually only those with the rank of colonel or above could acquire their own apartments in civilian neighbourhoods. The virtual apartheid separating officers from both enlisted soldiers and civilians was epitomised in the rules governing elevators in military buildings: one set of lifts used by officers and another for civilians and lower-ranking soldiers.

EMILIO MIGNONE, *'The Military: What is to be Done?'*, NACLA Report on the Americas, July 1987

In the absence of combat experience, most Latin American armies place enormous importance on educational qualifications as the path to promotion. The standard of education in military schools is often higher than in civilian life, reinforcing the officers' sense of innate superiority.

But education has not prevented graft. In Paraguay General Stroessner kept his officers happy by cutting them in on the smuggling trade with Brazil; in Panama General Noriega bought his men's loyalty and silence by involving them in everything from protection rackets to prostitution; in El Salvador local commanders left soldiers killed in action on the battalion's books and pocketed their wages. As one army leader in the Mexican revolution of 1910 commented, 'there is no general who can withstand a bombardment of 50,000 pesos'.

From the early days of import substitution, some of the region's most developed armies began to assemble a military–industrial complex which gave them enormous economic muscle. In Brazil and Argentina, military conglomerates came to control everything from arms manufacture to petrochemicals. Brazil came to rival Israel as the Third World's foremost arms exporter, exporting weaponry worth US$1 billion a year during the 1980s. In Chile, the Pinochet regime sang the virtues of privatisation, except when it came to the lucrative state copper company, which is still obliged to give 10 per cent of its income directly to the armed forces. The military's growing economic power further strengthened its political autonomy from central government.

The social gulf between officers and men in Latin America's armies is exacerbated by the widespread use of conscription. Many of the young men who shivered in the Argentine trenches during the Falklands/Malvinas war of 1982 were conscripts with little interest in fighting. Non-commissioned officers, or young officers who have not yet acquired the privileges that go with senior rank, are traditionally a source of unrest within the military, often leading uprisings against the military hierarchy.

The Spectre of Communism

Following the Second World War, Latin America's military forces increasingly adopted a Cold War ideology. This world view was refined at the military staff colleges, where high-flying young officers were prepared for the high command. In Brazil, the military set up the Higher War School (*Escola Superior de Guerra*, ESG) in 1949, where young officers studied not only military tactics, but also politics, economics and sociology. From the outset, the ESG also recruited among the civilian elite – business leaders, top civil servants, politicians and judges, who by 1966 comprised half the graduates. The ESG thus served both to train the future military top brass and to establish firm links between them and Brazil's civilian rulers.

The ESG was instrumental in developing what became known as national security doctrine, an all-embracing viewpoint which saw the military as the guardians of order in the broadest sense, including economic development and the prevention of internal political or social division. The enemy of the continent's social order was the spectre of international communism, which was supposedly conducting a stealthy war of internal subversion against pro-western governments throughout Latin America.

National security doctrine became established as the linchpin of military thinking following the Cuban revolution of 1959, which the generals saw as proof of the international communist conspiracy. The doctrine provided the intellectual justification for the military to make the defeat of 'internal subversion' its top priority. Subversion was defined as anything that threatened the status quo – trade unionism, peasant movements, socialist politics, or student protest. Since this was a 'Third World War' against the communist menace, human rights considerations and the rule of law became redundant, clearing the way for the atrocities, disappearances and bloodshed that followed.

Some of the wilder excesses of national security doctrine had a tragicomic air: in the late 1970s the Argentine junta reportedly burnt books on Cubism under the mistaken belief that they expounded the philosophy of Fidel Castro. Junta members were much given to describing themselves as the defenders of western Christian democracy, despite their aversion to elections. The Argentine military's perception of what constituted a threat to western Christendom has always been broad; in the 1960s General Onganía defended the sanctity of the family by outlawing miniskirts.

Until the Second World War, US influence was greatest in its traditional backyard of Central America and the Caribbean. In the early years of the 20th century, Washington regularly sent in the marines to overthrow governments, before setting up client armies such as General Somoza's National Guard in Nicaragua, enabling US forces to retreat to bases in the Panama Canal zone. Further south, in Brazil, Chile and Argentina, the

German army had considerable influence in the early professionalisation of regular armies.

The Second World War destroyed Germany as a regional influence and established the US as the supreme foreign power throughout Latin America. US military missions spread across Latin America to supply and train the region's armies, ensuring in the process that future military leaderships would be firmly pro-US. As the Cold War gathered pace, US influence was crucial in forging national security doctrine.

In addition to sending military missions to the various countries, the US trained thousands of Latin American officers and future military leaders, either in the US or at the School of the Americas in the Panama Canal zone – earning it the name 'School of the Dictators'. Pupils included Major Roberto d'Aubuisson, godfather of El Salvador's death squads, and the Panamanian dictator General Manuel Antonio Noriega. In 1996, the Pentagon provoked a scandal when it declassified documents showing that Spanish-language training manuals used at the school in the 1980s recommended to its Latin American trainees using threats, bribery, blackmail and the torture of guerrillas.

As a result of President Carter's short-lived human rights policy in the late 1970s, brutal military regimes in Latin America found their arms supplies from Washington reduced or cut off. Their response was to look elsewhere for suppliers and develop their own armaments industries. This undermined US supremacy in the region, as arms suppliers from the UK, France, Italy, Germany, the Soviet Union and Israel broke into the market.

In 1981 President Reagan took office, determined to end Carter's human rights policy, which he blamed for the US 'losing' Nicaragua as a client state through the 1979 revolution. One of the key right-wing thinktanks behind Reagan's new policy, the Council for Inter-American Security, painted a lurid, and farcically incorrect, picture of the challenge facing the US in Latin America: 'World War III is almost over. The Soviet Union, operating under the cover of increasing nuclear superiority, is strangling the Western industrialised nations.... America is everywhere in retreat. The Caribbean, America's maritime crossroad and petroleum refining centre, is becoming a Marxist-Leninist lake.'

President Reagan chose to 'draw the line against communism' in Central America and the Caribbean. US marines invaded Grenada in 1983 and overthrew its left-wing government, while in Nicaragua and El Salvador US strategists refined Vietnam-style counter-guerrilla tactics into a more general technique known as 'low intensity conflict'. This attempted to defeat the guerrilla movement in El Salvador and the Sandinista government in Nicaragua through the use of proxy armies in order to avoid the use of US troops, which might lead to an anti-war backlash at home. In El Salvador the army was encouraged to 'win hearts and minds' among the peasantry, but at the same time had the conflicting objective of striking at anyone considered sympathetic to the guerrillas. In the end repression took precedence over reform. In Nicaragua the Contras played a significant part in the downfall of the left-wing Sandinista government by sabotaging the economy and forcing the government to divert scarce resources into defence.

Despite pouring US$6 billion in aid into El Salvador, the war ended in stalemate and a 1992 peace agreement which effectively removed the military from politics and made way for the guerrillas to re-enter civilian politics. In Nicaragua, Washington's war of attrition undermined public support for the Sandinistas, who were voted from office in 1990.

Relief at the end of the fighting was tempered by the problem of what to do with the newly unemployed soldiers from both sides. In El Salvador the UN accused the army of having links to armed robbery and murder; in Guatemala the military is widely believed to be involved in crime rings which steal cars and run the drug trade; in Nicaragua, banditry became endemic in the countryside. More generally, the militarisation of the 1980s left the legacy of a more violent society, littered with left-over guns. As one former member of an elite Salvadoran anti-guerrilla battalion commented in an unguarded moment ,'I need to kill'. Having been fired from the army, and tormented by nightmares from his years behind guerrilla lines, the man was about to cross the US–Mexican border on his way to join a gang in Los Angeles – one small example of the violence sown by US anti-guerrilla tactics coming back to haunt it.

General Unrest

The quintessentially Latin American phenomenon of the military coup and military government long preceded the invention of national security doctrine, stretching back to the Spanish and Portuguese roots of the region's political systems. Prior to the Second World War, military interventions usually aimed to return power to the military's civilian allies, or took place in response to threats against the military as an institution, such as government attempts to interfere in the promotion system or cut the military budget. However, with national security doctrine came not only the notion that government was a legitimate role for the military, but that squabbling civilian politicians were often less fit to govern than well-educated military men with only their country's interests at heart. When the Brazilian military took power in 1964, even the US ambassador expected it to hand over power to a suitable civilian government within the year. Instead it ruled for two decades.

In most cases, military coups took place with the support of at least a section of the civilian political elite. In Chile Christian Democrat leader Patricio Aylwin openly supported the coup that brought General Pinochet to power in 1973, presumably hoping that once his socialist rival, President

Salvador Allende, was removed, the army would then hand power to Aylwin's party before retiring to the barracks. Instead Pinochet kept power for himself and remained in the presidential palace for the next 17 years, until a chastened Aylwin led the campaign that secured his departure.

The military's willingness to interfere, and civilian leaders' readiness to encourage it, destabilised democratic civilian politics by offering politicians a short cut to power, which seemed more seductive than the prospect of long years in opposition. Parties no longer needed to succeed by developing sound policies to win more support than their rivals, but could gain power by currying favour with the high command. The art of conspiracy became the successful politician's chief weapon.

The generals who seized power declared themselves to be 'above politics', disparaging all civilian politicians as corrupt incompetents. Instead, they saw the problems facing the continent as essentially technical, and cast themselves as 'iron surgeons', who would carry out profound re-structuring operations for which few anaesthetics were available. In the larger countries, the military ruled as an institution, seeking to avoid the temptations of caudillismo in Argentina by governing by committee – the junta – or in Brazil by rotating the presidency among the top generals.

The military's low opinion of politics did not include the state itself. It saw an efficient, well-managed state as essential to the achievement of

---

A Rich Man's Coup

'The evening of that mild spring day, Tuesday 11 September, General Augusto Pinochet had been in power for a few hours. The guests were assembled in the main hall of the Hotel Carrera, a sumptuous room three storeys high....The new regime had decreed a curfew. The doors were barred.

People sat around on the sofas or at the little copper-topped tables. They talked animatedly, the suave men and the elegant ladies. They laughed and joked and drank noisily, the sound of their celebration bouncing and echoing off the shiny walls. Every so often there was an expectant hush when the television came up with a *bando*, some new message from the new masters of Chile. When it was ended there were cheers, more champagne corks popped and from ladies' slippers toasts were drunk to Pinochet and his brave companions.

In the corner the service door opened from time to time and groups of waiters peered timidly out. The juxtaposition of the stylish carousers and the apprehensive serving staff was dramatic and served like nothing else to bring home the social impact of the putsch above and beyond the patriotic and martial music that the radio and the television were broadcasting. The waiters and the rest of those below stairs knew what military rule was going to bring and they were afraid.

Hugh O'Shaughnessy, *Latin Americans*, London: BBC Books, 1988

national security and development, and if anything, increased the state's intrusion into every nook and cranny of society: in Argentina even the head of the national ballet was a military officer. Boosting state arms industries also proved popular with the generals. Only in Chile under General Pinochet, and to a lesser extent in Argentina after the coup in 1976, did military governments abandon state-led development in favour of a ferocious pursuit of the market. In the name of free trade and boosting competitiveness, both governments suddenly removed any protection from local industries, with the inevitable result that cheap imports flooded in, undercutting and bankrupting much of the industrial base so painstakingly assembled over the previous 40 years.

The military's belief in its economic prowess proved seriously mistaken. Military governments showed themselves to be, if anything, even less competent than their predecessors, running up vast national debts during the free-spending 1970s, squandering resources on prestige megaprojects such as dams and nuclear power programmes and neglecting the nuts and bolts of long-term economic success, such as health and education.

In the longer run, the military's attempt to stamp out politics backfired. Banning political parties in countries such as Argentina, Chile and Uruguay created a political vacuum into which a new generation of grassroots movements grew, led by human rights and neighbourhood organisations. These were the first groups to fight back against military rule, becoming the catalyst for a broader opposition which brought about the military's eventual downfall. The new movements brought new sections of the population into politics, such as women and slum dwellers, creating a richer, more plural spectrum of social organisations that augured well for the future.

Military rule was at its starkest in the southern cone countries of Argentina, Chile and Uruguay, along with Brazil. The development of the state elsewhere was more varied. In Venezuela and Mexico, the proceeds from oil exports helped governments to soften the impact of the crisis of state-led industrialisation, preventing the kind of political crisis which could have precipitated a military coup. Colombia pursued a more cautious role for the state, running up fewer debts and avoiding the worst of the collapse that afflicted the others. Paraguay looked more like Central America, as it languished under the rule of General Stroessner for 35 years from 1954. In Peru and Bolivia the recalcitrance of the landed elite blocked political change, eventually precipitating a revolution in Bolivia in 1952, and a modernising military take-over in Peru in 1968, when General Juan Velasco seized power, promising sweeping reforms. Within months his government nationalised the property of the US transnational, International Petroleum Company, and began a radical land reform. These two measures marked the high point of military radicalism in Peru. Soon the government became engulfed in economic crisis and internal divisions, and just before Velasco's death in 1975, a conservative faction within the military seized power. Velasco's reforms, however, left a radically altered rural society, where the feudal powers of the hacienda owners had in many cases been destroyed for ever.

In 1992, a section of the Venezuelan military demonstrated a similar strand of left-wing nationalism when Lt Col Hugo Chávez led a military revolt by the Revolutionary Bolivarian Movement. The uprising was swiftly crushed, leaving 70 dead, but not before Chávez's opposition to the government's economic austerity programme had turned him into a folk hero, a status that later propelled him to the presidency.

Yet most military regimes have been firmly on the right, following the example of Brazil, whose generals, when they seized power in 1964, attempted to revitalise the economy as import substitution was running out of steam. By cutting real wages (by 35–40 per cent in the first four years of the government), opening the economy to foreign investors and transnational companies, and investing massively in state companies and economic infrastructure, they succeeded in temporarily galvanising the Brazilian economy, before the debt crisis of the 1980s forced the military's long and orderly withdrawal from politics. Direct elections for a civilian president finally took place in 1989.

Costa Rica has succeeded in ridding itself of its military altogether. After a brief civil war in 1948, Costa Rica's rival political parties agreed to abolish the army. Free of the military burden, Costa Rica now has a much higher standard of living than its Central American neighbours. In Bolivia the revolution of 1952 also radically weakened the army, but within four years the government had agreed to re-establish the armed forces as a condition for a vital US$25 million loan from the International Monetary Fund.

By the end of the 1990s, the international political climate had changed following the end of the Cold War. The US government concluded that military governments were both politically destabilising and economically less competent than civilian ones. Washington showed its new resolve by pressurising the Salvadoran and Guatemalan militaries to accept deep cuts as part of the peace agreements that ended the civil wars in those countries. The US also effectively abolished the armies of Panama and Haiti following its military occupations of those countries in 1989 and 1994. Military leaders found themselves subject to prosecution, and throughout the 1990s the public mood moved steadily against the idea of military power and embraced such concepts as human rights and democracy.

Transitions to Democracy

Just as the nature of military regimes varied enormously between different Latin American countries, so did the way they handed over power to elected governments. In many cases, the outgoing military government tried to cover its retreat by passing legislation giving its officers immunity from prosecution over human rights violations. Success in achieving immunity depended on the degree of military unity during withdrawal to barracks and the pressure exerted by the civilian opposition. The regimes in Brazil and Uruguay both managed an orderly exit, not only acquiring immunity for crimes committed in government, but retaining considerable political power. However, the accession of left-wing governments in both countries at the turn of the century threatened the future immunity of the retired generals. Elsewhere, investigation and prosecution for past atrocities remains one of the main areas of civilian–military conflict everywhere from Chile to Honduras.

The Argentine military's humiliation in the Falklands/Malvinas war forced it into a shame-faced flight from power, giving the incoming Alfonsín government the chance to waive immunity; in 1985 five military leaders, including President Videla, were found guilty and given long prison sentences. Alfonsín thus achieved a Latin American first – never before had officers of a defeated military dictatorship been brought to trial. The trials were followed by a new law confining military activities solely to defending the nation's frontiers. Nationalist officers responded with a wave of military uprisings between 1987 and 1990, which ended only when incoming president Carlos Menem amnestied the 300 jailed officers, and found new roles for the military in UN peacekeeping forces and 'civic action' programmes of public improvements. The 2003 election of Néstor Kirchner, a Peronist who had been jailed by the military junta in the 1970s, marked a significant change in Argentina, as he promised to push for justice for fellow victims.

The assault on military privilege has also been financial. Under pressure from Washington, the IMF and the World Bank to cut spending, governments have cut military budgets and privatised the military industries set up under import substitution. Across the region military spending per head of the population halved between 1985 and 1994, and has remained at a fairly constant 1.3 per cent of GDP since then.

Reviled by the public and former allies, confused over its role and facing falling wages, the military in many countries has entered a profound crisis of identity and morale. Where guerrilla insurgencies have continued to operate, in Colombia and Peru, joined in 1994 by Mexico following the Zapatista uprising, the military role has been clear, if bloody. Elsewhere, less introspective officers have turned to crime, creating a military mafia involved in drugs, car theft rings, and kidnapping. Many of the army's more talented members have left. The small number of military thinkers that remains has struggled to define a new role that can restore the military's legitimacy with the general public and provide a renewed sense of purpose as an institution.

There have been many suggestions. Some governments have opted for civic action programmes to restore the army's reputation, covering everything from traditional road-building to environmental campaigns such as cleaning up piles of rotting garbage in Lima, or soaping down oil-soaked penguins in Argentine Patagonia.

In Venezuela, military engineers have been employed in a civic role, while the line between policeman and soldier has been significantly blurred. Washington has prodded insistently for the military to take a higher profile in the fight against the narcotics trade but the military leadership fears that entering the 'war on drugs' opens the door to corruption, as soldiers on ever-lower wages are tempted by the vast sums at the drug traffickers' disposal. Drug-related corruption is already on the increase in several Central American armies, while two former military leaders, Bolivia's General García Meza, and Panama's General Manuel Antonio Noriega, are currently serving long prison sentences for drug trafficking.

The Left in Latin America

The Guerrillas

In the 1970s no western student bedsit seemed complete without its poster of Che Guevara, with beret and beard, gazing mistily off into the middle distance. Che personified the myth of the guerrilla fighter, caricatured by Peruvian novelist Mario Vargas Llosa in *The Real Life of Alejandro Mayta:*

> His beard had grown, he was thin, in his eyes there was an unconquerable resolve, and his fingers had grown calloused from squeezing the trigger, lighting fuses and throwing dynamite. Any sign of depression he might feel would disappear as soon as he saw how new militants joined every day, how the front widened, and how there, in the cities, the workers, servants, students and poor employees began understanding that the revolution was for them, belonged to them.

Che was heir to a long Latin American tradition. In 19th-century Argentina the cowboy Montoneros of the pampas fought an unsuccessful civil war to free the interior from the stranglehold of Buenos Aires. Elsewhere, irregulars helped to win independence from Spain. As the century wore on, such exotic bands passed into folklore as they were replaced by regular standing armies.

The guerrilla tradition was rediscovered in the 1920s by Augusto César Sandino, the Nicaraguan rebel whose distinctive ten-gallon hat became the symbol of revolutionary Nicaragua. When US marines occupied Sandino's homeland in 1912, Sandino, who as a young man had worked in the Mexican oilfields and been influenced by the anti-yankee and socialist ideas of the Mexican revolution, returned to Nicaragua. With a band of 29 fighters, he began to harass the US forces. When conventional tactics led to a series of defeats, reducing his company to just six, he developed a new style of fighting which became the blueprint for guerrilla warfare. According to Sandino, guerrillas should:

- avoid set-piece confrontations where the enemy's superior firepower will give it an advantage

- use hit-and-run tactics and surprise rather than defend fixed positions. The objective is not to seize and defend territory, but to make the costs of staying unacceptably high to the enemy

- stay in small groups to avoid detection and increase mobility

- rely on superior knowledge of the terrain and contacts with local people to outwit the enemy.

Sandino's movement gathered force, giving the Nicaraguan brief fame as a romantic hero at the head of 6,000 fighters. When the Guomintang marched into Beijing in 1928, they named a division after Sandino, and a thriving anti-war movement in the US sang his praises. For the first time, the US experienced the frustration of facing an enemy that wouldn't 'fight fair'. In the words of the writer and former Sandinista vice-president Sergio Ramírez: 'The well-trained and elegantly uniformed yankee soldiers could find only one phrase to describe it: "damned country". Rains, mosquitoes, swamps, swollen rivers, wild animals, the horror of suddenly falling into an ambush, fevers, an always invisible enemy.' The words could just as well describe the US nightmare in Vietnam, and the US forces in Sandino's Nicaragua reacted in much the same way, venting their anger on civilians they suspected of supporting the guerrillas and thereby swelling the numbers of Sandino's supporters.

In 1933 the US changed tactics, withdrawing from Nicaragua and setting up a National Guard which soon came under the control of Anastasio Somoza. Sandino's fight had always been primarily a nationalist one, so when the marines left he accepted partial disarmament and peace talks. In 1934, as Sandino and his generals were leaving a dinner in the presidential palace, they were ambushed and shot dead by Somoza's men.

The world forgot about Sandino, and the ensuing Somoza dictatorship did its utmost to wipe out his memory in Nicaragua, but his example inspired a group of radical students in the 1960s, who formed a new guerrilla band, the Sandinista National Liberation Front (FSLN), and took to the hills in Sandino's old strongholds. There they found many ageing Sandinistas willing to help them. One guerrilla leader, Omar Cabezas, recalls the time when a young Sandinista came for the first time to an old farmer's hut. 'See, I knew you'd come back', the campesino said with a grin, 'I've got something you left behind last time'. He then dug up an Enfield rifle from the time of the marines, buried for 50 years since the days when Sandino roamed the mountains.

Castro, Cuba and Che

While Sandino's memory smouldered in the Nicaraguan hills, it was the Cuban revolution of 1959 which marked the start of the modern guerrilla era. Cuba under the Batista dictatorship combined misery in the countryside and urban slums with a millionaire's playground of casinos and brothels for US tourists and organised crime. Cuba's guerrilla war began in 1956 when Fidel Castro and 81 men, including the young Argentine Che Guevara, squeezed on to a motor launch with the unlikely name of Granma and set off from Mexico to invade Cuba. The mission was a disaster; Castro's 26 July Movement had already been infiltrated by Batista's secret service, and the Cuban troops were waiting for them. Fewer than 20 survivors fled to the mountains of the Sierra Maestra to lick their wounds and begin a two-year guerrilla war. Batista's ferocity and intransigence fuelled peasant support for the guerrillas; in 1957 he attempted to forcibly relocate the rural population of the Sierra Maestra. By 1958 opposition political parties, landowners and businesses had joined in, while the guerrilla force had grown into a rebel army which was attacking the government forces on three separate fronts and was able to take and hold fixed positions. Castro mounted a nationwide offensive, during which Che Guevara's soldiers succeeded in splitting the country in two. Batista fled to the Dominican Republic in early 1959 and Fidel Castro swept into Havana.

Cuba had a huge impact on the thinking of the Latin American left, convincing it that revolution could be triggered in underdeveloped countries by *focos* (small nuclei) of guerrillas. Previously the Communist Party had dominated the debate, insisting that revolution could be achieved only when the 'objective conditions' were present. This entailed the creation of a 'bourgeois democracy' and the growth of an industrial proletariat which would then form the vanguard for a predominantly urban revolution.

There followed a wave of unsuccessful attempts to repeat the Cuban experience across Latin America. Many of the young men and women who took to the guerrillas' harsh life in the mountains did so because they had

Ernesto 'Che' Guevara

The 20th century's most famous guerrilla fighter was born Ernesto Guevara in Argentina in 1928 to middle-class parents, and qualified as a doctor in 1953. Guevara became a committed communist from the time of the 1954 CIA-instigated overthrow of the reforming Arbenz government in Guatemala. In that sense, he was much more radical than Fidel Castro, who embraced communism only when US hostility forced revolutionary Cuba into the arms of the Soviet Union.
Guevara, a tall asthmatic man, became a Cuban citizen a month after the revolution. Castro made him President of the National Bank and Minister of Industries. Always a hardliner, he argued that Cuba should seize the Soviet missiles when Krushchev agreed to withdraw them to end the 1962 missile crisis. In 1965 he left Havana on an eight-month tour of revolutionary movements around the world. Itching to return to the guerrilla struggle, he embarked in 1966 on the Bolivian episode which led to his death the following year.

Part of Guevara's legacy to Cuba has been insistence on the need for a 'new man', motivated not by profit but by moral commitment to the cause of progress and equality:

'The process is a conscious one. The individual perceives the impact of the new social power and perceives that he is not completely adequate to it. He tries to adjust.... He is educating himself. We can see the new man who begins to emerge in this period of the building of socialism.... The [new men] no longer march in complete solitude along lost roads towards far-off longings. They follow their vanguard, composed of the party, of the most advanced workers, of the advanced men who move along bound to the masses and in close communion with them.... The reward is the new society, where human beings will have different characteristics: the society of communist man.... He will thus achieve total awareness of his social being, which is equivalent to his full realisation as a human being, having broken the chains of alienation.'

Ernesto Che Guevara, *Man and Socialism in Cuba* (trans. Margarita Zimmerman), Havana: Book Institute, 1967

seen all peaceful means for bringing about change blocked by a combination of electoral fraud and physical repression. In El Salvador the military denied electoral victory to a reforming coalition of political parties in the 1972 and 1977 elections, thereby triggering a spiral of frustration and violence which was to plunge the country into a decade of horror during the 1980s.

The rise in the guerrilla movement was partly driven by another social change: the extraordinary expansion of higher education in Latin America after 1960. In Mexico and Brazil, the student population increased 15-fold by 1980. Universities became centres of political and cultural ferment. The growing gulf between the expectations raised by education and the economy's inability to meet them turned the universities into prime recruiting grounds for future guerrilla leaders.

Guerrilla war, especially *foquismo*, suited student idealism and impatience in its offer of a short-cut to power. A few young heroes with sufficient courage and political clarity could go up into the mountains and lead the people to inevitable victory, it was thought. For the region's angry and disenchanted middle-class youth, this was a far more exciting prospect than years of toil in the trade union and peasant movement.

Young radicals formed guerrilla groups in Brazil, Venezuela, the Dominican Republic, Colombia, Argentina, Peru, Bolivia, Guatemala and Nicaragua, all of which met with failure or were forced radically to rethink their tactics. A generation of young radicals, poets, students and peasant leaders lost their lives.

Guevara's own attempt to bring revolution to Bolivia in 1966 showed many of the fatal errors of *foquismo*. Choosing Bolivia because it was the poorest country in Latin America and 'ripe for revolution', Guevara set off with a team of 16 Cubans and headed for a remote south-eastern province to set up their foco. The obstacles proved insuperable; although the guerrillas managed to recruit a few Bolivians, the leadership was entirely Cuban. As none of them could speak Guaraní, the local indigenous language, local people viewed the outsiders with suspicion. Furthermore, the region they chose was more prosperous than surrounding regions, and was so cut off that it had almost no contact with the capital, La Paz, and therefore no one had suffered directly at the hands of central government.

With intensive counter-insurgency training from the US, the Bolivian army soon tracked down and defeated the isolated 'freedom fighters', and Guevara was shot. Following his death, foquismo came in for severe criticism, as new wars in Vietnam and later Nicaragua provided alternative models for guerrilla war.

The late 1960s and early 1970s saw a new phenomenon – urban guerrilla movements. In Argentina, the Montoneros named themselves after the horseback irregulars of the 19th century, while in Uruguay the Tupamaros took their name from Peru's 18th-century indigenous rebel leader Tupac Amaru II. Similar movements sprang up in Brazil and Colombia. These groups concentrated on spectacular actions, described as 'armed propaganda', intended to win publicity and popular support. Some kidnapped prominent politicians, ambassadors and businessmen. In Colombia the M-19 guerrilla group showed a keen sense of history by symbolically stealing the sword of independence hero Simón Bolívar. Such actions, however, won little lasting support and frequently led to severe repression at the hands of the military, who aimed far beyond the guerrillas to attack the whole popular movement. In Argentina, 90 per cent of the 5,000 Montoneros lost their lives. Such groups have been criticised for their lack of political direction and tendency to use methods little different from terrorism.

After the failure of the *foquistas* and the urban guerrilla movements, the

The face of the Zapatista uprising: Subcomandante Insurgente Marcos. *(Latinphoto)*

armed left continued to seek the elusive magic formula which would enable them to overthrow the state. Learning from the US defeat at the hands of a guerrilla army in Vietnam, organisations such as the Popular Liberation Forces (FPL) in El Salvador embarked upon a strategy of 'prolonged popular war', involving a patient long-term programme of political work with the peasantry. As a result, guerrilla organisations became less dominated by students, and instead evolved into genuine peasant armies.

Other experiences enriched guerrilla thinking; the Nicaraguan revolution of 1979 showed the need for unity between different ideological currents on the left and demonstrated how a combination of rural guerrilla warfare and urban insurrection could produce a quick victory. In Peru, the Sendero Luminoso (Shining Path) showed that an authoritarian and violent movement built around a god-like leader in Abimael Guzmán ('President Gonzalo') could win over the oppressed indigenous communities of the Andes with a combination of intimidation and the promise of unheard-of security. Following Guzmán's capture in 1992, Sendero went into decline as a serious threat to the government, though it has recently re-emerged as a player in the cocaine trade.

The left-wing guerrilla group in the region which continues to stimulate revolutionary fervour abroad is Mexico's Zapatista National Liberation Army (EZLN). The Zapatistas burst on to the scene in spectacular fashion on New Year's Day 1994, when 1,500–2,000 fighters simultaneously occupied four towns in the impoverished southern state of Chiapas. The action stands out as by far the largest inaugural operation by any guerrilla movement in Latin American history. Following the initial weeks of warfare, the Zapatistas holed up in their strongholds in the Lacandón jungle, conducting interminable and frustrating talks with the Mexican government and playing host to endless visits by the great and good of the European and US left, from Danièle Mitterrand to Oliver Stone.

The Zapatistas are governed by a council of representatives from the region's indigenous communities. Their main demands are for the defence of indigenous culture and peasant agriculture. The group seems largely confined to Chiapas, and most of their fighters are indigenous, many speaking little or no Spanish, but the Zapatistas' most prominent leader is a *mestizo*, the charismatic 'Subcomandante Marcos', a former philosophy professor whose witty and biting communiqués and press interviews have made him a household name and Robin Hood figure in Mexico.

The Zapatistas disavow the guerrilla organisations' traditional aim of seizing state power. Instead, the EZLN explain that they see themselves as only one part of a broad-based effort to make Mexico more democratic.

Despite the idealism and courage of generations of Latin American guerrillas, the only two outright victories they have to show for 40 years of fighting and bloodshed are Cuba and Nicaragua. In both instances, the brutality and intransigence of the previous regime had at least as much to do with eventual victory as the guerrillas themselves. In Nicaragua, the Sandinistas were toppled in 1990 with the aid of the Contras, themselves midway between a genuine guerrilla group and a band of hired thugs. Fidel Castro, on the other hand, has survived every challenge, from a 40-year economic embargo imposed by the US to a crippling recession following the collapse of the Soviet Union, from mass defections of sports teams to semi-comic but deadly serious CIA-sponsored assassination attempts. The real difficulty for Cuba will come with the inevitable succession of power. The Cuban government appears to be in some denial over this: when a journalist at a press conference asked a government official what would happen when Fidel died, he was politely corrected, '*if* Fidel dies'.

In Central America the guerrilla wars came to an end in the 1990s with negotiated peace agreements between government and guerrillas in El Salvador (1992) and Guatemala (1996). The Central American wars had been particularly bloody, as brutal counter-insurgency campaigns by the Guatemalan and Salvadoran armies accounted for 100,000 and 70,000 lives respectively, although such totals are only the roughest of estimates. The FMLN guerrillas' military strength in El Salvador enabled them to achieve greater concessions at the negotiating table, largely demilitarising the political system. Human rights abusers in the armed forces were purged (though not put on trial), the police were removed from army control, and the military establishment halved in size. Yet the unequal economic system which had prompted the guerrillas' uprising remained largely untouched, and when the FMLN took part in elections in 1994, they lost heavily (although subsequently won a number of local government elections, including in the capital, San Salvador). In Guatemala, the guerrillas were much weaker, and so extracted fewer concessions from the government in return for laying down their arms.

A number of factors account for this dismal record of guerrilla achievement:

• The state and army invariably possess an overwhelming advantage in firepower, troops and logistical support.

• It is difficult to reconcile military and political work, both of which are needed for eventual victory. Military success requires a small tightly disciplined group, able to keep mobile, preferably in secret, not defending fixed positions. Political support requires steady contact with the 'masses', staying put to build up a relationship, and being able to defend them against any ensuing attack by the army.

• The US has placed enormous importance on preventing first 'another Cuba' then 'another Nicaragua' in its hemisphere. Since Vietnam, the Pentagon has tried to develop effective counter-guerrilla strategies – 'low intensity conflict'. These have combined elements of reform ('winning hearts and minds') with anti-guerrilla military tactics. Counter-insurgency has often involved severe repression of civilians judged sympathetic to the guerrillas, and Washington's readiness to support human rights abusers in El Salvador and Nicaragua has lost it many friends in the region. The relatively successful EZLN has never been challenged by US troops, whose presence in Mexico would not be countenanced by even the most Washington-friendly government.

Nicaragua and Cuba show that military victory only heralds the start of a revolution's problems. Both governments managed to survive a US economic and political siege only by turning to the Soviet Union for oil and other supplies. Radical governments in Bolivia (1952–56) and Chile (1970–73), which did not have eastern bloc support, soon fell or caved in to a combination of pressure from the US and local economic and military elites. Since the collapse of the USSR, Soviet aid is no longer an option. Instead, any future revolutionary government in Latin America will have to assuage historic US hostility to radical regimes or find another sponsor in Europe or Asia. Neither option looks likely as long as Latin America remains firmly in the US sphere of influence, although the end of the Cold

War has seen slightly more tolerance in Washington. It would have been hard to imagine US troops during the Cold War invading a country to force a military government to restore the presidency to a radical priest, yet that is what they did with Jean-Bertrand Aristide in Haiti in 1994.

In Colombia, the Fuerzas Armadas Revolucionarias Colombianas (FARC) have been key players in the country's internal war, and control much national territory. Formed in the countryside, the FARC have never been very strong in the cities. They are very different from the media-savvy Zapatistas in Mexico, who have expertly publicised their case through a canny use of technology. FARC's doctrines, insofar as they exist, are vague. They pay respects to the revolutionary experiences of the Soviet Union, Cuba and Vietnam, but say that they are blazing their own trail.

From the time they were founded, the FARC sought to control territory, and in doing so to amass funds. In the 1990s drug money began to overtake kidnapping and extortion as a source of funding for the organisation. In recent years the FARC have lost much popular support due to widespread disapproval of their authoritarianism, human rights violations, kidnappings and extortion.

Social Movements

Recent decades have seen an upsurge of social movements in Latin America. Social movements are broad-based coalitions of the powerless who demand access to a political system that often excludes them. They had a key role to play under military dictatorships, for example when the white headscarves of Argentina's Madres del Plaza de Mayo – the mothers of the disappeared – became an icon for human rights around the world.

In recent years social movements have tended to form around struggles against neoliberalism and the governments that impose it. Contemporary social movements to make headlines in recent years are the coca-growers in Bolivia, the Indigenous People's Council (CONAIE) in Ecuador, and the largest social movement in the world, the Movimento Sem Terra, the landless rural workers of Brazil.

While often characterised as resistance movements, social movements do far more than resist: they push forward real social change, and work pro-actively to expand the range of rights that democracies in Latin America have hitherto often failed to provide for citizens. It is social movements, and not formal politics, that have often given Latin America its political dynamism – although some commentators would call it 'instability'. It is true that they have played a leading role in destabilising elected governments, most recently in Bolivia, Argentina, and Ecuador, ousting presidents and calling for constitutional reforms (for more on social movements see Section 4).

The Left in Power

Latin America's left has long had an ambivalent relationship to democracy. In the heyday of revolutionary socialism, left activists derided 'bourgeois' democratic structures, portraying them as little more than a confidence trick played by the elite, which did nothing to achieve real participation and empowerment for the region's poor majority. Since the failure of the guerrilla movements and the barbarities of military rule, however, many have changed their views and come to accept the virtues of elections. Activists who suffered repression and exile under military rule decided that formal democracy and the rule of law were not so bad after all, while the fall of the Berlin Wall and the collapse of state socialism in Eastern Europe convinced many doubters of the importance of accountability and democracy in ensuring that politicians remain in touch with the people.

Nicaragua under the Sandinista government (1979–90) encapsulated many of the arguments and dilemmas over the left's attitude to formal democracy. The Sandinistas came to power in 1979 as a small guerrilla organisation whose structure and ideas had been forged in the underground war against the Somoza dictatorship. Throughout the period of Sandinista rule, the party itself remained a small, vanguard organisation of hand-picked activists which sought to provide leadership to a wider popular movement.

At first the FSLN appeared to disparage electoral democracy, preferring more direct forms of participation. The party's leaders toured the country conducting face-to-face talks with peasants and workers to hear their complaints, and popular organisations such as trade unions, peasants and women's groups were given seats on a consultative Council of State, established to advise the FSLN in government. The party's cadres were told to act as the eyes and ears of the government, keeping it in touch with ordinary Nicaraguans.

The results were mixed. The emphasis on participation and organisation transformed a large part of Nicaraguan society. Many of the poor gained self-confidence as they learned to read and write and became involved in myriad 'mass organisations'. Since these organisations were largely controlled by the party, however, they were often forced to put party or national interests before those of their members. Participation dropped off as people became exhausted by endless meetings, the growing economic crisis and the rigours of the war against the US-backed Contra rebels.

In 1984 the FSLN held presidential elections to try and win international recognition as a legitimate government, but failed to convince Washington to stop funding the Contras. From 1984 to 1990, the FSLN ruled Nicaragua in the dual role of a government that had been freely elected and as an extra-parliamentary vanguard party working directly with mass organisations. Over time, its views changed. From being a tactical measure designed to forestall US pressure, elections became more central to Sandinista philosophy.

In February 1990 the FSLN was stunned when it lost the elections to Violeta Chamorro's UNO coalition, but passed the democratic test by accepting the result. The revolutionary vanguard assumed the role of opposition in a party political system. Its credentials were further tested in 1996, when it again lost the elections, this time to right-wing populist Arnoldo Alemán.

Many of the same dilemmas faced the Brazilian left as the Worker's Party (PT) grew in strength throughout the 1990s. The PT won the giant city of São Paulo and 35 other major towns in November 1988. Although it lost São Paulo in 1994, it was re-elected in several large cities such as Porto Alegre, and by the late 1990s the tensions between grassroots activists and the party leadership had been largely overcome. The PT built up a reputation as a trustworthy and 'safe' electoral alternative by governing at municipal, city and state levels before Lula's success in the 2002 presidential elections. This victory was of great significance for the Latin American left, and heralded a regional realignment toward the left in Argentina, Ecuador and Uruguay.

The ideology of the 'New Left' is far from revolutionary; instead it combines a desire for social justice with a commitment to a measure of economic liberalism and an adherence to the existing geopolitical 'rules of the game'. By reaching out to unions and social movements, Lula in Brazil and Néstor Kirchner in Argentina sought to combine political stability, economic growth and a degree of economic justice through increased spending on social services and some success at tackling extreme inequality.

Venezuela has undergone a unique leftward shift of its own. Hugo Chávez, the paratrooper who in 1992 had led an armed insurrection against the corrupt party system, captured the public imagination with his 'Bolivarian' program of deep social change and the devolution of power to the masses. After reinventing himself as a populist civilian politician, he stormed to a landslide victory in the 1998 presidential election, and soon implemented far-reaching constitutional and social legislation, funded by a timely flood of oil revenues. Predictably, his regime faced a conservative backlash, including charges of cronyism and a disregard for legal procedures. In 2002, Chávez was briefly deposed in a coup organized by media and business leaders with close links to the old parties which had been swept away by Chávez' 'revolution'. But to the consternation of the plotters, the army remained largely loyal to the elected government, and amid much confusion and rioting, Chávez was re-installed as president.

The left is by now well-rooted at local government level, reflecting the dynamism and local nature of the social movements. In 1997 just 60 million Latin Americans were governed by the left at municipal level; by 2003 this number had risen to more than 200 million. However, leftist local governments have had to work within severe constraints, since their budgets were usually determined by hostile national administrations. Even so, many acquired a reputation for efficiency and honesty, and introduced ground-breaking experiments in local democracy and accountability. In 1990 the Frente Amplio (Broad Front) broke Uruguay's two-party duopoly to take control of the capital city, Montevideo, and introduce innovative programmes to decentralise services and make them more accountable to residents. As in Brazil and, potentially, Mexico, success at local level paved the way for national breakthrough. The Frente's Tabaré Vázquez won the Uruguayan presidency in November 2004.

The Brazilian PT gained a good reputation through innovations such as the participatory budget in Porto Alegre, whereby voters were involved to an unprecedented extent in directly deciding how local government should set its spending priorities (see box on p 83).

By 2005, Colombia's President Álvaro Uribe was the only clearly right-wing, pro-US leader in the whole of South America, as well as host to its only significant surviving guerrilla movement. Both aspects gave the impression that Colombia was somehow frozen in the 1980s. When the armed left attempted to re-enter electoral politics, the bloody result demonstrated why such polarization persists. Within a few years of its creation, the Unión Patriótica, a political party set up by the FARC guerrilla group in 1985, had had over 3,000 leaders assassinated by the paramilitaries. The victims included mayors, governors and two very capable presidential candidates. Not surprisingly, this attempt to move into the formal political arena was eventually abandoned and armed conflict continued to dominate Colombian politics.

Democratisation

Despite massive recessions, economic crises and corruption scandals, which in earlier decades would have had the generals champing at the bit, the military has mostly stayed in the barracks over the past two decades. Isolated bouts of sabre rattling, when commanders have sent tanks on to the streets of Lima or Santiago, have been easily seen off, not least because US support for military interference in politics largely ended with the fall of the Berlin Wall. In consequence, the 1980s and 1990s were decades of unprecedented political stability under civilian governments. When Argentina's Raúl Alfonsín handed over the presidency to Carlos Menem in 1989, it was the first constitutional transfer between Argentine presidents of rival parties in the 20th century. One result was a series of constitutional amendments to allow presidents such as Carlos Menem (Argentina), Fernando Henrique Cardoso (Brazil) and Alberto Fujimori (Peru) to run

Porto Alegre: the Dynamism of the Organised

When Tarso Genro assumed, for the second time, the *prefeitura* (mayoralty) of Porto Alegre in January 2001, the city became home to the first four-term *Partido dos Trabalhadores* (PT, Worker's Party) administration in Brazil, and one of the longest-running leftist city governments in Latin America.

The city of Porto Alegre stands at the centre of a metropolitan area of almost three million people. Literacy rates of over 90 per cent are among the highest in the country for a large city, as is its life expectancy (72 years). But Porto Alegre is also a highly socially segregated city. Almost a third of its population lives in irregular housing, such as slums or 'invaded' areas. By the time the PT administration was voted into office in 1989, the city had experienced, like much of Brazil, an exacerbation in urban poverty and a decline in service provision throughout the 1980s. The Participatory Budget revolves around the OP (*Orçamento Participativo*) meetings, which alone drew over 20,000 people in 2000. Budget meetings provide the bulk of citizen participation and have been in place since the PT's second year in government. Over the years they have evolved into a structure of councils where citizens deliberate all year round and decide on both district-specific projects and broad municipal investment priorities. The city has recently achieved a sort of 'global status' for this participatory scheme, being recognized by activists, international organisations and policy makers from North and South alike. Most recently, as host city for the World Social Forum, Porto Alegre has continued to attract attention from progressives around the world.

Gianpaolo Baiocchi in Daniel Chávez and Benjamin Goldfrank (eds), *The Left in the City. Participatory Local Governments in Latin America*, London: LAB, 2004

for a second (in the case of Fujimori, a third) term in office. Until the 1990s, most presidents had struggled to finish even one term in office without being forcibly ejected from the presidential palace.

In recent years, Latin American leaders have shown a new-found vulnerability to public opinion and the law. Corruption scandals have seen national parliaments and public pressure combine to oust Brazil's Fernando Collor in 1992, Venezuela's Carlos Andrés Pérez in 1993 and Peru's Alberto Fujimori in 2000. Ecuador gets through presidents at regular intervals, either through legal avenues or street protests – the most recent, Lucio Gutiérrez, was shown the door in April 2005, when he was impeached by his own Congress for authoritarianism. Argentina famously had five presidents in a fortnight during the economic collapse of December 2001. What were once highly centralised presidential systems have become significantly more accountable to public and political pressure.

Optimists see all this as evidence of a lasting transition to democracy, but there are also ample grounds for pessimism. The early hopes of a better life following a return to democracy in the 1980s swiftly foundered, as living standards dropped across the region. Many Latin Americans have become particularly disillusioned with professional politicians, although they no longer believe that the army could run the country any better. In many countries the left too seems to have lost its self-belief and political appeal. The result has been a political vacuum into which has stepped a new breed of authoritarian populist. In one of its regular surveys of Latin American public opinion, the Chilean polling organisation Latinobarometro found that in 2004 some 55 per cent of respondents (up from 50 per cent in 2002) said they 'wouldn't mind a non-democratic government if it could solve the economic problems', while 48 per cent said they preferred order to liberty.

Foreign observers spend a great deal of time assessing Latin America's democratic credentials. Some concentrate on form, lauding regular elections, peaceful handovers of power, and the absence of military coups as proof of a lasting shift in the continent's politics. They also applaud the growing diversity and complexity of Latin America's social and political spectrum.

Sceptics, on the other hand, stress the lack of democratic content, pointing to the authoritarian style of many presidents, the prevalence of corruption, and the failure of legal systems to uphold the law. Party political systems are fragile and volatile. New parties rise and sink without trace at an increasing rate, while parliamentary politics is often chaotic and corrupt. Brazil has probably the most unstable party system in the region. During one term in office in the 1990s, 170 out of 513 members of the lower house switched parties, some of them more than once – one defected seven times. Party loyalty is almost non-existent, a nightmare for any president and an almost certain guarantee of pork-barrel politics, as political managers seek to buy the votes of deputies on key issues.

Other critics, especially in Brazil, stress the lack of true citizenship, believing that real democracy is impossible when rising inequality, crumbling social services, the crime wave, and police intimidation and immunity from prosecution are so widespread. In many countries, the apparently abstract notion of citizens' rights has galvanized the popular movements in seeking to put real content into the newly achieved democratic forms.

But there is still a long way to go. A functioning democracy relies on a degree of social consensus; people have to accept the legitimacy of the system. Yet according to Brazilian political scientist Paulo Sérgio Pinheiro, 'in almost all Latin American countries, the poor see the law as an instrument of oppression at the service of the wealthy and powerful.... According to Brazil's pastoral land commission, of the 1,730 killings of peasants, rural workers, trade union leaders, religious workers and lawyers between 1964 and 1992, only 30 had been brought to trial by 1992, and only 18 convictions achieved.' In Venezuela, 18,800 of the country's

Evo Morales, Bolivia's first
indigenous president.
(Latinphoto)

25,000 prisoners have not been sentenced, while 92 per cent of Venezuelans
say that justice does not apply equally to rich and poor, and 51 per cent say
people should take the law into their own hands. This is hardly the basis
for a functioning democracy, where disputes and conflicts can be settled
through a judicial system that everyone believes in or at least accepts as in
some sense legitimate.

The Future

Latin America has to some extent achieved democracy by default: the Cold
War has ended and for the time being Washington and foreign investors
see democratic regimes as the best route to political stability (though they
are happy to turn a blind eye to undemocratic practices in strategically
important countries such as Mexico); the military has withdrawn to the
barracks to lick its wounds after disastrous performances in government;
the left is still searching for a convincing alternative to neoliberalism. There
are now enough leftist governments in the region to declare a resurgence,

and some good results: administrations have been creative, responsive to the needs of the grass roots, and have made some headway against corruption.

Winning a presidency was itself an epic achievement for the Latin American left, but in many cases it marked only the beginning of a difficult road. Once in office, left-wing presidents of even large countries such as Brazil or Chile swiftly found how constrained their options were. With economies deeply integrated into international capital markets, any move that 'unsettled the markets' – too high an inflation figure, a spat with the IMF, or a decision to shelve privatisation plans – could lead to a sudden exodus of capital, precipitating a run on the currency and economic collapse, as happened in Mexico in 1994 and Argentina in 2001.

Governments also need to find capital for investment, to create jobs and deliver the kind of benefits their supporters have long campaigned for. But if they pursue a traditional 'tax and spend' approach, the elite is likely to spirit its wealth out of the country. Instead, governments have mixed tax reform with efforts to build 'public–private partnerships', which have acquired a distinctly mixed track record.

Finally, governments have sought to increase trade in order to generate the foreign exchange needed to pay for vital imports. But trade too is dominated by large private businesses, forcing governments to build alliances with the private sector, even if it entails going slower on other reforms. Only Hugo Chávez has been insulated from such constraints by Venezuela's booming oil receipts, although high gas prices may allow Bolivia's Evo Morales to follow suit.

Commentators have always claimed that the latest Latin American trend was going to last for ever: in the 1950s the modernisers claimed that Latin America had finally made it on to the road to industrial development; in the 1960s the future was revolutionary after Cuba; in the 1970s and early 1980s, Latin America would forever remain grimly authoritarian. Each prediction was promptly disproved by events. Now foreign pundits and politicians alike once again rashly affirm that Latin America is irreversibly democratic. If history is any guide, it is more probable that the future will see the twin threads of authoritarianism and democracy once more combine to create a more complex and quintessentially Latin American brand of politics.

Land, the City and Environment 3

CONTENTS

Promised Land: Land Ownership, Power and Conflict

The priest is holding an open-air mass for the indigenous coffee pickers. Women in their bright traditional costumes listen on rough benches under the hot sun; the men sit on the ground, hats in hands. Round about are their tents, made of transparent plastic sheets stretched over sticks. Maize grinders, essential for the staple food, tortillas, are mounted on branches stuck into the earth. A few possessions are hung from other branches, clear of the pigs.

In Guatemala such scenes are re-enacted every December, as the coffee harvest starts and indigenous villagers are trucked down from their tiny plots of land in the highlands of Chimaltenango to live rough and pick coffee for several months. The wages are US$3–4 a day, the food is worm-ridden and insufficient, but they come every year because they have no choice. Their land does not grow enough food to keep them going all year round, so they must pick coffee.

As the priest says mass, the owner of the coffee plantation, Loren, opens a beer on the veranda of his estate house. He has driven out in his jeep from his town house in Guatemala City to visit his farm, a crumbling but still beautiful building with whitewashed walls, palm trees and a stagnant swimming pool full of tadpoles. Green fields of coffee bushes cloak the hillsides.

Loren is white, owns a great deal of land, speaks French, English and Spanish, and is very rich. Back in Guatemala City, he plays the international coffee market by computer. 'His Indians' inhabit a different world; they own minute plots of land, are mostly illiterate, speak Kekchi and broken Spanish, and will probably never see either a computer or Guatemala City. Loren makes his excuses: 'I can't give them meat and vegetables on top of everything else or I'd go bankrupt. Anyway, those people are not used to it – they don't want it.' Outside, the priest exhorts the coffee pickers to 'work hard and be humble'.

Guatemala is an extreme example of the abyss that separates peasant from large landowner in most of rural Latin America. In this essentially apartheid system, the struggle for land and the other farming essentials such as water, credit and roads, has been a source of political conflict and instability throughout the 20th century, producing revolutions, massacres and innumerable simmering disputes. The recent wave of market reforms in the region has further exacerbated such tensions.

In 2002, 23 per cent of Latin Americans lived in the countryside. Of these 121 million people, just over half lived below the poverty line. The continent has vast under-used areas of cultivable land, climates and soils to suit every crop, and good water resources, yet at least six million children are malnourished, a million of them severely so. Rural children are three times as likely to live in extreme poverty as their counterparts in towns and cities. The roots of this hunger amid plenty lie in the patterns of unequal land ownership established from the first days of the Spanish conquest.

Before the conquistadores came, most land was communally owned and largely used for arable crops. The most advanced civilisation, the Incas in Peru, had large-scale irrigation systems, crop terracing whose remnants can still be seen today, and a sophisticated storage and distribution system.

The Spanish and Portuguese introduced cows, sheep, horses, wheat and sugar-cane, and raised them alongside traditional crops like maize, beans, tobacco and potatoes. Both Spanish and Portuguese monarchs rewarded their troops and settlers with grants of land and indigenous slaves. Under the *encomienda* system in the Andes, conquistadores had the right to exact forced labour from specified indigenous communities. In return they had to send a percentage of the proceeds to Madrid and, in theory, convert the natives to Catholicism.

From these massive land grants, three main forms of land ownership became established during the colonial period:

Plantations: these were large farms geared to exports, often using foreign capital and slave labour (the first slaves were brought from Africa to Brazil in 1538). They were mainly in areas where the indigenous population was less advanced and soon wiped out by the European conquerors. The first great plantation crop was sugar in north-east Brazil, coastal Peru, parts of Colombia, and the Caribbean. On the plantations African slaves worked in gangs, often in the harshest of conditions, watched over by armed guards. Plantation owners were businessmen, motivated by profit, and their farms were usually both efficient and brutal.

Haciendas: (known as *fazendas* in Brazil) these produced for the domestic market, rather than export. They grew food crops for pack animals and raised cattle to feed the Spanish armies and mine-workers. The haciendas were mainly in regions with advanced indigenous civilisations at the time of the conquest, such as Peru, Ecuador and Mexico. Rather than profits,

Life on a Sugar Plantation

'I saw many horrific punishments in slavery. That's why I hated that life. In the boilerhouse were the stocks, which were the most cruel. There were stocks which made you lie down, and others which kept you on your feet. They were made from wide boards with holes where they forced the slaves to put their feet, hands and head. They kept them stuck like that for two or three months, for any unimportant misdemeanour. They used to whip pregnant women as well, but lying face down with a hole in the earth to protect their bellies. They used to really give them a good beating! They took care not to damage the child because they wanted them unharmed.

The rowdiest days on the plantations were the Sundays. I don't know how the slaves had so much energy. That's when slavery's biggest fiestas took place. On some plantations the drums started at midday. The hubbub started as soon as the sun rose, and the kids started to run around and get underfoot. The slave quarters were throbbing from early on, it felt like the end of the world! And to think that after all that work, people woke up happy.'

Miguel Barnet, *Biografía de un cimarrón*, Havana, Instituto de Etnología y Folklore, 1966, (author's translation)

hacienda owners valued the power and status conferred by land ownership; they more closely resembled aristocrats than businessmen and their farms were frequently under-used and inefficient. The workers on the hacienda had a feudal relationship with the landlord, renting land in return either for a share of their crop (sharecropping), or for cash, or more often paying by working on the landowners' estate for a certain number of days a year. Hacienda owners controlled every aspect of their lives – some even ran their own local police and jails. The hacienda was a closed world where the owner was the main channel for contact with the outside.

Smallholder Communities: residual indigenous communities in inaccessible areas tried to carry on as before, despite the heavy tribute and labour payments exacted by the colonial authorities. The indigenous farmers retained many pre-Columbian practices, such as communal ownership of land, a strong spiritual bond with the soil, and the use of simple technology such as hoes and digging sticks. As time went by, their numbers were swelled by poor mestizo (mixed blood) farmers, many of whom spoke Spanish.

A typical peasant family today still lives in a one- or two-room shack made of wood or adobe. They own a few animals and handtools, and plough by hand or rented oxen from a better-off local family. Families are large, sons helping from an early age in the fields, while daughters work both on the land and in the home. They usually grow traditional food crops such as beans, maize or potatoes. In recent decades, such households have

---

Life on the Hacienda

On the haciendas of Bolivia, prior to the revolution of 1952, *pongos* were peasant farmers who did three or four days of unpaid work a month for the owner in exchange for the right to farm a small piece of often substandard land.

'The pongo must bring his own food, even though he has a right to the leftovers from the master's table. So when he goes to fulfil his obligation, he takes with him an earthenware or copper cooking pot, quite covered in soot, a faggot of kindling wood and a sack of llama turds for fuel, and some supplies of food.

The pongo is given a spot in the great house for his quarters, some alleyway near the mangers and pigsties, and here he builds a fire to prepare his soup, boil up his corn-grits or toast his corn. But like a watchdog he must sleep in the lobby ready to open the door for the master's children and for the master himself if he is a night bird and likes to spend his time at the club or in a tavern.

His work occupies him from dawn until far into the night, amongst his labours are the following: to help in the kitchen, to look after the harness and mind the poultry. He must sweep out the rooms, the courtyards, clean the stables and pigsties and do the garden. The traditional colonial estate house is a little world, a kind of Noah's ark with every kind of animal in it. The pongo is builder, messenger, nanny and brewer of *chicha* (corn beer). He fills in the gaps in the phalanx of servants during the day. And at night he has other tasks to complete the dark rosary of his obligations: spinning, weaving, husking corn, *mukeo* (chewing corn for chicha, fermented with saliva) and of course, minding the doorway'.

Rafael Reyeros, *El Pongueaje*, La Paz, 1949

---

depended on income from labour on neighbouring large farms and from family members migrating in search of work. Almost half of the income on such small farms now comes from non-agricultural sources.

Unbridgeable Gulf

The legacy of the colonial system has been an extreme and growing concentration of land, wealth and power in the hands of big landowners, who are a tiny minority, while the vast majority of rural people have insufficient or no land, and are poor, hungry and excluded from the political system. In Mexico at the start of the 20th century one per cent of farmers owned an extraordinary 97 per cent of the land, while as recently as 1962 one per cent of Peruvian farmers owned 80 per cent of the land. These dry statistics hardly convey the almost unbridgeable cultural and economic gulf which still divides the rich elites from peasant farmers.

After independence, and especially in the second half of the 19th century, Latin America became increasingly bound in to the world economy. Foreign investment from the new industrial powers such as Britain and the US started to arrive, turning the old plantations into modern capitalist farms. Waged labour replaced slavery, which was abolished everywhere in Latin America by the end of the 19th century, and farmers began to invest more capital in machinery and fertilisers. This model proved extremely profitable, and grew at the expense of the traditional but inefficient hacienda system. As each new crop was introduced, the plantation system and the power of the plantation owners grew.

At the end of the 19th century, US companies started to buy up land themselves, rather than work through local farmers. The pioneers were the multinational banana companies, like United Fruit, which set up banana enclaves in Central America and the Caribbean. On these enclaves workers lived in barracks, permanently in debt to the company store, while the multinational built its own railroads to take the bananas to ports and its waiting ships. The system brought scant benefit to the host country, which usually received very little tax income from the banana trade.

The concentration of land in very few hands, which grew as capitalist agriculture expanded, made Latin America the most unequal continent in the world. Big farmers, whether local or foreign, became rich and used their influence to ensure government policies favoured their interests. Governments duly encouraged exports, kept taxes low on the luxury imports the elites desired, and made sure that the big farmers received the lion's share of state spending through bank loans, investment in roads and railways, and training and technical advice for their administrators. As they grew richer, the big farmers bought more land, whereas the peasant farmers were deprived of state help, credit and social services like health care and education. The gap between rich and poor grew ever wider. In her autobiography I, Rigoberta Menchú, the Guatemalan indigenous leader and Nobel Peace Prize winner Rigoberta Menchú recalls how

'We Too are Falling'

In the black community of Vertente, in the Brazilian northeast, 60 families live crowded on to five hectares of drought-stricken land. It is April, and six months since the last rain fell. The only water supply is a trickle of a stream, where it can take four hours to fill a bucket. Dusk is falling and a shining green hummingbird hovers in front of an enormous purple bud on one of the few banana trees that keep the community going. As it grows dark, sounds seem louder: children's voices, birdsong, the rustle of banana leaves. 'The banana trees are falling, because they only have one leg', says one old man. 'A man has two legs to support him, but now we too are falling.' The pot-bellied children gather round to dance, as the adults talk of their endless struggle for farms big enough to feed their families. At the moment they are sharecropping, so large portion of whatever pitiful crop they harvest must go to the landlord. There is good soil lying idle nearby, but they dare not farm it for fear of reprisals. A greater proportion of Vertente's children die than anywhere else in northeastern Brazil.

A Green Prison

'In the midst of a dense undergrowth of brambles, reeds and tall grasses that choked the abandoned banana fields, the clearers made their machetes whistle through the air as, bent double and breathing noisily like cattle, they hacked their way through the tangle. Clouds of thistledown flew up and settled again, sticking into their reddened, sweaty skin as they plodded along like sleepwalkers, heavy with weariness and enervation. And, amidst all this confusion of labourers and banana trees, sun and pestilence, sweat and machines, creeks and malaria, rang out the cocky shouts of the foremen, the whistling of the overseers, and the arrogant, all-powerful gringo slang.

So it went on all day long. The peasants' exhausting toil stretched out until nightfall when, their legs buckling under them with weariness, they quit the green prison of the banana plantations only to be engulfed in the dispiriting prison of their soulless, barrack-like quarters.'

Ramón Amaya Amador, *Prisión Verde*, Mexico, 1950 (translated by Nick Caistor)

---

her parents lost their land to incoming ladinos (Spanish-speaking Guatemalans of mixed race):

> They weren't exactly evicted but the ladinos just gradually took over. My parents spent everything they earned and they incurred so many debts with these people that they had to leave the house to pay them. The rich are always like that. When people owe them some money they take a bit of land or some of their belongings and slowly end up with everything.

As the rural population grew, families had to subdivide their land between their children. Broken up, their small plots proved unable to sustain a family, and both adults and children were forced to seek work on the plantations at harvest time. Millions more abandoned the countryside for the shantytowns that were springing up around the major cities. The combination of peasant farming and seasonal labour, known as semi-proletarianisation, has become the norm in much of the countryside. In Central America, seventy per cent of the rural population are seasonal migrants, joining the coffee pickers of Guatemala in their annual trek to the plantations at harvest time. For the plantation owners, this system provides a cheap labour force at harvest time, with no need to pay year-round wages to regular employees.

Factory Farms

After the Second World War many politicians and economists saw further modernisation as the solution to Latin America's inadequate agricultural system. This meant increasing productivity and making Latin America's

Land inequalities in Honduras

'Standing on a hillside above the melon farm in southern Honduras, I am surrounded by foot-high maize plants that belong to Samuel, a local farmer. The valley below is criss-crossed with neat green lines of honey melons. Although it is only 6.30 in the morning, the large farm is a hive of activity, with workers applying water and pesticides to the fruit destined for export to Europe and the United States.

The slopes around me are a mosaic of maize plots and remnants of the dry forest that used to stretch in a continuous band along the Pacific coast from Mexico to Panama. Once farmers clear the forest to grow crops, the soil loses its protective cover and, on exposure to the intense rains, the result is soil erosion. As the land degrades, production falls. Some farmers will clear more patches of forest or eke out a living on the original plot; others will migrate to the cities to find work.

The melon farm exemplifies the type of agriculture that emerged during the Green Revolution, an agricultural system that relies on large and expensive technical inputs such as irrigation, pesticides, herbicides and fertiliser to restore and maintain soil productivity. The Green Revolution has undoubtedly led to a substantial increase in production, but it has also bypassed millions and millions of farmers, such as Samuel, who simply cannot afford the costly inputs.

Inequalities in land distribution in countries such as Honduras mean that resource-poor farmers have few alternatives but to cultivate marginal agricultural areas such as hillsides. Driven off prime land in the valley floors, small farmers in small, densely populated areas have been forced to cultivate steep slopes, leading to soil erosion.'

Jon Hellin (ed.), 'Better land husbandry: from soil conservation to holistic land management', Oxford: Oxford Brookes University Press, 2006

farms more like the capital-intensive farms of the United States and Canada. Since the 1960s, a new wave of state and foreign investment has transformed Latin American agriculture. In Colombia, state spending on agriculture increased 50-fold between 1950 and 1972. Most of the money went on grandiose schemes favouring large-scale export agriculture; for example, the Mexican government irrigated the arid north-west of the country, which subsequently became a major producer of fruit and vegetables for the US market.

Driving through the rich Cauca valley of Colombia, one passes through mile after mile of lush new sugar and sorghum fields, punctuated by billboards advertising the latest in tractors and pesticides. In Mexico's Northwest, the fast-growing fruit and vegetable industry has transformed the fertile river valleys into a vast patchwork of irrigated fields and packing sheds resembling those of California's Imperial Valley. In southern Brazil, more than a dozen multi-million dollar soybean processing plants owned by US multinationals are scattered through the region, surrounded by large-scale mechanised soybean farms, none of which existed two decades ago. While a few countries such as Brazil, Colombia, Mexico and Argentina are clearly in the forefront of the agricultural revolution, no part of the countryside has been left untouched by capitalist development.

ROGER BURBACH AND PATRICIA FLYNN, *Agribusiness in the Americas*, New York, Monthly Review Press, 1980

Following the military coup of 1964, Brazil provided the most dramatic example of government involvement in boosting agro-exports. Through lending, tax concessions, state investment and a guaranteed minimum price for farmers growing export crops like soybeans, southern Brazil has been transformed into one of the most modern agricultural regions in the hemisphere and a leading global exporter of crops such as soybeans. Although a few Brazilian families have grown very rich in the process, they remain heavily dependent on foreign banks and multinationals to finance and buy their crops. For the mass of the population, the new crops have meant yet another round of land concentration, increasing inequality of wealth and growing malnutrition as food crops are once again squeezed out by commodity exports. Rather than abolishing hunger in the countryside, modernisation has often made it worse.

In some cases foreign investors have bought and farmed land, but in recent years transnational companies have largely drawn back from the direct control that made them so unpopular in the past, leading to extensive nationalisation of their operations in the 1960s and 1970s. Instead, they prefer to sign contracts with local farmers, under which the companies provide credit and agricultural inputs such as fertilisers and equipment in return for buying the farmer's crops at a guaranteed price. This leaves the transnational in control of the profitable processing and marketing of a product, while the local farmers must deal with the local labour force and run the risk of a failed harvest. The transnationals lose little through this arrangement: in 2003, of each US$1 earned by bananas in the marketplace, only 10 cents found its way back to the producer country, and just 1.5 cents went to the workers on the banana plantations.

In today's Latin America, high-tech farms coexist with traditional peasant agriculture. The two worlds are intimately connected: peasant farms provide seasonal labour and often sell their produce to local agribusinesses. But power lies firmly in the hands of the big farms, with their near-monopoly on capital, credit, state support and access to world markets.

In some countries, farming has to some extent moved on from the triple stereotype of plantation, hacienda and impoverished smallholder. In parts of Colombia, Central America and Brazil, for example, some small farmers have absorbed technology and have gained limited access to credit,

Canned Imperialism in Mexico

'When Del Monte first sent its technicians to look at the Bajío [valley in Mexico] in 1959, they found a region ill-suited to the needs of the world's largest canner of fruits and vegetables. Grain production predominated, with corn and beans serving as the mainstays of the local diet. In Del Monte's own words, "vegetable production was small and limited to a few crops grown exclusively for the local fresh market."

The Bajío's land tenure system was also incompatible with Del Monte's needs. Due to the valley's population density, and the break-up of the large landed estates under Mexico's agrarian reform laws, the average land holding was small – 10–20 acres. Some of the land was held in *ejidos*, large state-owned farms that are subdivided into many small plots and worked by peasants. Mexican law prohibited the sale of these lands, and it also placed restrictions on land ownership by foreign corporations. For a company used to owning plantations and working with US growers who own hundreds or even thousands of acres, the conditions in the Bajío did not appear auspicious.

But Del Monte found the perfect tool for changing the valley's agriculture: contract farming. Under the contract system, the farmer or grower agrees to plant a set number of acres of a particular crop, and the company in return provides financial assistance, which usually includes seeds and special machinery, as well as cash outlays for purchasing fertilisers and hiring farm labour. All these costs are discounted from the farmer's income when the crop is delivered to the cannery.

In a country like Mexico, where agricultural credit is limited or non-existent, contract farming is a powerful instrument. Del Monte revealed just how influential its crop financing was when it noted that 'in the early 1960s Productos Del Monte was practically the only source that many of its growers could turn to for short-term crop loans'. By skilfully using its financial leverage, Del Monte affected the valley in several ways: it introduced crops that had never been grown there, favoured the development of the larger growers at the expense of the smaller more marginal producers, and gained operating control over large tracts of land.'

'Canned Imperialism', in NACLA *Report on the Americas*, New York, September 1976

notably to produce horticultural products for the growing urban markets, or even for export. In other cases, cooperativisation has helped smallholders to gain access to credit and markets. But most regions of Latin America still manifest the threefold structure. Some recent changes have made life harder for small farmers. Increasingly, the farm trade in Latin America, like that in the US and Europe, is dominated by large supermarket chains that use their market clout to drive down prices and impose ever higher standards of uniform quality that are particularly hard for small, low-tech farmers to meet.

Fighting For Land

Plantations, haciendas, and peasant farms have competed for land, and the expansion of one form at the expense of the others has generated conflict, land seizures, political unrest and even war.

As commercial agriculture has spread on to lands traditionally farmed by peasant families, the big landowners have forced them out through a combination of money, legal trickery (for example, over the deeds to the land) and brute force. In the Brazilian Amazon, landowners commonly hire gunmen to expel peasant farmers from land they want to turn over to cattle. Peasants have responded by seizing land left idle by the landowners and organising political movements to demand agrarian reform and access to social services.

On the plantations, disputes have been over wages and conditions, rather than demands for land and credit. Since plantation owners are determined to keep wages as low as possible, these disputes have frequently been bloody, often involving the army and police on the side of the owners. One of the worst-hit areas has been Colombia's banana-growing Urabá region.

> A typical incident was the arrest by members of the [local army] battalion of 19 banana plantation workers in the municipality of Apartadó in March 1989. They were taken to the battalion headquarters in Carepa and twelve were later released. Four others were released after several days during which they were tortured, and three needed hospital treatment for their injuries. The bodies, or rather the remains, of two other workers were found on 4 April. They had been killed by having charges of dynamite attached to their bodies and exploded.
>
> JENNY PEARCE, *Colombia: Inside the Labyrinth*, London: LAB, 1990

In many cases, when local disputes were met with repression, they have escalated into national political protest movements. In El Salvador in the 1970s frustrated peasant activists decided they could not improve conditions in the countryside without a radical change of government. As a result, many joined new guerrilla movements, fighting in a bloody civil war in which over 70,000 people died, mostly at the hands of the army and their associated death squads.

Since the mid-20th century, governments have tried to alleviate pressure on the land through colonisation programmes. These have consisted largely of irrigation projects to reclaim arid land in countries such as Mexico and Peru, and the deforestation and occupation of the Amazon basin in Brazil and the neighbouring Andean nations of Bolivia, Peru, Ecuador and Colombia. Governments have often seen these programmes as an alternative to agrarian reform, since they can ease pressure on the

Peasants harvesting coca leaves, the primary ingredient in cocaine, on a Colombian hillside. *(Latinphoto)*

land by sending landless peasants off to colonise new areas. Unfortunately, rainforest land being colonised has often been unsuitable for sustained agriculture, and has been in remote areas, making it expensive or impossible for small farmers to get their produce to market. Colonisation programmes have often been chaotic and violent, as in Brazil, where large landowners have moved in to throw peasants off the land, once they have cleared it for farming. In her autobiography, *Mi Despertar* (My Awakening), Ana María Condori, a Bolivian indigenous woman describes the colonisation programme of the 1950s:

> My father went there because our farm at home was all divided up and wasn't producing enough for all the children. Going on the colonisation seemed like a solution to him, because the government at that time promised people heaven and earth. They gave out publicity at the fairs in the Altiplano [high plateau region of the Andes where most Bolivians live] trying to get people to sign up – leaflets, posters, adverts on the radio offering ready-made houses, a hectare of land already cleared, schools, hospitals, paved roads, technical assistance and credit for the farm. But once people got to the colonisation zone, they found nothing of all that; the government handed out food to make sure people didn't actually starve to death, but apart from that they were left to their fate.

The conflicts generated by growing inequality in the countryside have made agrarian reform one of the hottest issues in Latin American politics. For both rich and poor, land is literally a matter of life and death.

The first and greatest Latin American agrarian reform followed the Mexican revolution of 1910–17. Over the ensuing decades, especially during the radical presidency of Lázaro Cárdenas (1934–40), Mexico's vast haciendas were broken up and given out to 1.5 million families in the form of *ejidos* – communally owned land administered by indigenous communities along traditional lines. The reform consolidated the ruling party's grip on the countryside, laying the foundations for 50 years of one-party rule.

The Mexican government gave out land, but failed to back up the programme with a reform of credit and investment to benefit the peasants. Credit is the financial oxygen for farmers because of the cyclical nature of agriculture. Every year a farmer has to borrow cash to buy seeds and fertiliser, pay employees, and hire or buy equipment before the harvest brings in the money to pay off debts and maintain the farmer's family until the next harvest. Even after the agrarian reform in Mexico, big farmers have continued to receive most of the credit, and government spending on roads and irrigation has benefited their farms most. Agrarian reform provided the security that goes with owning a piece of land, but did little to improve the living standards of Mexico's peasantry.

The Bolivian revolution of 1952 also led to a radical reform of its almost feudal rural society, directly benefiting three quarters of the country's peasantry. Large estates were divided up among the sharecroppers, who had previously been forced to give the landowner a large proportion of their crop in exchange for farming the land. Titles were established for indigenous communities, and the worst forms of labour exploitation were made illegal. In Guatemala a similarly radical land reform after 1952 came

---

Peasant Life in the 1960s

'In the early 1960s I visited Peruvian haciendas where corporal punishment was still arbitrarily administered by estate owners and managers for minor infractions of rules. On some estates, indigenous tenant workers were expected to kneel and kiss the *patrón's* poncho as a symbol of submission and respect. Even in Chile, many large estate owners in 1960 strictly regulated who could enter or leave the property, and used an iron hand to maintain control over the goods and printed information available to debt-ridden residents through the estate's commissary. Until 1956, Chilean estate owners could effectively direct the votes of their tenants, workers and other clients to the candidate and party of their choice. Union organisation of agricultural workers was for all practical purposes prohibited by law until 1967.'

Solon Barraclough, *NACLA Report on the Americas*, New York, November 1994

to an abrupt end when the Arbenz government was overthrown by a US-backed military coup.

Agrarian reform at a continental level took off in the 1960s. Following the Cuban revolution in 1959, the US government decided that it had to end social unrest in the countryside of Latin America if it was to pre-empt further revolutions. In 1961 President Kennedy launched the Alliance for Progress, a joint Latin American–US initiative under which the US gave money and advice for agrarian reform programmes in countries such as Chile, Colombia and Venezuela.

Agrarian reform as understood by Washington, however, had two often incompatible aims: it sought to increase productivity by modernising agriculture along capitalist lines, and at the same time to redistribute land and wealth to the rural poor. In practice, modernisation came first, often causing further land expulsions and impoverishment for the peasantry. Landlords successfully resisted US pressure to reduce their influence, and instead benefited from the drive for modernisation. Landlord opposition and government incompetence meant that even when apparently progressive reform laws were passed, they were seldom implemented. Such laws have become a focus of discontent, as peasants in countries such as Honduras and Brazil occupy idle lands and try to force the government to enact its own laws, expropriating the lands and distributing them among landless peasants.

Brazilian governments have historically made extravagant promises of agrarian reform that have not been kept. Both democratic and military governments have sought to quell peasant discontent with pledges of solidarity that come to nothing. The Landless Peasant Movement (*Movimento Sem Terra*, MST) claims that today there are 15 million desperate Brazilian peasant farmers currently without any land. Even under the Workers Party government, land conflicts continue to exact a deadly toll in Brazil: in December 2004, three landless peasants – all members of the MST – were assassinated in the state of Pernambuco. According to an article in the *Folha de São Paulo* on November 25, 2004, 'about 15 armed men, wearing masks, descended upon the MST encampment, machine gunning at random and burning down the barracks'. Few of the landowners and gunmen responsible are ever brought to trial. Three years into Lula's presidency, critics were pointing out that less land had been handed out to the poor than under his predecessor.

Where agrarian reforms have worked to the advantage of the rural poor, they have generally been associated either with revolution (Mexico, Bolivia 1952, Cuba 1959, Nicaragua 1979) or with an elected left-wing government (Chile 1970–73, Guatemala 1950–54). In both Chile and Guatemala, the governments were overthrown by military coups, in part because of the hostility of the landed elite to agrarian reform. In Peru, one of Latin

The MST

Testimony of Maria Joaquina de Nascimento (Nazinha)

'I'm 57 years old. I was born on Agua Branca in Ceará. My father had a small plot of land. We were lucky because it had a spring, so we always had water. I was the only girl, but I had five brothers. I went to school for a short while. I had to get up, cook lunch for my parents and then walk the four kilometres to school. I really only learnt to sign my name. When I was 22 years old, I married. My husband didn't have land of his own so he worked with my father.

We all left Ceará because my father got ill. One of my brothers lived in Petrolina, so we went there. We found it difficult living in a town. We had to buy everything, even gas for cooking. Before that we'd always used wood from the countryside. We found it strange to have to buy fuel to cook. It was difficult. I went hungry for the first time in my life in Petrolina. My husband got a job on a building site. I had seven children, but three died. My first-born died when he was 11 months old. Then I had twins, who were born dead. But the other four – three girls and a boy – survived.

We were living in Petrolina with all these problems when some lads came to the door and invited us to a meeting. They said they were from the MST and they could help us win land. We were so pleased! So we all took part in the occupation of Safra estate. It was six years ago – August 7, 1995. I felt so happy when we arrived. I had two of my daughters with me. I left the other one in Petrolina because she was completing her last year at school. We had to take everything – black polythene, mattresses, bedclothes, hammocks, pots, food. It was difficult because we didn't have much protection from the wind and the rain. But we didn't care. In the town you suffer without hope, but here we were suffering with hope. That makes all the difference.

We spent five months in this camp. But there wasn't enough land in Safra for all the families. So on January 5, 1996 we went with 105 other families to occupy Ouro Verde estate and that's where we won land. We were evicted once from here, on January 31, 1996. The police came and it was really frightening. But we reoccupied again, on February 18, 1996, and in the end we won the land. Everything is fine now. I've got a nice house, with a veranda. We sit out here in the evenings. It was my dream, to have a house like this. My parents had a house with a veranda. It was better than the one I've got, but I'm going to make this one as good as theirs one day. I've planted lots of trees in the garden and I've got flowers in pots. It looks like a real home.

We can grow all our food now. That's so much better. The only bill we have to pay is for the electricity, for the house and for the water pump for the grapes. We only have two crops to sell on the market – grapes and *açerola* (a tropical fruit). They don't really bring in enough money. We still suffer, but life is so much better.'

Sue Branford and Jan Rocha, *Cutting the Wire: The Story of the Landless Movement in Brazil*, London: LAB, 2002

America's few radical military governments, the regime of General Velasco (1968–75), also transformed the country's semi-feudal land system with a radical reform.

In the 1990s agriculture was deeply affected by the wave of neoliberal reforms which tried to open up the Latin American economy to market forces. As part of the drive to encourage private investment in agriculture, especially in non-traditional agro-export crops, governments in countries such as Peru, Mexico, Ecuador and Nicaragua put past reform processes into reverse in a new wave of 'modernisation' that had disastrous implications for many peasants. Credits were cut back and private buyers began to acquire the land, causing outbreaks of violence such as the 'First National Indigenous Uprising' in Ecuador in 1990. In 1991, the earlier gains of the Mexican peasantry were eroded by President Carlos Salinas, whose constitutional reforms allowed for the break-up and privatisation of the communal *ejidos*. Since then, *ejidatarios* have been able to sell their land or go into joint ventures with private companies. The reform, coupled with the structural requirements of NAFTA, has placed great pressure on millions of peasant families, pressure that in part contributed to the Zapatista uprising of 1994.

In Venezuela, just five per cent of the population have historically owned three quarters of farmland, with the vast majority owning no land at all. The landslide election of Hugo Chávez in 1997 was due in part to his promises of land reform, and within months the *Chavista* parliament introduced legislation to hand out land. By 2005, however, there was little to show for the fiery rhetoric beyond a small number of high-profile expropriations.

Although the growing urbanisation of the continent has reduced the relevance of rural questions to many Latin Americans, a quarter of the region's people still live in the countryside, where they suffer the consequences of unequal land distribution and a system that invariably favours the rich farmers over the peasants. The modernisation of agriculture seems only to exacerbate the situation, while half-hearted colonisation programmes and agrarian reforms have done little to change the system, and in some cases may have made matters worse. Experience shows that initiatives such as agrarian reform can work only when they are carried out democratically, in consultation with their supposed beneficiaries, and governments are willing to challenge the power of the big landowners. Even then, the change must be locked into the constitution, protected against future government policy, otherwise the gains may be lost, as in Mexico or Nicaragua. Only if such reforms take place is there hope that a more just society can grow in rural Latin America, one which does not perpetuate poverty, hunger, sickness and an endless flight to the cities.

Mean Streets: Migration and Life in the City

The tourist hotels along Ipanema beach in Rio de Janeiro are some of the most expensive real estate in the world. Luxury tower blocks, their balconies bursting with foliage, overlook beaches strewn with perfect brown bodies sporting skimpy swimsuits known locally as 'dental floss'. Far above the beach, dozens of hang-gliders circle lazily down from one of Rio's extraordinary bare-rock mountains, to which clings the Rocinha *favela*, a shantytown which is home to 350,000 of Rio's poor. Shimmering in the heat haze, Rocinha looks down on the beaches like a bad conscience.

Shantytowns surround most Latin American cities, bulging with migrants from an economically stagnant countryside or the city's youth, fleeing the overcrowded tenements of the inner city in search of a house of their own. In Peru the poor have built their settlements on the barren desert around Lima. In Ecuador, 60 per cent of Guayaquil's population have built shacks over the muddy and polluted water of the swamps, their houses suspended on stilts. Some homes are a 40-minute walk along rickety boardwalks to dry land.

The growth of the cities has been astounding. In 1930, Latin America's total urban population was 20 million, out of a total population of around 100 million. Now around 400 million Latin Americans live in cities, out of a total of 525 million. Since the 1930s, millions of peasant families have left their farms and villages and joined the great trek to the cities. The driving forces behind this human tide include war, famine, the shortage of land and the often illusory glitter of the city, with its promise of jobs, education and excitement. By the early 21st century, much of Latin America was more urbanised than the US, and if present trends continue South America will be among the world's most urbanised regions by 2030. Already the majority of people live in towns and cities in all but two Latin American nations – Haiti and Honduras.

Contrary to the common image of poor, desperate peasants trailing into the cities, most migrants are literate young adults, frustrated with the lack of opportunity in the countryside. In Latin America, unlike Asia and Africa, women migrants outnumber men, reflecting women's lesser role in agriculture compared to the other continents. Catastrophes like war and famine, however, change the pattern, as people of all ages and educational backgrounds flee to the cities en masse.

The way people migrate has been determined by the changes in public transport. As roads and bus and truck services have improved, migration has become a less daunting prospect. Not only has it made it easier for people to move to big cities from once remote rural villages, but better transport now means that the move need no longer be a definitive break with the past. Increasing numbers of poor Latin Americans now divide

Favela overlooking downtown Rio de Janeiro. *(South American Pictures)*

Table 3.1:
Percentage of population living in urban areas, 1960–2000

Country	Urban population as % of total population		
Most Developed*	1960	1993	2000**
Argentina	74	88	89***
Costa Rica	37	49	59
Uruguay	80	90	93
Chile	68	84	86
Intermediate			
Colombia	48	72	76***
Brazil	45	77	81
Ecuador	34	57	63
Paraguay	36	51	57***
Least Developed			
Honduras	23	43	46
El Salvador	38	45	58
Nicaragua	40	62	57
Haiti	16	30	36

*Most developed, intermediate and least developed categories based on Human Development Index ranking, see table, page xi **Source:** *World Development Report,* 1996
****Source:** United Nations Statistical Division, 2000
*****Source:** World Bank, 2001

their time between town and country, visiting the family farm at weekends. The distinctions between urban and rural lifestyles are becoming blurred. As the rural population has declined in relative terms, the driving force for growth in urban areas has increasingly come from residents having children and moving between towns, rather than traditional rural–urban migration.

The increased contact between town and village has in turn stimulated further migration, as one Aymara indigenous woman in Bolivia recalls:

> At that time I was nine years old, and was already seeing the older girls coming back from working as servants saying: 'I'm happy in the city. Life is great there'. To me they seemed physically happier; they talked beautifully, they had lovely clothes with embroidered shawls, with luxurious skirts. Pretty Indian girls, they looked. So I said 'Ah! I'm going too'.
>
> ANA MARÍA CONDORI, *Mi Despertar*, La Paz: Hisbol, 1988 (author's translation)

Unless driven by war or natural disaster, migration is usually a carefully planned operation; for example, a family will send an eldest daughter on ahead to find work and establish a base before other family members follow. Since they are mainly young people, migrants then have their children in the city, further boosting urban population growth. For those that stay behind, money sent by relatives in the city, or increasingly from abroad, has become vital to the survival of many rural communities. One study of Mixteca communities in Mexico showed that remittances from family members working in New York now pay for everything from a new drinking-water system to the religious festivals which bind the villages together.

The numbers are huge and growing. In 2004, total remittances from the estimated 25 million Latin Americans living overseas came to US$46 billion, more than overseas aid and foreign investment combined. Mexico took a third, followed by Brazil and Colombia, but proportionally the impact was often greatest in small economies in the Caribbean and Central America, where remittances often exceed total export income.

The growth of the cities is a consequence of Latin America's drive for industrialisation. As industry grew from the 1930s onwards, the prospect of jobs pulled in the rural population. In addition, as commercial agriculture spread further into the countryside, peasants were forced off the land and left with the choice of seasonal labour on the plantations or moving to the city in search of a better life. Although many migrants never found regular employment, they still lived better in urban squalor than in rural poverty. Their children were more likely to get some schooling, and there was more chance of winning eventual access to basic services like water and electricity. At a national level, wealth in Latin American countries is disproportionately concentrated in the urban areas, especially

Table 3.2:
Population of Latin America's largest cities (incl. urban areas), 2003

City	Population (thousands)
Mexico City, Mexico	20,267
Buenos Aires, Argentina	11,298
São Paulo, Brazil	10,009
Bogotá, Colombia	6,422
Lima-Callao, Peru	5,681
Rio de Janeiro, Brazil	5,613
Santiago, Chile	4,788
Caracas, Venezuela	2,784
Salvador, Brazil*	2,331
Havana, Cuba*	2,192
Belo Horizonte, Brazil*	2,154

Source: www.citymayors.com/features/urban=areas1.html (*city only)

the capital. This enduring inequality is the driving force behind the continued drift to the cities. One of the consequences of the debt crisis of the 1980s has been a sharp rise in urban poverty, which has tarnished the glitter of the cities and reduced migratory pressures in many countries.

The lopsided division of wealth between urban and rural areas also occurs between countries. Table 3.2 shows that those countries which remain predominantly rural, such as Bolivia and Paraguay, are among the poorest in the continent, while the more urbanised countries are among the best off.

Even though it is generally easier and cheaper to provide health, education and water to people clustered in towns, rather than dispersed across the countryside, the speed of urbanisation is a serious headache for Latin America's planners, swamping existing services, and stretching such resources as water and food dangerously thin. In recent years pollution and congestion have added to their problems. Governments' attempts to check urban growth have had little impact, however, since they have failed to question the logic of the development model that was fuelling migration. The only exception has been Cuba, where the Castro government used its central planning of jobs, housing and food distribution to dissuade would-be migrants to Havana, while investing in other, smaller cities and rural improvements. As a result, it managed to reverse the growth in Havana's share of the population. In some giant cities like Buenos Aires, congestion and pollution have started to make life so difficult that some companies are relocating to nearby cities.

Portrait of a Migrant

Sergio, 19, is from Guadalajara. A stocky, scruffy youth in black jeans and T-shirt with a skimpy moustache, he is excited about his planned 'jump' this afternoon and cannot stop talking. When the 'migra' – the US immigration patrol – changes shift at 2.30 p.m., Sergio, along with hundreds of other Mexican youths, will jump the chain-link fence that separates the US from Mexico in the border town of Tijuana. If he can make it across a stretch of waste ground to the burger bars on the far side, he can pay for a ride to Los Angeles in the trunk of a car waiting on the US side of the border. Tijuana is the main crossing point into the US. The San Diego border patrol say they make 500,000 captures a year, and reckon that for every person they catch, two or three get through. They say 85 per cent are men, and nearly all are Mexican.

Crossing is so easy that Sergio has just been home to visit his family, and is now on his way back to work. Since he first crossed over three years ago, he has worked loading vans and serving coffee in San Bernardino, California. He works all hours and earns US$350 a week. In Guadalajara, where he worked in a cobbler's workshop, he was earning about US$20 a week. He lives cheaply, sharing an apartment with six other Mexican men, and wires his savings to his family from the local Western Union office. He calculates that in four or five years he can save the US$6–7,000 he needs to open his own shoe workshop or clothes shop back in Guadalajara.

Crossing the Border

Many migrants, especially those from Mexico, Central America, the Caribbean and Colombia, decide to leave their country altogether. Their usual destination is *El Norte*, the promised land of the US, where they work illegally in factories, on farms, or in restaurants in the hope of one day acquiring the coveted green card, or work permit. The route to the US is uncertain and dangerous, and involves running the gauntlet of unscrupulous *coyotes* or guides, as well as US Immigration Service patrols. Migrants caught at the border are swiftly returned to their home country, often to begin another attempt to head north and find safety in the anonymity of the Hispanic quarters of major US cities.

The influx has changed US society. By 2002 an estimated 13 per cent of the US population – some 37 million people – were 'Hispanics', over two-thirds of them hailing originally from Mexico. Hispanics are concentrated in a few states, notably California and Texas, where by 2002 they made up over a third of the population, and New Mexico, where they account for almost half. Successive immigration amnesties have swelled the number who hold green cards to prove legal citizenship and the right to vote, and Hispanics are finally beginning to have an impact on national politics. The latest member of the Bush dynasty, George P. Bush, campaigned on behalf of his uncle, George W. Bush, using his Mexican heritage to reach out to the increasingly important Latino electorate. After re-election in 2004, Bush nominated two Hispanics to his cabinet – Cuban-born Carlos Gutierrez to Commerce, and Alberto Gonzales (the Texan-born son of Mexican immigrants) as Attorney General. However, while Cuban émigrés dominate political life in Florida and high-profile Hispanic mayors have governed major cities such as Los Angeles, the Hispanic community has not found a united voice or national leaders to match Jesse Jackson's role in galvanising black voters. The 2004 elections saw the total of three incumbent Hispanic senators cut to two, when Richard Romero in New Mexico was defeated. Part of the reason is that the Hispanic community is fragmented – Puerto Ricans and Dominicans dominate in New York, whereas Mexicans and Central Americans are the main groups in Los Angeles.

Within the US, attitudes to Hispanic immigrants have depended on the state of the economy. After the Second World War, when US agriculture was suffering a labour shortage, Mexicans were encouraged to migrate on the *bracero* farm-worker programme. In recent years, however, a rising tide of anti-immigrant feeling has prompted discrimination and attacks against Hispanics. In a largely unreported sideshow to George Bush's re-election in 2004, voters in Arizona approved 'proposition 200'. This requires Arizonans to prove citizenship when seeking public benefits or when registering to vote and was targeted at the state's estimated 300,000–350,000 undocumented immigrants who, Latino leaders fear, may be forced further underground.

Politicians have been swift to capitalise on the issue. In March 2005, Representative Steve King, a Republican from Iowa, and 57 additional members of Congress introduced the English Language Unity Act of 2005, which would make English the sole official language of the United States government.

Not all Latin American migrants head for the US; inequalities of wealth and opportunity between neighbouring countries often force migrants over the nearest border. In Buenos Aires the people of Ciudad Oculta (Hidden City) are shorter and darker than the rich white inhabitants of the city centre. High-cheek-boned indigenous features and darker skin denote the thousands of Bolivians and Paraguayans who have come to Argentina in search of a decent living. City-centre stores are full of the latest labour-saving gadgets, yet the women of Ciudad Oculta cook in mud ovens, and watch over scruffy, barefoot children. Infant mortality is four times the national average – one child in ten never reaches its first birthday.

Builders and Squatters

Migrants recently arrived in Latin America's cities frequently stay with friends and relatives until they get used to their new surroundings and find some way of earning a living. With space at a premium, however, they soon come under pressure to find a place of their own. Choices are limited. They can rent a tiny room in an overcrowded inner-city tenement, but the development of bus and other mass urban transport networks in the last 50 years has given them another option – joining the increasing number of squatters in the shantytowns on the outskirts of the cities.

Shantytowns have transformed Latin America's urban landscape. In Rio de Janeiro the first were recorded in 1920. Today they house over a third of the city's inhabitants. In Caracas that figure is nearer two-thirds. Each country has a different word for them – in Brazil they are *favelas*, in Argentina the evocative term is *villas miserias* (towns of poverty), in Peru the progressive military regime which came to power in 1968 insisted on the more dignified *pueblos jovenes* (young towns). In Chile they are simply *callampas* (mushrooms), springing up overnight on the outskirts of Santiago.

Shanty-town homes are built by their residents and are nearly always illegal, either because the squatters do not own the land, or because they have no planning permission to build. Many squatter settlements begin with a 'land invasion'; a group of the urban poor, often including recent migrants, invades a piece of ground at night and hastily raises temporary shacks. If they succeed in fending off initial attempts by the authorities or the landlord to evict them, the temporary homes stand a chance of becoming permanent.

As time goes by and the settlement's prospects improve, residents start the long struggle to improve their homes. The improvements take up much of their spare time and money. The first cardboard and plastic shacks are replaced by planks or corrugated iron. Over the years brick houses start to appear, some even acquiring a second storey. Eventually they come to resemble other parts of the city, and become absorbed into the city's economy as increasing numbers of the houses are sold or rented out by their original inhabitants.

Squatter settlements face enormous initial problems. Often the land they have occupied was empty precisely because it was unsuitable for building. In Rio the poor cling to sheer hillsides, risking landslides every time it rains. In El Salvador's capital, San Salvador, shantytowns are strung terrifyingly close to railway lines or huddled into ravines, often side by side with the local rubbish tip. In Lima the pueblos jovenes are built into the desert, leaving the new arrivals at the mercy of private water suppliers. Typically, the most urgent problems are water and sanitation. In São Paulo, over a third of the city's houses, mainly in the peripheral shantytowns, have no sewer connections or cesspools. People use open holes or dry latrines, which often contaminate the shallow wells that provide their only water supply.

The key to improving living standards is organisation, and squatter settlements have produced some of Latin America's best-organised and

Building a Self-help Home

'Alfonso and Isabel Rodríguez live with their three children in a low-income settlement in the south of Valencia, a Venezuelan city with around 800,000 inhabitants. The population has grown rapidly as manufacturing plants have moved to the city in preference to the crowded conditions found in Caracas. Alfonso works in the Ford plant. He was born in the mountain state of Mérida and arrived in Valencia in 1975 after an uncle told him that work was available. He stayed with his uncle for a while in a consolidated self-help house in the south of the city and then moved into rental accommodation nearer the centre. He met Isabel, who had been born in Valencia, six months later. They rented a new home together and stayed there for 18 months. Two years later, he managed to obtain a plot of land through an invasion. The invasion was organised by an employee of the local authority who was trying to win support for a councillor who was hoping to be re-elected that year. One hundred and twenty families established rudimentary shacks early one Sunday morning. Because of the protection given by the councillor there was little trouble with the police and the settlers soon began to improve their accommodation. Since Alfonso had a reasonably well-paid job, he could afford to buy cement and bricks with which to improve the house. In addition, he sold half of the 20 by 35 metre plot he had obtained to two other families; this was sufficient to buy the rest of the materials he needed. He could also employ, on an occasional basis, a friend who worked in the construction industry. Progress on the house was slow but steady. Since he had to work at his paid job during the week, he could do little except at weekends. Even then there were interruptions, family visits, the occasional fiesta, demands by the children to go out. Isabel helped with some of the lighter jobs when she could, but three rapid pregnancies and a miscarriage limited her participation in the actual building.

By 1985, five years later, the house had three rooms. It was not pretty to look at but it was solidly built and the roof kept out the rain. It had electricity, stolen from the mains by a neighbour who worked for the electricity board. Water had been provided by the government during the last election campaign, but sewerage was still lacking. There was a school in the next settlement, and the eldest child would start to attend it in a couple of years' time.'

Alan Gilbert, *The Latin American City*, London: LAB, 1990

most vocal neighbourhood organisations. The list of demands is dispiritingly long: roads, drinking water, sewers, electricity, schools, rubbish collection, health clinics and bus routes. Another major battlefield concerns their illegality, since without proper legal title to the land, the inhabitants will never be secure in their homes. Once a settlement is established it can grow rapidly. In Lima 500 people organised a land invasion in 1960 and founded the Cuevas settlement. By 1970, 12,000 people lived there.

Shantytown women in Peru

'At the settlement Márquez del Callao, hundreds of children line up in front of the dining hall. They begin two hours before noon, every day, plate and spoon in hand. They beg and shout in hopes of getting a free portion from the mothers who organised this communal kitchen. Forty mothers cook 400 portions a day, half for member families and half for the hungry children.

These organisations depend on donations of oil, oatmeal and flour, and on their own purchases. In their search for better prices, the women will frequently contact the producers directly. This form of organising has proven so successful that, by 1986, 800 *comedores* (communal canteens) were represented by a National Commission of Comedores. Some are independent while others may be funded by the Church, the state, political parties or development agencies.

Rosario de Meléndez, recently laid off from a stocking factory, is a new member of the Glass of Milk committee of the neighbourhood of El Carcamo. When it is her turn, she gets up at five in the morning, turns on the stove and begins to heat a huge pot of milk, oatmeal, some sugar, cloves and cinnamon. She knows that at seven the children will begin lining up at the door of her house waiting for the hot milk. Each member of her committee contributes less than 10 cents a week for the purchase of kerosene, cocoa and cloves.

By working together, these women come to see their oppression as a social ill and open up new horizons for themselves. The voice of the women, before silent, is making itself heard. Formerly taboo subjects are now discussed. The mere fact that they are no longer shut up in their houses cooking for their husbands transforms relationships within the home. The women like to talk about the time one leader arrived at a meeting barefoot because her husband had hidden her shoes to keep her from going.'

Carolina Carlessi, 'The Reconquest', in *NACLA Report on the Americas*, New York, November 1989

The authorities may respond to land invasions with violent attempts at eviction, but in the long term many recognise that illegal settlement and self-build housing are the only solution to the shortage of accommodation. In cities like Lima and Mexico City, local politicians support squatters in exchange for votes, while political parties frequently try to co-opt the neighbourhood organisations' leaders. In Argentina, on the other hand, the military government bulldozed the villas miserias while cleaning up the city for the World Cup in 1978. Bolivian and Paraguayan migrants were beaten up, then herded on to trains and trucks for deportation. Often, however, the settlements' successes produce a spirit of optimism and self-confidence which is lacking in the gloomy tenements of the city centre.

The only alternative to the current uneasy coexistence between authorities and squatters is serious urban land reform. There are many parallels between the rural land crisis and that in the cities. Like agrarian reform, urban land reform requires far more than mere distribution of land if it is to succeed. Settlers also need access to credit to enable them to buy building materials, physical infrastructure such as roads and electricity, and technical advice on building. Just as in the countryside, the big urban landowners resist any attempt to challenge their control, and are usually successful in their efforts.

Visitors to Latin America may see little of life in the shantytowns and tenements, since tourists' hotels and friends or contacts are usually in the wealthier areas, either pleasant suburbs or modern city centres. In the middle-class areas, families lead a relatively comfortable existence, aided by servants and access to household appliances. As a proportion of the total population the middle class in Latin America is far smaller than in Europe or the US, and a vast gulf separates it from the poor masses of the slums. The middle-class enclaves are often little more than islands of 'modernity' in vast surrounding expanses of poverty. Along the main road north out of Recife, in northeastern Brazil, car drivers are even spared the sight of the long lines of cardboard and wooden shacks. A municipal billboard hundreds of yards long apologises for the 'inconvenience caused by temporary housing'. The billboard can hide the houses from view, but not the hot stench of the canal passing through the encampment. Scrawny children swim in the polluted waters. In places the canal banks are made up entirely of rubbish.

Scraping a Living

New Year's Eve on the road to Mexico City's airport: when the cars pull up at the traffic lights, a fire-breather steps out in front of the queue. A jet of flame lances across the night, lighting up a shiny face, glazed eyes and a hand clutching a bottle of petrol. After the show, the ragged performer goes up the line of car windows, hand outstretched. On New Year's Eve the drivers are in a good mood and he does well.

Although many migrants come to the city looking for regular paid jobs in industry, few find them. Despite Latin America's attempts at industrialisation, most of the investment has been in capital-intensive industry where machines do the work instead of people. Consequently, manufacturing employment has failed to keep up with the demand for jobs. In most Latin American nations, social security provisions apply only to those in regular employment for the state or big companies – unemployment and maternity benefits or pensions are not available to the majority. Without the safety net of a welfare state, migrants unable to find a way of earning an income face starvation, and most of the inhabitants of the shantytowns are forced to find work in what has become known as the 'informal sector' of the economy.

An Informal Sector Success Story

'At a busy traffic intersection in the Honduran capital of Tegucigalpa, Don Alfonso is an example of the informal sector in operation. Now a grizzled patriarch of 68, Don Alfonso has spent 15 years steering his family through the rapids of the Central American economy. He sits on the pavement next to stacks of today's newspapers, as six of his sons and daughters weave through the choking traffic. When the lights turn to red, the children move up and down the lines of cars in search of customers. Periodically they return to Don Alfonso to exchange their haul of grubby notes for a new supply of papers. The family makes a profit of about eight cents on each paper sold, and business is brisk.

When the time comes, Don Alfonso packs his various children off to school, scattered across the morning and afternoon shifts of the creaking Honduran education system. Franklin, 15, goes to night school from 6 p.m. to 8.30 p.m., even though he has to be up and on the streets by 5.30 the next morning for another seven-hour stint at the traffic lights.

Fifteen years ago, Don Alfonso abandoned his barren farm and headed for the city. By working together with his family, he can keep a firm eye on his children, and has succeeded in keeping the family united when many others have collapsed. With the proceeds of 15 years at the traffic lights, he has steadily upgraded his shanty-town hut into a solid house, with a new tin roof, cement floor and electricity. The walls are hung with family photos and their children's diplomas. Don Alfonso is proudest of his eldest son, who trained as a mechanic and now has a prized regular job in a factory.'

Duncan Green, *Hidden Lives: Voices of Children in Latin America and the Caribbean*, London: LAB, Cassell and SCF, 1997

The informal sector is the umbrella term for a mass of different tasks including street selling, domestic service, odd jobs, casual building labour, small-scale industry – recycling tyres into sandals, for example – picking through garbage for tin cans and paper, or even firebreathing at traffic lights.

Such work is in stark contrast to the formal sector of waged jobs more familiar to those in the industrialised nations. Formal-sector jobs are provided by large private and state-owned businesses, subsidiaries of multinational companies, and the public sector. Such jobs generally take place in the westernised centres of the cities, with their office blocks, government departments and shops, while economic life in the poor fringes of the city operates through the networks of the informal sector. Perhaps the clearest distinction between the two is over the level of protection: if someone in the informal sector is injured or sacked, they are on their own. Increasingly, the deregulation of workplaces and spread of activities such as subcontracting to sweatshops by textile companies means that the informal sector is encroaching on what were formal sector occupations.

To the visitor, the street traders are the most striking members of the informal economy. In La Paz, the Avenida Buenos Aires and adjoining streets are the site of the capital's biggest street market. Young men dressed in denim sell the latest line in microwaves or stereos smuggled in from Brazil while, one street along, indigenous women sit patiently in their bowler hats and ponchos, selling dried llama foetuses which are buried under the foundations of most new houses in Bolivia to bring good luck. Herbal remedies, BMX bicycles, imported disposable nappies, toiletries and pots and pans – the list of available goods is endless.

As the numbers of the urban poor have grown, so has the informal sector. During the recession of the 1980s and the subsequent neoliberal reforms, the informal sector has acted as a gigantic sponge, soaking up those who have been sacked, or who are entering the work force for the first time. The comparison between formal and informal sectors has led some economists to talk of two parallel circuits existing within the urban economy. The first circuit is a formal, western-style world of banks, factories and supermarkets, existing alongside a second circuit of street traders, money lenders and casual labourers. The two worlds are linked, however, since the informal sector provides low-cost services which often benefit the formal economy. The system resembles agriculture, where modern capital-intensive commercial agriculture exists alongside traditional labour-intensive peasant farming, which supplies cheap labour at harvest time.

In Latin America as a whole, the percentage of informal employment in urban areas has climbed by over five percentage points (nearly 20 million individuals) since 1990. New jobs in the informal sector rose from 67.3 per cent in 1990–94 to 70.7 per cent in 1997–99. Of every ten jobs being created now, seven are in the low-tech, low-wage economy. When the Argentine economy bounced back from a deep crisis in 2001–2, economic output returned to pre-crisis levels, but the nature of employment had shifted radically away from waged jobs towards the informal sector. As Latin America's streets have become clogged with vendors desperately seeking customers, incomes have fallen. In La Paz, where 60 per cent of the workforce is now in the informal sector, there is one street trader for every three families – there are just not enough buyers to go round. Informal-sector work impacts heavily on women, especially single mothers or those without family support; long hours spent ravelling to work mean that some single mothers have no choice but to leave even young children locked up at home alone. In an equally wasteful middle-class variant, the informal sector also absorbs Latin America's surplus lawyers, doctors and architects into its fleet of overqualified taxi drivers.

Future Cities

Latin America is now an urban continent, and will remain so. In many ways, its cities have been remarkably successful, absorbing nearly 400 million new inhabitants over a 70-year period. The fact that more keep arriving is proof that, whatever the difficulties of city life, for many it is still preferable to the struggle for existence in the countryside.

Yet if a better future for the region is to be forged in the cities, much has to change. The energy and dynamism of the self-help housing movement must be channelled into community development; governments must help rather than hinder the process, by passing urban land reform laws, providing support for the informal sector and ensuring that the next generation gets adequate education and health care. The ability of city authorities and national governments to provide such a future for their citizens is largely determined by the performance of the economy and the role of the state. The millions who have moved to Latin America's cities in search of a steady income will find work only if economic stability, jobs and effective welfare can be developed in tandem. There are causes for hope, such as the spread of public participation in setting local government budgets; what began as an experiment in a left-wing administration in Porto Alegre in southern Brazil has been replicated in numerous towns and cities across the continent. Yet such efforts still swim against an economic tide of instability, deep-rooted inequality and sluggish economic growth.

A Land in Flames: the Environment

The burning season starts in June in the Brazilian Amazon. The sky turns a dirty ochre, as a pall of smoke closes local airports and cuts off whole towns from the outside world. Each year the flames engulf a vast and irreplaceable area of virgin rainforest. By 2005, the forest was disappearing at the rate of 4.5 hectares a minute; in recent years an area as large as France, 17 per cent of the forest, has been felled – and some studies believe this figure could be much greater.

Although many people in the industrialised nations see environmental questions in Latin America as synonymous with the Amazon rainforest, the damage stretches to every corner of the continent, blighting cities and countryside alike.

In Costa Rica, resort developers have filled in and built upon the fragile mangrove swamps which form a buffer against the wind and waves. Furthermore, shrimping is poorly regulated and intense aquaculture is not prohibited under Costa Rican law, meaning that those areas of mangrove swamp unaffected by construction and development have found themselves open to overfishing and degradation. In 2000, a landmark ruling ordered a company to repair the environmental damage it had caused during a construction project, but little has been done to prevent further breaches.

The economically booming border zone where Mexico meets Texas has been blighted by pollution and disease on both sides of the border, although US settlements are in a far better position to deal with these problems. Tuberculosis and dysentery are particularly problematic for residents of the maquiladora towns on the Mexican side of the border, while ozone pollution has made the air in large towns unsafe. Another critical issue is hazardous waste, which is supposed to return to its country of origin, which for maquila goods would be the US. It is estimated, however, that less than one third of waste is actually transported, while less than 12 per cent is treated in accordance with environmental agreements.

In Ecuador, the rainforest region has been polluted by oil companies. The area known as *el Oriente* is one of the most biologically diverse in the world, but also provides the oil which furnishes Ecuador with 40 per cent of its export earnings. Around five million gallons of untreated toxic waste are dumped into this fragile environment every year, while the temptation to cut corners in the extraction process causes an average of two large oil spills each week..

The Conquest of Nature

The Conquest of the Americas lessened one kind of environmental pressure, but introduced many new ones. Recent archaeological evidence suggests that indigenous agriculture in Mexico and the Andes was in a state of crisis when the Spaniards arrived, as population pressure and soil erosion combined to produce a food crisis which may have been an important factor in enabling the Spaniards to win against the odds. The ensuing collapse of the indigenous population, through disease and forced labour, did much to ease the immediate pressure on the ecosystem. The population of Latin America did not return to pre-conquest levels until the 19th century.

However, the subsistence economies of the great indigenous civilisations were replaced by a colonial gold-rush mentality which aimed to plunder Latin America's resources, whether mineral or agricultural, as quickly as possible and send them abroad. When one resource was exhausted, another was found, with no attempt to build long-term sustainability. The philosophy was even applied to people: when indigenous labourers began to die out on Brazil's sugar plantations, the plantation owners chose to ship in Africans to do the job, rather than try and reduce the death rate among the indigenous population. As the centuries have passed, and Latin America has become ever more enmeshed in the world economy, natural resources have been raided to pay for imports of manufactured goods.

In the 20th century, an urban environmental crisis took off following the aggressive industrialisation programmes introduced in the 1930s and 1940s. As cities sprang up, sucking the rural poor into shanty-towns with few facilities, unregulated industry has poured effluents into the air and water, and millions of dilapidated cars have choked the cities with carbon monoxide.

Big is Beautiful

Since the Second World War, governments and international lenders have added to the damage done to Latin America's environment through their predilection for 'pharaonic' projects. Especially attractive to military governments, giant dams, huge road-building programmes, nuclear power, and vast mining complexes have wrought enormous human and environmental damage on the continent.

Roads are the kiss of death for the rainforest. Amazonian roads can be seen from the air to be bordered by a corridor of deforested land, spanning roughly a day's walk either side, due to the peasant farmers who move in as soon as a road is built and start hacking back the forest.

Dams were originally hailed as a clean and renewable energy source – every environmentalist's dream. Small-scale dam projects, such as those of Costa Rica, which relies on hydro-schemes for 99 per cent of its energy, are indeed environment-friendly. They affect a small area, and do not create the social, economic or environmental disruption caused by the great dams. Elsewhere, notably in Brazil and Argentina, governments have built gigantic constructions, flooding vast areas of the countryside, displacing indigenous peoples and local farmers, and causing unpredictable climatic change.

On the border between Brazil and Paraguay, the Itaipú dam has been described as 'a monument built of raw superlatives'. For five years Brazilian construction companies poured enough concrete every day to build a 350-storey building. The construction contract alone weighed 220 lbs. The dam began operation in 1984, straddling the giant Paraná river which flows out to sea as the River Plate between Argentina and Uruguay. Itaipú produces as much electricity as ten average nuclear power stations.

Dams on this scale carry costs not associated with smaller projects. The initial investment adds enormously to the country's debt burden – Itaipú cost Brazil US$20 billion, roughly 20 per cent of its entire foreign debt at that time. Dams are usually accompanied by other developments, such as industries using cheap energy. Since they are often built in relatively untouched parts of the country, this can cause great environmental damage. A prime example is the Grande Carajas project, for which Brazil built the Tucuruí dam, fifty per cent bigger than Itaipú. Furthermore, flooding leads to a massive loss of forest, and kills wildlife. The Tucuruí dam flooded 216,000 hectares in 1984, killing 2.8 million trees which were first sprayed with chemical defoliants. In populated areas the valleys flooded by dam projects are often the most fertile farm land. In some regions, the sudden increase in standing water has led to epidemics of parasitic diseases such as malaria, and can even substantially alter the local climate. Finally, deforestation upstream can increase siltation rates, shortening the dam's lifespan and turning it into a huge loss-maker, even before environmental costs are included in the balance sheet.

Extractive Industries

Latin America is now the recipient of the world's largest share of mining investment. At the start of the 1990s, the region attracted 12 per cent of worldwide investment in mining. But by the early 2000s this amount had nearly tripled to 33 per cent. The main mining countries, such as Chile, Peru and Brazil, have seen their exports boom to an all-time high. Price rises, Chinese demand and the tax breaks and relaxed labour laws approved in the 1990s as part of structural adjustment programmes have driven the new boom, which has shifted the continent back towards its traditional role as a producer of raw materials for the world's industries.

The environmental threat posed by such a boom is serious. Mining in forest areas leads to deforestation, while the tailings and other waste products of mineral extraction pollute rivers and farmland downstream from the mines.

Massive foreign mining projects are not the only environmental villains. Following a steep rise in the price of gold in 1979, 500,000 impoverished gold prospectors (*garimpeiros*) poured on to lands occupied by the Yanomami people on Brazil's northern border. The Yanomami were previously one of the largest and most isolated of Brazil's indigenous groups. The miners brought guns, diseases such as malaria and TB, and mercury, which they used in a crude process to separate gold dust from mud. According to Survival International, 1,500 of the 9,000 Yanomami died over a two-year period, while in settlements near the mining camps there were almost no children under the age of two.

Fight for the Forest

Deforestation has galvanised the green movement outside Latin America. Public opinion has been horrified at the spectacle of vast tracts of rainforest falling under the chainsaw, and the possible implications for the global

Slash-and-burn, the destructive method of clearing rainforest for pastureland in the Amazon.
(South American Pictures)

climate. Latin America contains 62 per cent of the world's remaining tropical rainforest, chiefly in the Amazon Basin countries of Brazil, Peru, Colombia, Venezuela and the Guianas. There are also smaller areas in Mexico and Central America, where the process of deforestation is both more rapid and much more advanced.

In the Amazon, forests are burned in order to turn the land over to pasture for cattle. The huge, inefficient cattle ranches have been encouraged by the Brazilian government with a variety of tax concessions and other incentives as part of its scheme for colonising the Amazon. One study in the 1970s showed that each ton of beef received US$4,000 in subsidies, yet earned only US$1,000 on the international market. Although the farms made little commercial sense, they were seen as an inflation-proof investment by companies or individuals living in the industrialised south.

The forest is also hacked down by poor peasant colonisers using 'slash and burn' methods. The precise division of blame between peasants and cattle barons is controversial. Up until 1980, cattle ranching accounted for 72 per cent of the deforestation. Since then, however, hundreds of thousands of peasants have marched in along the new roads like an army of leaf-cutter ants, while some of the tax incentives for cattle ranching have been removed in response to international pressure. Many of the peasant colonisers are themselves environmental refugees from soil erosion elsewhere or have lost their land to the onward march of soybean and other agribusiness in the south. Frequently they migrate following government advice to seek their fortunes as pioneers in the Amazon. What the government fails to tell them is that rainforest soil is unsuitable for sustained agriculture. Stripped of its trees, the fragile ecosystem rapidly collapses, nutrients are washed out of the soil, and within two or three years, declining fertility forces the peasant farmer to move on and cut down more forest. Most recently, Brazil's development of new strains of soybean suitable for more tropical climates has led to a new wave of deforestation, this time to make way for giant agribusiness producers of soybeans destined for animal feed.

The destruction of the Amazon has reached a critical point. By the end of 2005 in some areas the river has fallen to the lowest levels ever recorded. Several districts had been declared disaster areas and the army was having to bring in emergency supplies to towns and villages. And so many years after the murder of Chico Mendes, environmentalism can still carry a heavy price tag in Brazil: in February 2005 an American nun who had lived and worked on social and environmental issues in the Amazon basin for 20 years, Dorothy Stang, was shot by gunmen sent by local landowners.

In Central America the hamburger, epitome of US consumerism, is the driving force behind the breakneck pace of deforestation. Unlike their Brazilian counterparts, whose meat is destined largely for domestic consumption, cattle ranches in countries like Costa Rica are commercial ventures aimed at the US fast-food market. As in the Amazon, peasant farmers enter the forests and do the work of clearing the land for agriculture, but are soon squeezed out by declining fertility and pressure from cattle ranchers coming in behind them. Under cattle, the soil deteriorates further over 7–10 years, leaving an increasingly barren scrubland supporting fewer and fewer animals per hectare. By one calculation, Costa Rica loses 2.5 tonnes of topsoil for every kilogram of beef exported.

The Cost of Deforestation

• Deforested land is quickly eroded, and tons of topsoil are washed into watercourses, silting up streams and rivers, clogging hydroelectric installations and disrupting marine ecosystems along the coast. In Panama, deforestation has increased soil erosion, threatening to silt up the Panama Canal.

Fight for the Forest

The fight by local people to defend the Amazon gained world-wide attention when Chico Mendes, the leader of the Brazilian rubber tappers, was assassinated by a landowner in 1988. Mendes pioneered the idea of 'extractive reserves', using the forest sustainably to produce fruit, rubber and nuts.

'We realised that in order to guarantee the future of the Amazon we had to find a way to preserve the forest while at the same time developing the region's economy.

So what were our thoughts originally? We accepted that the Amazon could not be turned into some kind of sanctuary that nobody could touch. On the other hand, we knew it was important to stop the deforestation that is threatening the Amazon and all human life on the planet. We felt our alternative should involve preserving the forest, but it should also include a plan to develop the economy. So we came up with the idea of extractive reserves.

What do we mean by an extractive reserve? We mean the land is under public ownership but the rubber tappers and other workers that live on that land should have the right to live and work there. I say "other workers" because there are not only rubber tappers in the forest. In our area, rubber tappers also harvest brazil nuts, but in other parts of the Amazon there are people who earn a living solely from harvesting nuts, while there are others who harvest babaçu and jute.'

Cachoeira ('rapids') was the name of the rubber estate in the forest outside Xapuri where Chico Mendes was brought up and started life as a rubber tapper. He worked on the Cachoeira estate from the age of ten until his early thirties, when he began devoting most of his time to the rural workers' union.

In 1987 Cachoeira was bought by Darli Alves da Silva. Using a mixture of inducements and threats, he tried to drive out the 60 families of rubber tappers who had lived and worked on the estate for generations. Chico Mendes invested a great deal of effort and all his powers of persuasion and leadership to convince the rubber tappers of Cachoeira to stay where they were, and Darli issued death threats against him. In the second half of 1988, following the shooting of two youths during the *empate* [confrontation] at the Ecuador rubber estate in May and the assassination of Ivair Higino in June, the federal government sought to defuse the situation by signing expropriation orders for three extractive reserves. One of these was Cachoeira, where 15,000 acres were allocated to the rubber tappers.

This victory for the rubber tappers was also the death sentence for Chico, as the family of Darli Alves sought to avenge their defeat. The attempts on his life became systematic and on 22 December 1988 he was murdered.

Chico Mendes, *Fight for the Forest*, London: LAB, 1989

- Deforestation disrupts the local climate, since the trees regulate the storage and release of rain water. By returning water vapour to the atmosphere, trees also encourage further rainfall. The loss of forests therefore makes both drought and flooding as well as mudslides more likely.

- Many of Latin America's poor rely on firewood for fuel. As the forests become depleted, they must travel farther afield to scavenge for supplies, and in the towns the price rises reflect wood's increasing scarcity.

- Indigenous peoples who live in harmony with the forest have little hope of surviving sustained contact with incoming settlers, although some indigenous groups are now fighting to survive and even benefit from the environmental onslaught.

- The rainforest is a repository of plant and animal species which, besides their intrinsic value, are a vital source of new genetic material – a quarter of all pharmaceutical products are derived from rainforest products, even though only one per cent of all Amazon plants have been intensively investigated for their medicinal properties. Tropical forest plants have provided treatments for leukaemia, Hodgkin's disease, breast, cervical and testicular cancer and are currently being used in AIDS research.

- A number of investigations show that the commercial potential of the forest is far greater than that of the pasture which replaces it. In addition the forest can be farmed in a sustainable way, yielding rubber, brazil nuts and many kinds of fruit.

- Most western attention has centred on the issue of global warming. The burning itself releases greenhouse gases (especially carbon dioxide, which accounts for half the global warming effect) into the atmosphere, and the forests are no longer there to absorb carbon dioxide through photosynthesis. However, developing countries point out that 75 per cent of the world's carbon dioxide emissions come from the factories and cars of the industrialised nations, who long ago destroyed their own forest environments. They say the North has not yet put its own house in order, and therefore has little moral authority to tell Latin America what to do with its rainforest.

Soil erosion

Over-intensive agriculture can produce just as much soil erosion as deforestation. In Central America 40 per cent of all lands suffer a degree of erosion which undermines their productivity. The worst case is El

Salvador, where an estimated 77 per cent of arable land is eroded. Ravaged by years of civil war, this tiny country is the most densely populated in Latin America and has an extremely unequal system of land distribution. In the Salvadoran countryside peasant farmers hand-tend tiny plots of maize and beans on steep hillsides, while down below on the fertile valley floor the rich landowners' tractors prepare the land for cotton or sugar.

The El Niño weather pattern has increased the frequency of hurricanes and floods in recent decades, with catastrophic results. The effects of these natural disasters have been magnified by both deforestation and over-intensive farming, leading to enormous landslides in parts of Central America and the Caribbean. Now, without the stabilising root systems of forest trees, rural settlements can be washed away in an instant.

Downstream the silt, often laden with pesticides, devastates the marine environment. Siltation, pollution and wood-cutting have reduced El Salvador's 300,000 acres of mangrove estuary to a pitiful remnant. The loss is also an economic one: mangroves provide a rich breeding ground for marine life, and one square kilometre of mangrove estuary is worth US$100,000 a year in fish and shellfish. Siltation has also greatly reduced the lifespan of a number of hydro-electric dams in the region by clogging up the lakes that feed the generators.

Despite efforts to show poor farmers the virtues of terracing, crop rotation and tree-planting, hard-pressed families are likely to continue to plough up hillsides or cut down trees unless serious land reform gives them better lands elsewhere.

Pesticide Poisons

All over rural Latin America glossy roadside billboards peddle the wares of the big agrochemical multinationals. Names like Bayer, Ciba-Geigy, Shell, Monsanto and Du Pont adorn adverts promising farmers prosperity if they administer just one more dose of chemicals to their crops. In jeeps and village bars, the plantation owners sport brand names such as Tordon or Gramoxone on their T-shirts and baseball caps. The pesticide companies claim to sell their wares in philanthropic pursuit of an end to world hunger, and that, in the words of one Bayer annual report, 'emotional attacks against conscientious agrochemicals research are attacks against humanity.'

In fact, nearly all pesticides are used on export crops, not food for local people, and the cotton and banana plantations of Central America provide some of the worst examples of pesticide abuse in the world. In the 1970s Central America consumed 40 per cent of all US pesticide exports. Chemicals like DDT, which were illegal in the US, were routinely exported and sold in the region, where about 75 per cent of the pesticides used are

Biopiracy: The Battle for the Yellow Bean

'The term "biopiracy" was coined in 1992, and has since gained wide usage in the controversy over scientists and businesses that simply take biological material from developing countries and patent it back home. With his red beard and swashbuckling manner, Colorado bean broker Larry Proctor even looks like the stereotype of the old-fashioned pirate, and has spurred a cross-border turf war in the long fight against biopiracy. The little yellow bean he claims to have invented has become emblematic of the inequities between the North and the South in an age that measures riches not in buried treasure but in the multidigit patents that form what the biotech industry likes to call its "intellectual property estate".

Proctor's use of patent laws to take over an emerging US market for Mexican yellow beans highlights both the inequities and the injustices in the current intellectual property regime. In this case the victims are not poor farmers but a well-organized group of modern Mexican producers seeking to take commercial advantage of NAFTA's opening of cross-border trade.

In 1994, Larry Proctor bought a bag of bean seeds in Sonora, Mexico, and took them home to sow. He began to breed a yellow bean, and in 1996 he applied for a patent from the US Patent and Trademark Office. Patent number 5894079, issued on April 13, 1999, gives his company, Pod-ners, LLC , exclusive monopoly rights to market what he calls the "Enola" bean – after his wife's middle name.

Meanwhile in the northwestern state of Sinaloa, Mexico, the farmers who have been producing the yellow bean for generations learned that it was no longer theirs. Proctor's patent bars them from what had become a lucrative market for the beans in southern California. But the powerful Rio Fuerte Growers Association (RFGA) of Los Mochis, Sinaloa, has vowed to fight back. As one member put it, "What Mr Proctor has done is plagiarism of years of research in Mexican experimental fields."

As the ink flows and the accusations fly, policymakers and dealmakers view the yellow bean patent as a precedent-setting case within the murky realm of international biotech protection. Across borders, lawyers, scientists, farmers, activists, trade officials, and now even the United Nations, have all taken up arms in the battle of the bean.

Timothy A. Wise, Hilda Salazar and Laura Carlsen (eds), *Confronting Globalization*, Bloomfield, Conn: Kumarian Press, 2003

either banned, restricted or unregistered in the US. In 1990 the US Congress finally took action and passed laws preventing the 'dumping' of banned pesticides on third-world markets. Over the next decade, however, Central American pesticide imports more than doubled. By the turn of the century, the Pan American Health Organization estimated that 400,000 cases of pesticide poisoning were occurring in Central America every year.

Pesticide pollution even finds an echo in the cocaine boom, as aerial spraying of anti-coca herbicides funded by the US Drug Enforcement Agency has led to serious health concerns in rural Colombia and Ecuador.

Lost Volcanoes

The cities of Latin America are losing their volcanoes. In Santiago, Chile, people recall the days when the snow-capped Andes loomed over the city. Now they rarely break through a dense blanket of smog. The Chilean government has even proposed blasting a hole through the mountain chain to allow the wind through to clear away the murk. 'They think it's easier to move mountains than to control the bus drivers,' explained a resident.

In Mexico, the two great volcanoes of the Aztecs, Popocatépetl and Ixtaccihuatl, have similarly been lost to sight. Average visibility has dropped from 12 kilometres to just 3 in the last 40 years. Air pollution exceeds internationally acceptable levels in São Paulo, Buenos Aires, Santiago, Caracas and Mexico City. Mexico is probably the worst, as any visitor will agree who has had the misfortune to be there on one of the 225 days of the year when a thermal inversion prevents the city's filth from escaping. Pedestrians weep as they walk through the streets in air that does as much damage as smoking 40 cigarettes a day. Mexico is uniquely damned by geography – it lies in a natural bowl where pollution collects, and at its high altitude of 7,400 feet car engines produce twice their sea-level amount of carbon monoxide. For the inhabitants of such cities, air

---

Pesticide Contamination Among Farm Workers

'An early morning bus ride through the cotton-growing area of Central America provides a stinging glimpse of everyday reality. As the bus passes plantations, its windows film over. Most of the passengers, knowing what to expect, close their eyes, slow their breathing, and cover their nose and mouth with a scarf. Those riders caught unaware feel their eyes begin to smart, their lungs involuntarily contract, and a bitter chemical smell starts to clog their noses.

Visitors to the area will likely rush off the bus to change clothes and to wash their stinging skin with soap and water. The local population is not so fortunate; their exposure to agricultural chemicals for the day has only begun. They will toil long hours in the fields, drenched with chemicals that crop dusters sprayed earlier that morning. Three out of four farm workers have no running water in their homes to wash off the day's accumulation of pesticides. Many bathe in irrigation canals or streams contaminated with still more agrochemicals, or try to wash off with water stored in a discarded pesticide drum.'

Tom Barry, *Roots of Rebellion*, Boston: South End Press, 1987

pollution is far more than an irritant. Seventy per cent of all babies are born with unacceptable levels of lead in their bloodstreams.

Following the Great Depression of the 1930s, all of the larger Latin American nations embarked on a programme of industrialisation aimed at reducing their dependence on commodity exports and manufactured imports. The consequence was a sudden surge in unchecked industrial growth and a chaotic exodus of impoverished farmers from the countryside to the cities. Latin America's cities rapidly became some of the biggest in the world – Mexico City had about 20 million inhabitants by 2003.

Three quarters of Mexico City's pollution comes from millions of cars and the city's huge and filthy industrial complex. 'If the [US] Environmental Protection Agency standards were applied to this country,' comments one US embassy official, 'Mexico would surpass the highest tolerable levels for sulphur dioxide, cadmium, lead, zinc, copper and particulate matter.' What he omits to mention is that many US and other multinational companies have been quick to relocate some of their dirtiest factories to Latin American countries precisely to avoid those EPA standards and the increased costs they imply.

The growth of the cities seems inexorable, but could be slowed if governments undertook serious agrarian reform in the countryside and used regional planning to decentralise the economy. In the towns, the environmental damage could be reduced if factories and vehicles were regulated, and there have been some encouraging signs in recent years, with the Brazilian city of Curitiba offering some impressive lessons to city planners around the world. City schemes to encourage lead-free petrol and make people leave their cars at home for one working day a week have helped to cut air pollution in Santiago, Mexico City and São Paulo.

Climate Change

Latin America is already suffering the effects of global warming. In the Andes, many glaciers are rapidly retreating, as they melt faster than new snowfalls can replenish the ice. Huge chunks of the Antarctic ice shelf are breaking off and floating out to sea. But scientific studies predict that worse is to come. Further north, semi-arid areas could be turned into deserts, destroying the livelihoods of already vulnerable smallholder farmers in places such as northeast Brazil. Perhaps the most immediate overall threat is an increase in the catastrophic weather cycles known as El Niño and La Niña, periods of warm and cold water currents off the shores of the Americas that produce severe droughts and floods. As with many other so-called 'natural disasters', poor and vulnerable communities are the most likely to be harmed by such phenomena.

Exports

The squeeze on the environment accelerated with the debt crisis, as governments stepped up exports to meet escalating repayments to the western banks. As time went on, the broader processes of 'structural adjustment', which pursued an 'export-or-die' approach to development, have further increased pressure on the ecosystem.

Governments desperate to find new sources of hard currency have shown little interest in longer-term issues such as environmental protection. In Guyana, largely untouched forests have come under the hammer as part of an adjustment programme agreed with the International Monetary Fund (IMF) in the late 1980s. Guyana has duly parcelled out its forests and rivers to an unholy alliance of Canadian, Brazilian and Asian mining and logging companies. In return for a 50-year licence on a 4.13-million-acre concession, the notorious Sarawak-based logger Samling Timbers promised to export 1.2 million cubic feet of Guyanese timber a year (compared to national exports of just 94,000 cubic feet in 1989).

One of the growth areas has been so-called 'non-traditional exports' of higher-value agricultural products such as cut flowers or fresh fruit. These require enormous doses of pesticide and fungicide in order to reach supermarkets in the North in pristine condition.

Genetically modified crops, involving gene splicing across species rather than traditional forms of selective breeding, have spread in several Latin American countries, particularly Argentina, where, as early as 1998,

---

The Cost of Exports

'In the Chilean port of Puerto Montt, a rich sweet smell of fermenting wood emanates from several huge mounds of wood chip, silhouetted against the dockside floodlights. Dwarfing the wooden houses and shops of the town, the mounds steam gently as they await loading onto the Japanese ship which rides at anchor in the bay. Each pile contains the remnants of a different species of Chilean tree, hauled from the country's dwindling native forest.

Along the Chilean coast, the wire-mesh tanks of innumerable salmon farms dot the picturesque fjords and inlets. On the beaches, the black strings of pelillo seaweed lie drying, before being sent to Japan for processing into food preservative. In the ports, the fishmeal factories grind mackerel into animal fodder. All these products will be shipped overseas as part of the Chilean export boom, a vast enterprise which has turned the country into the fastest-growing economy in Latin America and the flagship of the new market-led economic model which has taken the region's governments by storm.'

Duncan Green, *Silent Revolution: The Rise and Crisis of Market Economics in Latin America*, London: LAB, 2003

90 per cent of all soybeans were GM. Since then, Brazil has followed suit. GM has proved controversial in many consumer countries, especially in Europe, which has largely shunned them. In developing countries, while GM has enabled producers to reduce usage of pesticides and herbicides, there is concern that the widespread adoption of GM will displace local species (genetic erosion) and leave peasant farmers increasingly dependent on the seeds and linked chemical inputs controlled by large multinationals like Monsanto.

Green Guerrillas

In recent years, the environmental movement has taken off in Latin America and has already achieved some notable successes. Environmental groups were initially largely urban and middle-class, taking their cue from the burgeoning green movement in Europe and North America. They were

---

Dirty Industry

'Apart from raw materials, the other growth area in Latin American exports are the *maquiladoras*. These are assembly plants run by transnational companies in Mexico, Central America and the Caribbean which take advantage of low wages and lax environmental laws to produce goods for re-export to the US market:

"Twelve years ago we came to live here", says Maurilio Sánchez Pachuca, the stout president of the local residents' committee in a dingy *colonia* just outside Tijuana, Mexico. "We thought we'd be in glory because it was an ecological reserve – lots of vegetation, animals, birds. Two years later the maquiladoras started to arrive up there." A fat thumb gestures up at the plateau overlooking the colonia, with its clean blue and white maquiladora assembly plants. "Now many of us have skin problems – rashes, hair falling out, we get eye pains, fevers. My kids' legs are really bad – all the kids have nervous problems and on the way to school the dust and streams are all polluted. We've tried to stop them playing in the streams, but kids are kids." He flicks despairingly through a treasured folder full of blurred photocopies of the hand-typed letters he has written to the authorities and their replies, a nine-year exercise in Kafkaesque futility. "The first thing [the maquiladoras] do is buy the local officials. There are too many vested interests – dark interests, dollars. I have so many lovely letters from the government – but they aren't real."

Up on the plateau, huge container trucks are at the loading bays, gorging themselves on the products of the 189 factories – Maxell cassettes, a crisp new Sanyo plant, Tabuchi Electric de México. A security guard ushers unwelcome visitors from the site. A black and pink slag-heap of battery casings is piled up by the fence surrounding the factories, where truckloads of old batteries from the US are broken up to recycle the lead and acid. By law, the remnants should be returned to the US, but they are just dumped here on the edge of the plateau.'

Duncan Green, *Silent Revolution: The Rise and Crisis of Market Economics in Latin America*, London: LAB, 2003

also boosted by the 1992 UN 'Earth Summit', held in Rio de Janeiro, which by explicitly linking the two concepts of environment and development, gained general acceptance of the importance of 'sustainable development'.

The work of the middle-class environmentalists and the international green lobby can clearly be seen in the increased media coverage for green issues within the region and the 'greening' of political debate. Even ranchers and loggers now feel obliged to dress up their language in green rhetoric. Pressure from the urban environmental movement has also been instrumental in forcing the region's cities to begin to try and control air pollution. In some cases, governments and the private sector found that environmentalism could also be good for business. One of the most successful green industries is ecotourism, which in Costa Rica brought in US$500 million in 1993, as northern holidaymakers were lured by a combination of beaches and spectacular national parks.

Another wing of Latin American environmental activism comes from the grassroots, involving those directly affected, usually poor communities such as those championed by Chico Mendes. Often led by the region's burgeoning indigenous revival (see Section 4), these groups have led campaigns against polluting oil industries in Mexico and Ecuador and have taken up numerous other causes.

Such developments offer hope for the future, but there are also ample grounds for gloom. The greed and short-sightedness of both local and foreign interests have changed little since the conquest – they still mistakenly treat the New World and its people as an inexhaustible and indestructible source of riches. Since the 1980s, the region's uncritical adoption of a development model based on the unregulated market and ever more rapacious exploitation of its ecosystem has worked against attempts to improve the environment, forcing grassroots campaigners to swim against the prevailing economic tide. When, as part of its commitment to opening up the economy, the Brazilian government removed the tariffs which had protected domestic rubber producers, cheap Malaysian rubber flooded in. The price of latex in Brazil fell from US$1.80 per kilogram in 1980 to under 40 cents in 1992, and Amazon-grown rubber saw its market share slide from 85 per cent to just 28 per cent. The first to suffer were the rubber tappers, who in the wake of Chico Mendes' murder had pressured the government into establishing extractive zones covering millions of hectares. Their joy turned sour as they watched prices slump, and thousands of families have been forced to leave the new reserves in search of a living wage in the cities, or join the ranks of the *garimpeiros* in the ecologically disastrous gold rush. The blind forces of economics have turned them from defenders of the environment into its destroyers.

Tourism

Travel and tourism to Latin American countries has increased steadily over the last twenty years: Costa Rica, Peru, Brazil and Mexico are now favoured long-haul travel destinations from the UK and Europe. The 1990s saw tourism climb steadily up the list of foreign-exchange earners for many countries; in the case of Costa Rica it had replaced bananas and coffee by the end of the decade as the top earner of foreign cash. Much, but not all, of this tourism is centered around adventure, nature, or eco-tourism. Latin America's many pleasures and assets – a rich natural environment, diverse cultures, history and heritage, suggest that this trend will only grow.

Ecotourism, Greenwash and Ecotourism Lite

'Ecotourism in Latin America, as elsewhere, has become "big business", both as a label applied to a vast range of tourism destinations, products and experiences and as the focus of vigorous debate. Many examples of ecotourism focus exclusively on tourism that offers encounters with nature. Another definition, this one by the International Ecotourism Society, calls it "responsible travel to natural areas that conserves the environment and improves the well-being of local people."

The liberal and often unjustified claims for ecotourism have brought widespread accusations that many tourism operators and destinations are guilty of "greenwashing", a kind of deceitful public relations message suggesting that a business acts in a more environmentally responsible way than it actually does.

Martha Honey, in her article "Giving a Grade to Costa Rica's Green Tourism", in NACLA's *Report on the Americas* in May/June 2003, offers a nicely sceptical viewpoint based on her close acquaintance with the evolution of Costa Rica's highly publicised ecotourism industry:

"Today, everything in Costa Rica seems to carry 'eco' in its name. There is, for instance, 'Eco-Playa' (a typical beach indistinguishable from other grey/black sand beaches), 'Ecological Rent-a-Car' (which rents the same vehicles as Hertz, Budget or Avis), 'eco-gas' (super unleaded), 'eco-musica' (songs with environmental themes), and innumerable ecolodges, ecosafaris and ecological cruises. Many of these tourism enterprises can be categorised as ecotourism 'lite', meaning that the company's green rhetoric far outstrips the reality of its adherence to sound ecotourism principles. The classic example of this in Costa Rica as elsewhere is the growing number of major hotel chains that offer guests the 'eco-option' of not having their sheets and towels laundered every day. Such sensible but relatively minor environmental innovations are advertised with claims such as 'Keep your towels and help save the world!' The reality is that it is the hotels that are saving sizeable sums on their laundry bills."'

Martin Mowforth and Ian Munt, *Responsible Tourism in Latin America*, London: LAB, 2007 (forthcoming)

For many countries in Latin America, tourism creates jobs, generates foreign exchange, and raises tax revenues. But it also brings ills such as environmental mismanagement and waste, cultural 'pollution' such as travellers bringing unwanted habits like drug-taking, and in some cases tourism exacerbates already entrenched social inequalities. From the tourists' point of view, many Latin American countries are seen as security risks, with tourist-related crime rampant in some areas. In a sense, much tourism in Latin America produces a more acute version of the abrupt collision between the haves and the have nots which already takes place among the domestic population.

Identity and Rights 4

CONTENTS

Race and Ethnicity

Latin America has moved on from its colonial days, when a tiny white elite ruled over an indigenous majority. *Mestizaje*, or racial mixing, describes the intermingled nature of the majority of the continents' population today. Whites mixed with indigenous peoples created a *mestizo* race, whereas whites with black African-descended peoples produced *mulatos*. Black and indigenous mixes were often termed *zambo*, or 'black indian'.

While most studies of race still concentrate on the indigenous experience, increasing attention is being given to the history, culture and everyday lives of the continent's Afro-Latin Americans. There are significant populations of descendants of Africans in Cuba, the Dominican Republic, Central America – especially Nicaragua, Costa Rica and Panama – Colombia, Peru and Brazil. But there are also smaller numbers of Afro-Argentines, and Afro-Venezuelans.

Race – especially 'blackness' – is now seen as much a social and cultural construction as a matter of genetic inheritance. In today's Latin America, race, social and economic position, and gender are inevitably intertwined.

Indigenous Peoples

Cape Sunday (Cabo Domingo) is a lonely place. Low, dark hills under an enormous sky sink towards the ocean at the southern tip of the Americas. At this spot one Sunday in the 1920s a German landowner held a banquet for the local Yaganes people. When they were drunk, his hidden henchmen opened fire with a machine gun. The Yaganes died because, unaccustomed to the concept of private property, they had killed and eaten the landowner's sheep. The indigenous people of Tierra del Fuego were an almost stone-age people dressed in skins and using flint hand-tools. When the whites started to colonise the region in the 1880s, the tribes soon succumbed to disease and slaughter. Today only a few old folk remain of the people whose permanent camp fires gave Tierra del Fuego (Land of Fire) its name.

Several thousand miles north, Ecuador came to a grinding halt in February 2005, as the Confederation of Indigenous Nationalities of Ecuador (CONAIE) initiated national protests against the government of Lucio Gutiérrez, a president they had helped to elect after a similar uprising in 1999 had ousted the previous president. Gutiérrez had alienated his erstwhile indigenous allies by agreeing a structural adjustment programme with the IMF, initiating military cooperation with the US, and opening up indigenous regions to oil exploration, and was duly forced from office. In Ecuador, the indigenous people now decide the fate of presidents.

The Ecuadorean movement's dynamism belies the conventional western image of fatalistic indigenous communities calmly awaiting extinction. Latin America's history is full of the uprisings and resistance of peoples whose civilisations were in many ways far in advance of Europe's at the time of the conquest.

Modern Indigenous Life

The continent's indigenous survivors now make up five per cent of its total population and fall into two distinct groups. The first, and by far the largest, is that of the highland indigenous people, descendants of the Inca, Aztec and Mayan empires. The second are the lowland indigenous groups, largely confined to the Amazon basin and Central America. In both Guatemala and Bolivia, over half the population is indigenous, while the largest numbers live in Peru and Mexico. Although highland indigenous people number some 22 million, lowlanders do not exceed 1 million, of whom about a quarter live in Brazil, with smaller numbers in the other countries of the Amazon basin: Venezuela, Colombia, Ecuador, Peru, Bolivia and the Guianas. Isolated lowland groups also survive in the Central American countries of Panama, Nicaragua and Honduras.

When not tied to the *haciendas* of the big landowners, highland communities farm the land in much the same way as they did five centuries ago. They grow the traditional crops – maize, beans and squash in Mexico, potatoes and maize in the Andes, using mainly the simple technology of the digging stick and hoe. Communities are tightly knit, and members are encouraged not to sell land to outsiders and to marry within the village. Although their lifestyles are often romanticised by outsiders, indigenous farming communities lead harsh lives, suffering the high levels of infant mortality and insecurity common to all peasant farmers.

Where they have managed to retain a level of independence, such communities frequently enjoy a rich cultural life. In Guatemala, each highland village has its own distinctive costume, with unique designs passed on from mother to daughter for generations. Many traditional practices have survived the efforts of the colonial authorities. Faith healers combine herbal medicine and magic, and the religion of the European invaders has been fused with its predecessors into an original form of 'folk Catholicism'. Communities attach great importance to ritual cycles involving saints' days, feast days and ceremonies such as baptism, marriage and funerals.

In the course of the 20th century modern influences gradually encroached upon this traditional pattern. Improved roads have increased trading and involvement in the money economy; improved education and contact with the outside world mean that most indigenous people now speak Spanish; satellite television and the internet have found their way into the most remote villages; and growing numbers of Protestant missionaries have both converted indigenous groups and persuaded them to abandon their traditional customs. The old ways persist most stubbornly in Guatemala, where many speakers of the country's 21 indigenous languages still know no more than a few words of Spanish. In most areas men are assimilated into non-indigenous ways faster than women, who have become the custodians of traditional culture. Men have more contact with the money economy through wage labour, and women less frequently go to school, where Spanish is often the only permitted language.

Another major cause of what is known as 'acculturation', the loss of traditional culture, is urbanisation. The exodus to the cities brings contact with poor mestizos and indigenous people from other communities, and Spanish frequently becomes the common language. The disruption of the move can leave few vestiges of traditional culture intact.

War and repression also accelerate the process. In Guatemala, a ferocious army counter-insurgency campaign in the indigenous highlands since the early 1980s left 40,000 dead and over 400 indigenous villages destroyed. Many more fled their villages to seek refuge in the cities, where they sought anonymity by abandoning their traditional dress and customs. Over a million people were displaced from their homes in what bordered on a race war. In the mid-1980s one Guatemalan President warned 'we must get rid of the words "indigenous" and "Indian".' Peru's civil war between the Sendero Luminoso guerrillas and the army also drove many indigenous families into the swelling shantytowns around Lima. The economic difficulties of the 1990s pushed many smallholders in Bolivia, Ecuador and Mexico away from farming, with its unpredictable returns, to the grim certainty of urban life.

Violent racism persists in most countries with a significant indigenous population. In Guatemala the enormous divide between poor, non-Spanish speaking indigenous people and wealthy white landowners and entrepreneurs closely resembles apartheid. When indigenous activist Rigoberta Menchú won the Nobel Peace Prize in 1992, 'ethnic dolls' in indigenous dress speedily went on to the market in the US. Wealthy Guatemalans were torn between national pride and class hatred, and were heard to joke that at last Barbie had found a maid.

Indigenous Identity

'Our parents tell us: "Children, the earth is the mother of man, because she gives him food." This is especially true for us whose life is based on the crops we grow. Our people eat maize, beans and plants. We can't eat ham, or cheese, or things made by machines. So we think of the earth as the mother of man, and our parents teach us to respect the earth. We must only harm the earth when we are in need. This is why, before we sow our maize, we have to ask the earth's permission.

By accepting the Catholic religion, we didn't accept a condition, or abandon our culture. It was more like another way of expressing ourselves. It's like expressing ourselves through a tree, for example; we believe that a tree is a being, a part of nature, and that a tree has its image, its representation, its nahual, to channel our feelings to the one God. That is the way we Indians conceive it. Catholic Action is like another element which can merge with the elements which already exist within Indian culture. And it confirms our belief that, yes, there is a God, and, yes, there is a father for all of us. And yet it is something we think of as being only for what happens up there. As far as the earth is concerned, we must go on worshipping through our own intermediaries, just as we have always done, through all the elements found in nature.

When we evoke the colour of the sun, it's like evoking all the elements which go to make up our life. The sun as the channel to the one God, receives the plea from his children that they should never violate the rights of all the other beings which surround them. This is how we renew our prayer which says that men, the children of the one God, must respect the life of the trees, the birds, the animals around us. We must respect the life of every single one of them. We must respect the life, the purity, the sacredness, which is water. We must respect the one God, the heart of the sky, which is the sun. We must not do evil while the sun shines upon his children. This is a promise.'

Rigoberta Menchú and Elisabeth Burgos Debray (ed.), *I, Rigoberta Menchú* (trans. Ann Wright), London: Verso, 1984

Lowland Indigenous People

'No one sells his own son or his mother, because he loves them. In the same way, it is an absurd idea for an Indian to sell his land. We can't change our feelings for our land, which is where our ancestors are buried.'
Speaker from Taxáua people, Brazil

In contrast to the highlanders' stable agriculture based on herding and crop rotation, lowland indigenous groups have traditionally practised mobile slash-and-burn forms of farming, combined with fishing and hunting. Both groups, however, share an overwhelming and mystical bond with the land. Lowlanders, like the highlanders, have strong religious traditions in which worship of aspects of the natural world is mediated through shamans who speak to the deities in a trance.

Lowland groups traditionally live more communally than highlanders, often in communal houses, known as *malocas*, which can hold several hundred people. Malocas have been criticised by Protestant missionaries for encouraging promiscuity and in many cases have been abandoned in favour of family houses. Many hundreds of different language groups exist, some comprising only a few dozen speakers.

Whereas highland communities have been in contact with whites virtually since the first days of the conquest, lowland peoples have frequently lived in inaccessible areas, especially those in the Amazon basin, which outsiders have only recently penetrated. There are still believed to be a few groups, numbering perhaps a few thousand, of 'uncontacted' indigenous people in the area. When contact does occur, it is frequently as disastrous as it was in the 16th century, leading to epidemics of disease and violent confrontations with settlers, such as those that have recently befallen the Yanomami people.

Lowland peoples have suffered the same 'curse of wealth' as their highland relatives. In the rubber boom at the end of the 19th century, unscrupulous rubber companies trapped and enslaved large numbers of indigenous people as latex collectors. In the Putumayo region of Colombia, 40,000 were killed by these rubber barons between 1886 and 1919. After rubber came African palm, cattle and oil, each new commodity penetrating fresh areas of the forest and absorbing or driving out the local indigenous groups. Since the 1990s, indigenous groups in the Ecuadorean Amazon have started to fight back against the oil companies whose drilling is destroying their forest ecosystem. In 2003, after years of legal struggles in US courts had come to naught, they filed a billion-dollar lawsuit in Quito against the US oil giant ChevronTexaco, accusing the company of destroying large areas of rainforest and contaminating local land and rivers. They also alleged that the company's activities had led to an increased risk of cancer among the local population. In the Peruvian Amazon, fears of the impact of oil exploration have also galvanized lowland indigenous activism.

The other main source of encroachment on indigenous lands has been the colonisation programmes, either spontaneous or government-run, through which landless peasants have moved into the forest, cutting down the trees to make way for food crops. This has provoked frequent armed conflict between peasants and indigenous communities.

Government attitudes to the lowland indigenous groups have alternated between cynical disregard and a desire to 'integrate' them into national life, a process anthropologists condemn as 'ethnocide'. One Brazilian government official proudly described his policy to a visiting journalist:

We resettle them as quickly as possible in new villages and then remove the children and begin to educate them. We give them the benefit of our medicine and our education, and, once they are completely integrated citizens like you and me and the Minister here, we let them go out into the world.

Once out in the world, 'integrated Indians' often end up on the social scrapheap, surviving as beggars or prostitutes on the fringes of the frontier boom-towns of the Amazon. Sometimes the ethnocide was more deliberate. In Brazil in the early 1960s, a government enquiry found that corrupt officials of its own indigenous agency had connived with local landowners to massacre entire tribes using dynamite, machine guns and poisoned sugar. Other investigations showed that tribes in Mato Grosso had been deliberately infected with smallpox, influenza, tuberculosis and measles.

Debt Bondage in Colombia

'We called all the Indians together, along with their families, in a ravine or at the mouth of a river and there, in the presence of the Indian authorities, we advanced them: one shirt, one machete, some knives to make the cuts [in the rubber trees], a belt so that they didn't fall out of the trees, and of course, any goods they wanted. Throughout the year, we advanced them anything they, or their women, asked for. The women were their ruin and our business, because they fancied everything. Vanity does not respect colour, nor age, nor sex. They wanted combs, perfumes, mirrors and coloured beads, cloth and more cloth, high-heeled shoes and ribbons for their hair. The men asked for drink, Italian sweets and German radios. They liked music and partying.

Every day around 4 p.m. the line of Indians would arrive with the latex, which was weighed on scales and then each Indian's amount was entered in a book. The scales didn't measure the true weight, and the amount we wrote in the book wasn't the amount on the scales. The [German missionary] did a lot of damage because she taught the "cousins" figures and they began to cause trouble the whole time. When they got unhappy, they'd run away. So we had to invent the pass – no boss would give them an advance if the Indians couldn't show a pass signed by their previous boss to prove that they had paid off their debts. Some Indians managed to pay off their debts, and even earned some money on top, but others didn't. Everything depended on their boss. Some bosses fiddled the books so they never managed to pay it off. But others were very humane and only wrote down what the Indian asked for.'

Alfredo Molano, *Aguas Arriba*, Bogotá: El Áncora editores, 1990, describing Colombia's early 20th century rubber boom, (author's translation)

Rebellion and Resistance

The slow genocide of the indigenous nations provoked fierce resistance. In some cases, as in the Caribbean or Brazil, indigenous groups opted for mass suicide rather than bow to the dictates of the whites. Many others retreated into the most inaccessible areas of the continent to escape the burden of constant tributes and forced labour. Some took up arms against the Spanish authorities, the most famous being Peru's Túpac Amaru, the most persistent being the dogged resistance of Chile's Mapuche people, who kept the outsiders at bay until the late 19th Century, the most recent being the Mayan Zapatista uprising in southern Mexico. Yet neither indigenous revolts nor independence succeeded in re-establishing indigenous self-rule. In the endless cycle of revolt and defeat, the rebels learned the wisdom of the advice given by Quintín Lame (1880–1967), a Colombian indigenous revolutionary leader: 'Do not believe in the friendship of the white man or the mestizo; distrust gifts and flattery; never consult a white lawyer; do not allow yourself to be hoodwinked by the chattering politicians of any party.'

Elsewhere, indigenous resistance to oppression was more subtle, but no less stubborn.

The key battleground has been over culture, in particular religion and language, which are central to indigenous identity. 'Religion is a Spanish word. For us, the Mayan priests pass down culture, not religion,' explains Justina, a Guatemalan indigenous activist. Through the centuries, Latin America's indigenous peoples have proved extraordinarily able to adapt to outside pressure while safeguarding the essential aspects of their cultural identity. This stubborn, silent refusal to give in explains the reputation for passivity which they acquired in the eyes of outsiders, and goes back to the earliest days of the conquest. In 1534 Mancu Inca Yupanki, an Inca leader, told his followers:

> Give the outward appearance of complying with their demands. Give them a little tribute, because if you don't give it they will take it from you by force.... I know that some day, by force or deceit, they will make you worship what they worship, and when that happens, when you can resist no longer, do it in front of them, but do not forget your ceremonies ... reveal just what you have to and keep the rest hidden.

Through this combination of both passive and violent resistance, Latin America's indigenous peoples have achieved their most remarkable victory – survival. In the face of five centuries of a military, epidemic, cultural and economic onslaught, they have survived, and are now increasing in numbers. However, most remain outsiders in their own lands, condemned to poverty, racism and persecution. The last 35 years

The Last Inca: Túpac Amaru II

'In 1781 Túpac Amaru laid siege to Cusco. This mestizo chief, a direct descendant of the Inca emperors, headed the broadest of messianic revolutionary movements. The rebellion broke out in Tinta province, which had been almost depopulated by enforced service in the Cerro Rico mines. Mounted on his white horse, Túpac Amaru entered the plaza of Tungasuca and announced to the sound of drums and *pututus* [conch-shell trumpets] that he had condemned the royal *Corregidor* Antonio Juan de Arriaga to the gallows and put an end to the Potosí *mita*. A few days later Túpac issued a decree liberating the slaves. He abolished all taxes and forced labour in all forms. The Indians rallied by the thousands to the forces of the "father of all the poor and all the wretched and helpless". He moved against Cusco at the head of his *guerrilleros*, promising that all who died while under his orders in this war would return to life to enjoy the happiness and wealth the invaders had wrested from them. Victories and defeat followed; in the end, betrayed and captured by one of his own chiefs, Túpac was handed over in chains to the royalists. The Examiner Areche entered his cell to demand, in exchange for promises, the names of his rebel accomplices. Túpac Amaru replied scornfully, "There are no accomplices here except you and I. You as oppressor, I as liberator, deserve to die."

Túpac was tortured, along with his wife, his children and his chief aides, in Cusco's Plaza del Wacaypata. His tongue was cut out; his arms and legs were tied to four horses with the intention of quartering him, but his body would not break; he was finally beheaded at the foot of the gallows. His head was sent to Tinta, one arm to Tungasuca and the other to Carabaya, one leg to Santa Rosa and the other to Livitaca.'

Eduardo Galeano, *Open Veins of Latin America* (trans. Cedric Belfrage), New York and London: Monthly Review Press, 1973

have seen attempts to build a politics based on the indigenous peoples' growing sense of identity and self-confidence, producing an upsurge in indigenous resistance. Among highland groups, indigenous activists have organised peasant associations and taken up arms to become involved in civil wars in Mexico, Guatemala and Peru, while in Ecuador and Bolivia indigenous peasant groups have risen to dominate national politics. In the lowland areas a plethora of indigenous organisations has sprung up, demanding land and help from the government, and defending themselves against the invasions of agribusiness, mining companies and poor peasant colonisers. Lowland indigenous movements have achieved a political impact out of all proportion to their numbers: 'Five centuries of contact has produced only marginalisation, exploitation and misery for our highland colleagues. We're not volunteering for the same', says Evaristo Nugkuag, an Aguaruna leader from lowland Peru.

Mario Juruna, the first indigenous person to become a deputy in Brazil's parliament, made his people's demands quite clear:

Indian wealth lies in customs and communal traditions and land which is
sacred. Indians can and want to choose their own road, and this road is not
civilisation made by whites … Indian civilisation is more human. We do not
want paternalistic protection from whites. Indians today … want political
power.

Indigenous organisations typically rely on individual communities as their
basic building blocks. Federations of communities then grow to cover an
area, in some cases combining to form regional and even national
confederations. Cross border co-operation took off in the indigenous
campaign over the 500th anniversary of Columbus' first voyage to the
Americas in 1992. The anti-Columbus campaign reached its peak in
October 1991, when 500 indigenous delegates from every corner of the
Americas met in Guatemala. A year later their campaign received
international recognition when Rigoberta Menchú of Guatemala received
the Nobel Peace Prize. Many observers now see the Columbus campaign
as a watershed for the indigenous movement, a view that seemed to be
confirmed when the indigenous peoples of southern Mexico and Ecuador
rose in revolt in 1994.

Several problems have dogged these attempts at organisation. The first
has been the difficulty of building alliances between different indigenous
groups and between highlanders and lowlanders. But even more thorny
has been the problem of the relationship between indigenous and non-
indigenous organisations. Indigenous organisations are often rightly
suspicious of non-indigenous political parties and peasant organisations,
fearing that they see the world purely in terms of class divisions, and fail to
recognise and respect the indigenous peoples' right to be culturally
distinct. Conflicts between indigenous communities and poor colonists can
further sour the relationship. In Bolivia, one indigenous woman gave voice
to the extreme 'indigenist' position: 'To the Indian, the Spaniard is only a
tenant. And we have to hit him, complain about him and tell him to leave,
because we are the owners and we are going to return.'

Despite these obstacles, the political strength of indigenous organisation
has grown steadily in recent years, forcing parties, social movements and
governments alike to take their demands seriously. Besides Ecuador, where
the indigenous movement routinely makes or breaks presidents, some of
the greatest recent advances have been in Bolivia, where Evo Morales of
the Movement towards Socialism (MAS), comprising coca-growers and
other peasant allies, became President in 2006 after playing heavily upon
his Aymara heritage and promising a series of reforms designed to benefit
the indigenous poor.

In Brazil and Colombia new constitutions now enshrine a number of
indigenous rights. In Mexico, the Zapatistas signed an indigenous rights
accord with the government which recognises the 'autonomy' of Mexico's

Marketplace in La Paz, Bolivia.
(Latinphoto)

ten million indigenous people, and their rights to multilingual education and 'adequate' political representation. But the accord did not touch on the economic issues at the heart of the Zapatista uprising, such as land redistribution and control of natural resources. In Guatemala the government signed a similar accord with the URNG guerrillas prior to the peace agreement of 1996. Such paper guarantees do not always translate into real improvements on the ground, but they provide a rallying point for the indigenous movement.

For optimists, the indigenous people are on the way back. Many in the Andes are convinced that the *pachakut'i*, literally the 'balance upheaval' that legends and oral history have prophesied for centuries, has finally arrived, heralding an indigenous cultural and political renaissance that will transform Latin America. They point to the resurgence in indigenous identity and organisation as evidence.

Pessimists see the tide moving in the other direction and blame the region's new-found obsession with structural adjustment. With its focus on individualism and the market, neoliberalism stands diametrically opposed to the indigenous traditions of community, subsistence agriculture and reciprocal aid.

In the long term, the pessimists may be proved wrong. Latin America's indigenous peoples have showed extraordinary tenacity in surviving five centuries of cultural, political and economic assault by outsiders. The recent resurgence of indigenous organisation faces enormous obstacles, but may indeed herald a future where indigenous and non-indigenous learn to live in mutual respect, and different cultures can flourish side by side.

Black Latin America

In recent years, 'blackness' in many Latin American countries has gone from being solely about social exclusion to become a powerful marker of identity, and has also provided the impetus for a new political consciousness and for social movements, especially in Colombia. Some nations, notably Cuba and Brazil, have actively pursued racial integration and a notion of harmony – 'racial democracy'. Many Cubans and

---

Hair-straightening in the Dominican Republic

'In the Dominican Republic, a white woman's hair is described as blonde. Whether it is curly or straight, black or brown, it is said that she is blonde. About the "others", it is said that they have "bad hair".

"When I quit straightening," Chaki said, "a man told me: 'You look like you don't have a husband. You will see the beating your husband is going to give you!' Another person asked me: 'where are you going to work, as a cook or a washerwoman?'"

"Straightening" does not whiten a woman, straightening is about self-denial. Being black in the Dominican Republic has never meant anything else. Accepting oneself as black means recognizing oneself as oppressed and exploited. The construction of a creative and free identity evolves from a double denial: to recognize oneself in the act of "not being" and to affirm it.

A 45-year-old woman who recently decided to quit straightening commented: "When you quit you feel free, you break the chain that you used to carry in your head before." To quit is an affirmation, a symbolic act of going over to the other faction – the faction of the maroons. That is why it is interpreted as an act of rebelliousness and, in the case of women, it is double rebelliousness, because these two oppressions go together. Many women confess that they anxiously wait for the day to have their hair straightened, because they will then be beautiful and will be able to enjoy, for a few days, what they feel has been denied to them. At the same time they recognize themselves as non-whites who can be exposed at any time, when the roots begin to grow and be noticed, when it rains and they get wet.'

Casandra Badilo, 'Only my Hairdresser Knows for Sure: Stories of Race, Hair and Gender in the Dominican Republic', in NACLA *Report on the Americas*, 2001

Brazilians are uncomfortable discussing race and its implied counterpart, racism. Racism may be acknowledged, but often only as an ill inherited from a past marred by colonialism and slavery; allegations of racism are seen to undermine national unity. But race, and notions of race, influence relations among ordinary people in many ways. Recently Brazil has adopted its own form of affirmative action, creating quotas for black people in universities and government jobs.

Multicultural Latin America?

'For us race is not a biological concept. For us, it is something spiritual. It constitutes a sum of the imponderables that make us what we are and impel us to be what we should be, through our origins and through our destiny. It is what dissuades us from falling into the imitation of other communities whose natures are foreign to us. For us, race constitutes our personal seal, indefinable and irrefutable.'
Juan Domingo Perón, 1947

Latin America is a multi-ethnic region – besides indigenous ethnicities and the black populations there are also significant Chinese populations, descendants of indentured labourers brought to Latin America in the 19th century, as well as a later wave of Japanese emigrants, who mostly settled in Brazil and Peru. In Mexico, European planters held vast tracts of land, while in the Southern Cone, and especially in Argentina, European labourers have left significant cultural legacies – one in two Argentines is descended from an Italian.

However, the co-existence of so many ethnicities and cultures is far from harmonious. The recent economic downturn in Argentina has brought to the surface tensions between the urban unemployed and Bolivian immigrant workers. Throughout the 1990s Bolivians were encouraged to travel to Argentine cities to work for less than locals would accept. The scarcity of employment since 2001, however, means that the immigrants are now accused of 'stealing Argentine jobs'. The statistics tell a different story. The number of Bolivians in Argentina has remained between two and three per cent since the 1860s, though in hard times the migrant labourers have tended to move into urban areas in search of work.

Tension also exists between the close communities of Central America and the Caribbean. The Haitians who have managed to cross into the Dominican Republic have been ghettoised. They are poorer than their Dominican neighbours and speak a different language, but the most common divide between the two communities concerns self-perception – while Haiti is a self-consciously 'black' republic, the Dominican Republic has chosen to emphasise its Hispanic identity. Similarly, Guatemalans working in Mexico often choose to hide their indigenous heritage the better to fit in with the northward-looking Mexican national elite.

At the same time mestizaje is being celebrated, at least within official and academic circles. There is a new willingness at government level to recognize and support multiculturalism and the rights that ethnicity confers on groups. Within nations a search is under way to harness the social and political power of competing 'identities'.

Sceptics, however, are suspicious that the new recognition bestowed on ethnicities by national governments – 'neoliberal multiculturalism' is the term coined by US academic Charles Hale – is merely a nod to the official multiculturalism of many countries in the North, while seeking to neutralise the power of social movements based on ethnic identity.

Youth, Class and Racism: Interviews with Peruvian Teenagers in Lima

'The boys are fifteen: Lucas and Yuri. Violeta, still in the little blue uniform of her English-style girls' school, is sixteen, but fast developing into a woman. They are full of curiosity and bubbling with life.

They tell me that Lima is going to the dogs and that they come to LarcoMar because it is the only place they can get away from the *cholos*. They refer not to the trading *cholos,* but the comical variation who make a living by dressing up in fishnet stockings and plastic boobs, stuffing cushions down their bums, and then stomp around the streets in stilettos spanking men to get a few soles from drivers at the traffic lights. Ambulant Comics they are called.

"So what is a *cholo* supposed to be like?" I ask, feeling strange just staying the word, as if it were like saying "nigger" or "paki".

"My maid," blurts out Violeta instinctively. They look at each other and giggle. "I don't want more equality," says Violeta. "If we had more equality, we would have to share more and work harder to stay where we are. In Peru there is not enough wealth for everyone. You have to keep what you've got."

She complains that the newly rich *cholos* even turn up at their discotheques. "We go to a place and make it really happening. Then the *cholos* turn up and you think uuugh, and you have to start going somewhere else and then they turn up there, It's impossible."

It seems that Violeta and her gang spend the whole time escaping from the *cholos* as if they carried the plague, a quest that strikes me as slightly futile, since the large majority of the Peruvian population is of indigenous descent. They would have to run very, very far before they were rid of the *cholo* face, and even when they reached the USA they'd find them here, in baseball caps and Levi's jeans.'

Amaranta Wright, *Ripped and Torn: Levi's, Latin America and the Blue Jean Dream*, London: Ebury Press, 2005

Race and Politics

Racial identity has always been an issue in Latin American politics. Haiti declared itself a 'black republic' after rebel slaves achieved independence in 1804, while Ecuador and Bolivia are often described (and describe themselves) as 'Indian republics'. At the other extreme, Brazil prides itself on a rather false notion of racial harmony, while Cuba sought the eradication of racism after the 1959 revolution and has done more than perhaps any other nation to end social stratification based on skin colour. Official proclamations of equality have, however, frequently masked an enduring racism.

In Peru, the chequered career of Japanese-descended Alberto Fujimori reveals some of the ways in which race has been hijacked by opportunistic politicians. In 1990, he played upon his 'outsider' image in an attempt to forge an alliance between immigrants and indigenous peoples against the white elite. This approach was tailored to neutralise the popularity of his opponent, the author Mario Vargas Llosa, who represented urban, white conservatives. However, in 2000, the now-disgraced Fujimori was pilloried by supporters of the indigenous Alejandro Toledo, who chanted '*cholo* yes, *chino* no'. The *Nikkei*, or Japanese Peruvians, have been tarnished by association with Fujimori's corruption – where once they were admired for economic success, they are now viewed as a stereotypically exploitative class. Throughout the Andean region it has become politically expedient for leaders such as Toledo to proclaim their *cholo* credentials, reclaiming the formerly disparaging word for people of indigenous descent.

Gender and Politics

Penha is an imposing figure, a big confident woman who has risen to become president of the Alagoa Grande Rural Workers' Union in Brazil's drought-prone and poverty-ridden northeast. She recounts her life story, the words half lost in the drumming of a sudden downpour which turns the street into a river bearing rubbish from the nearby market. A broken home, starting work aged seven, a mother who died from TB when Penha was twelve, early marriage and struggling to feed her six children – the story of countless poor Latin American women. Then came transformation when she joined the union, inspired by a charismatic woman leader named Margarida Maria Alves. When Margarida was assassinated, probably by local landowners, Penha took over.

Earlier, out on her rounds, Pehna was trying to persuade an impoverished farming community to join the union. Pot-bellied children with skinny arms played at the feet of men and women as the banter and serious talk rolled easily along. Penha guided the conversation with a blend of authority, humour and kindness, letting others speak and enjoying the jokes, as the impromptu discussion developed into a full-blown community meeting about the causes of poverty in Brazil. As dusk fell, the meeting turned into music and dance, in honour of the visitors.

There are thousands of women like Penha up and down Latin America, inspirational grassroots activists breathing new vigour into the region's social and political life. Although generalisations are always dangerous in a continent with such a variety of cultures and lifestyles, there has been an undeniable transformation in women's lives over the last 40 years. In the past, descriptions of Latin American society have either ignored its women altogether or portrayed them as the submissive victims of a male-dominated order perpetuated by the Catholic Church. Women were shown as helpless figures, condemned to endless pregnancies which destroy their health and confine them to the house, subject to the burden of childcare and dependent on unreliable and often violent men. In the title of one book, they were 'the slaves of slaves'. But in recent years, as more women have gone out to do paid work, some, like Penha, have fought for recognition in male-dominated trade unions. Others have built a new form of politics through the social movements, bypassing traditional political parties.

Women's lives and expectations may have changed, but so far there is little evidence of parallel developments among Latin American men. A dictionary translation of the Spanish word *macho* captures the essence of Latin American masculinity. Besides male and masculine, the word means tough, strong, stupid, big, huge, splendid and terrific, and doubles as a slang term for a sledgehammer. *Machismo* is an extreme form of patriarchy, the social system of male dominance which exists throughout much of the world. The Latin American variety has its roots in Iberian culture and the Catholic Church's contorted attitude towards women. As Virgin and Mother, Mary combines impossible and contradictory ideals of Latin American womanhood. Machismo stresses the opposition between male and female; men are fearless, authoritarian, aggressive and promiscuous, while women are naturally submissive, dependent, quiet and devoted to the family and home. Machismo is often greater among the mestizo population, although indigenous communities have their fair share of domestic violence, often linked to the men's prodigious consumption of alcohol, as an indigenous woman from Chiapas in Mexico recalls:

> Before, when I was poor, my first husband had to go away to work on the hacienda. I went with him, and stayed there for a few nights, but the men always got drunk because the *patrón* gave them money for booze. When he

got drunk, he beat me a lot. I thought I would die from the blows. It was horrible. I would go back to our farm with my face all swollen, all beaten up. And I still had to look after the sheep, clean the house, go and cut wood, work on the maize patch, bring in the harvest. If I finished that, I had to sew, spin wool, weave. Like that, see, lots of work. Still, I was happy when I went home, because there were no more beatings. He gave me no food – no beans or meat. Just beatings. My life was very sad with the husband who went to the hacienda.

GUIOMAR ROVIRA, *Women of Maize*, London: LAB 2000

Women have their second-class status drummed into them from birth: in rural Peru the midwife receives a sheep for delivering a baby boy, while a girl merits only two chickens. Under the ideological barrage, women often internalise these ideas of femininity and submissiveness, giving rise to a female counterpart to machismo, known as marianismo, after the Virgin Mary. In some countries these traditional stereotypes have been overlaid by more modern versions of what constitutes the 'perfect woman'. In Argentina, girls as young as six or seven show signs of anorexia, part of a nation-wide obsession with thinness and the 'supermodel' look, resulting in extraordinary levels of cosmetic surgery and eating disorders.

Latin America's most famous women have often filled these submissive and maternal roles. Evita Perón, a gifted politician and the darling of the Argentine masses, described her relationship with her husband as 'He the figure, I the shadow', while Violeta Chamorro became president of Nicaragua in 1990 by playing on her position as the widow of a national hero and presenting herself as the healing mother of the nation who could reconcile her divided children. Venezuela's obsession with beauty contests spilt over into politics in the person of Irene Sáez, a former Miss Universe who was re-elected as mayor of the country's wealthiest suburb with an impressive 96 per cent of the vote. Sáez, who studied political science at the University of Central Venezuela, was widely considered the most popular politician in Venezuela, until she lost against Hugo Chávez in the presidential election of 1998.

Family Ties

Traditionally, girls are groomed from the cradle for their future role as wife and mother. Bolivian parents call their baby daughters 'mamita' (little mother), and within a few years they can be seen hauling their baby brothers and sisters on their backs around the villages of the Andes. In rural Latin America, families usually have numerous children so that enough will survive high child death rates to work the family farm and to look after their parents in old age. For women this has led to the health problems associated with frequent pregnancies, compounded by

Growing Up in the Countryside

'I learnt early on what suffering meant. My father thought that women and girls were nothing. He used to say *"mulher não gente"* ("Women aren't people").

At home I was locked up. I wasn't allowed to have friends either, not even woman friends, and I was often beaten. I hated having been born a girl and envied my brothers like crazy.

Then there was the poverty. We often went hungry. My father had to sell our little plot of land, so we were tenants on a big landowner's *fazenda* (estate). Half of the harvest had to be handed over to the owner as rent. What was left wasn't enough for all of us. Two of the children didn't survive. Hunger and death are everyday occurrences for most of the families in our area.

I thought school was great fun, but after four years my father stopped me going any more. Sending girls to school was like casting pearls before swine, he said.

At 16 I thought I could escape from my father by getting married, so I married the first man who came along. But what I'd let myself in for was worse than I could ever have imagined. It was hell. You see, my husband was an oppressor too. He made me the slave he'd always wanted. I had one child after another, and I was either shut up at home with the babies or had to slog out in the fields.

I had my children, who I had to feed, on one side and a husband who only gave orders on the other. How I suffered!

The worst thing was when he used to hit the children and I wasn't allowed to intervene. He never once hit me, but the endless mental beatings that I had were far harder. If ever I wanted to cry on my mother's shoulder, she used to say, "Take it easy, daughter, don't get worked up about it. Women are born to suffer. And they have to obey their husbands – *mulher não gente!*" '

Caipora, *Women in Brazil*, London: LAB, 1993

malnourishment and poor or non-existent medical care. Large families lack even the most basic services such as running water, and need constantly to make do and mend. Together, these pressures create the archetypal Latin American mother who never rests. Cooking, cleaning, changing nappies, looking after children through frequent illnesses, queuing for scarce food, mending clothes or making food to sell outside the home: these activities consume every waking hour. In rural areas fetching water or firewood and the long haul to sell left-over produce in the local market impose further strains on women's workload.

While this still describes reality for millions of Latin American women, their lives are changing fast. By the turn of the 21st century, women had made considerable strides in education and politics, and in family and fertility. The size of the average family has dropped at a startling rate over the last 40 years. In the 1950s, the average Latin American woman had six children. By 2003 this had dropped to 2.5 children and was still falling. The causes of such a rapid fall in childbearing include the more widespread availability of contraception, the increase in girls' education, and the rate of urbanisation. In the shantytowns, large families can be a liability: women have to go out to work as maids or in the markets and since they have left their extended families in the countryside, there is often no one at home to look after the children.

Diversity has increased both within and between countries. Poor countries such as Bolivia, Haiti and Guatemala still have large families, while Argentina, Cuba and Chile more closely resemble 'northern' family models. Within each country, family size depends greatly on income and women's education: poor, uneducated women have much larger families than better-off or more educated ones.

In recent years there has been a sharp increase in the number of female-headed households, which now stands at over 20 per cent in most countries and above 30 per cent in many. These are often among the poorest families, with women forced to perform a gruelling combination of housework and wage-earning, often in the informal sector, to keep their children from starvation. According to one study men are increasingly seen as shadowy figures, drifting in and out of the family and avoiding responsibility.' Latin Americans put it more bluntly in the often-heard phrase 'you've only got one mother – your father could be any sonofabitch.'

Access to contraception has transformed many womens' lives. In the 1980s the number of couples using contraception varied widely from 23 per cent in Guatemala to 70 per cent in Costa Rica, but by the turn of the century the average for the region was among the highest in the world, at 71 per cent. The commonest form of contraception is female sterilisation, followed by the Pill and intra-uterine devices (IUDs). Nevertheless, the issue remains far more controversial than in the US or Western Europe. Not only is the Catholic Church hostile to all forms of contraception, but the health problems provoked by the often unsupervised use of the Pill, IUDs and injectables such as Depo Provera have created widespread suspicion. Contraception is anathema to many Latin American men, who see their wives' regular pregnancies as proof of their virility. In only 6 per cent of couples do men take responsibility for contraception by using condoms or by sterilisation. In some notorious historical cases, foreign agencies were implicated in sterilising women without fully informing them of the consequences. Such incidents led to the expulsion of the US Peace Corps from Peru and Bolivia in the 1970s.

One consequence of suspicion, ignorance and the shortage of

contraceptives is a high abortion rate. Abortion on request is illegal in all Latin American countries except Cuba, forcing women unable to afford a medically safe abortion to resort to back-street practitioners or their own efforts. More than 4,000 women – one in every five maternal deaths – die every year in Latin America during or as a result of botched abortions. Not surprisingly, in view of its more liberal legislation, Cuba has one of the lowest maternal death rates in the region. By one estimate, there are four million abortions performed every year in the region, one for every three live births. Although huge numbers of women undergo abortions, it remains a taboo subject, as this woman from a Chilean shantytown explains:

> Women don't want to talk about abortion because it's against the teachings of the Church and also because it's against the law, but nearly all women have them. The difference is that the women from the *poblaciones* use a knitting needle, parsley twigs or rubber tubes and many end up in hospital or die, while the middle class go to a clinic and walk home afterwards. When we go to the hospital with haemorrhages the doctors slap our faces; they send their wives to the best clinics but they slap the faces of poor women.
>
> FROM JO FISHER, *Out of the Shadows: Women, Resistance and Politics in South America*, London: LAB, 1993

Literacy plays a vital role in empowering women, making it easier for them to find better-paid work, and to wade through the avalanche of printed information resulting from almost any contact with the state. Research by the World Bank and others suggests that women's education is also the single biggest factor in determining family size – the more years of schooling a woman has, the fewer children she ends up with. Illiteracy is higher among women than men in every Latin American country, in some cases reaching 90 per cent among elderly women. The figure for both sexes is higher in rural than in urban areas, since schools are more scarce, and parents may need the children to work on the farm. Many families prefer to keep girls at home to help with the household tasks and learn how to keep house, while believing that boys must study to prepare themselves for the outside world. However, the situation is improving rapidly due to the massive expansion in primary education, which has absorbed an extra two million children a year since 1950, even during the recession-hit 1980s.

Among the middle classes, the situation is already very different. Now half of all students in higher education are women, although a large number of them are concentrated in the traditionally female spheres of teaching and health care.

The ideology of machismo has influenced legislation affecting women. In most countries adultery is sufficient grounds for divorce only if committed by the wife, while divorce is available at all only in exceptional cases in countries such as Argentina, Brazil and Colombia. Such double standards were condemned 300 years ago by Sor Juana Inés de la Cruz, a Mexican nun and poet who has become a feminist icon in modern Mexico:

> Ignorant men who accuse
> Women wrongly
> Without seeing that you cause
> The very thing you condemn.
>
> Whose is the greater guilt
> In a sinful passion,
> She who falls to his lure
> Or he who, fallen, lures her?
>
> Or which is more rightly reproached
> Although both are guilty
> She who sins for pay
> Or he who pays for the sin?

Thanks to the work of women's lobby groups and the UN Decade for Women (1975–85), many governments have improved their legislation and established agencies to promote the status of women and ensure equal rights. Yet despite such paper safeguards, social attitudes and the implementation of equal rights laws lag far behind. Statutory rights on maternity benefits or equal pay are frequently ignored by both employers and male-oriented ministries of labour, and legislation often appears irrelevant to the poor. Most women work in the unregulated informal sector and so do not have even a theoretical right to maternity benefits. Since formal marriage is the exception among poor families, the niceties of divorce law hold little meaning.

Working for Wages

The number of women officially in the economically active population – a definition that excludes those involved in unwaged work in the home, on the farm or in the informal sector – more than tripled between 1960 and 1990, though the rate of increase slowed dramatically during the 1990s. In most countries, 30–50 per cent of girls and women over ten years old now work for money (in both the formal and informal sectors), the proportion being highest among 25–34 year-olds. Even these figures are underestimates, as women often do not describe themselves as wage earners when asked during household surveys, even though they may bring in money from selling food or taking in washing.

Despite this rise in numbers, the kinds of jobs have changed little, with a strong emphasis on 'women's work' which merely extends their caring role in the home. Proportionally fewer women work for money in rural areas than in towns and cities, where as many as half the women employed are domestic servants, most of them young unskilled migrants from the countryside who have had on average only three years of school education. The other main categories of paid women's work are the informal sector (market women, street sellers), caring professions such as teaching and nursing, and office work. Women's participation in agriculture and manufacturing actually fell between 1960 and 1980, as mechanisation reduced the proportion of unskilled jobs traditionally performed by women, although it has picked up in recent years in new export crops such as fruit and flowers, which have been promoted under neoliberal reforms. In manufacturing women are concentrated in industries such as textiles, clothing and the booming *maquiladora* assembly plants in northern Mexico and the Caribbean basin. Besides being segregated by job, women also earn 20–40 per cent less than men, even though their educational qualifications for comparable jobs are generally higher.

The Domestic Worker

Usually young unskilled migrants from the countryside, servants are among the most exploited and invisible of the region's women. Ignorant of their rights and of life in the city, isolated in their employer's house, they are on virtual 24-hour standby, and vulnerable to verbal, sexual and physical abuse by their employers. Young girls emotionally dependent on their employers often absorb their values, feeling self-loathing and contempt for their own families and backgrounds, especially in countries where the employers are white and the servants indigenous:

> The old lady explained everything to me, and little by little she made me aware of my class, using words like 'Indians' and 'Yokels' and saying 'You shouldn't be like that, you're going to get civilised here.'

> When you hear it that often you end up being ashamed and uncomfortable about your own class and finally you find yourself supporting the class of your boss. I thought she loved me because she told me: 'I love you like a daughter; here you have everything.' And I accepted it all.

> The truth is that the bosses use us even through love. Without realising, we end up loving them and so we say, 'Ay, my señora is good, she loves me a lot.' We look after her things as though they were our own, and after a while you start identifying totally with her mentality.

> ANA MARÍA CONDORI, *Mi Despertar*, La Paz: Hisbol, 1988, (author's translation)

The Street Seller

Market women and street sellers are perhaps the most conspicuous of Latin American women workers, lining the streets of major cities with stalls offering home-made cakes, vegetables, soft drinks or imported toiletries. Their numbers have been swollen by the impact of neoliberal reforms since 1980. By the early 1990s, there was one street vendor for every three houses in La Paz, Bolivia's chief city. Market women's daily contact with the public and unscrupulous wholesalers has made them self-confident and fiercely individualistic throughout the region. As Anita, a 28-year-old Nicaraguan market woman, explains: 'I'm better off working in the market. If I don't want to sell, I don't have to. I can go home whenever I want to, we can bring our children to work and no-one bosses you about and tells you when to come and when to leave. I don't want to work for a boss again.'

Maquiladoras

Since the mid-1960s, Mexican industry has been transformed by the growth of *maquiladora* plants along its northern border with the US. Others have sprouted elsewhere in Central America and the Caribbean. These factories, largely owned by US, Japanese and other foreign electronics or textile companies, use cheap local labour to assemble products for export to the US. In the Caribbean, women are also used to perform cut-price data processing for US companies. About 60 per cent of maquiladora employees are women, usually single and in their late teens or early twenties. Young women are ideal because, in the words of one plant manager, 'they are willing to accept lower wages', and 'girls are educated to obey at home. It is easier to get their confidence ... they are loyal to the company.'

> Martina, like many working-class Mexican women, has a hard exterior, a tough skin of nonchalance until you get to know her. She has worked in various maquilas in Ciudad Acuña but dislikes them intensely. Last Monday she started at a Korean-owned maquiladora called Kim Toys, where the employees sew small cheap stuffed animals to go inside the ironclaw machines in the American chain of Pizza Huts across the border. 'It's the worst place I've ever worked in,' she says, while making supper. 'Run down and dirty. And no air conditioning, just a couple of old fans in the whole place. It was so hot. Everybody just sat there sweating so much it looked as if someone had come in and thrown a bucket of water over them. I saw one supervisor get mad at a woman for taking too long in the bathroom. "Five minutes," he was saying. "All you've got is five minutes." She went back to her sewing machine and was crying.' Martina decided it wasn't worth US$30 a week and quit after just one day.
> AUGUSTA DWYER, *On the Line: Life on the US–Mexican Border*, London: LAB, 1994

Women's growing role in the workforce has brought them mixed blessings. Although paid jobs have often increased women's economic independence and self-confidence, there has been no compensating reduction in housework, with the result that working women are expected to perform what is known as a 'double shift'. A study of women in Chile during the early 1980s showed that working women did on average a 12-hour day, seven days a week, between workplace and home. When women did manage to reduce their housework, it was by employing poor women as domestic servants. Men did no more housework than before, despite the decline in their role as breadwinner. For any macho man, scrubbing floors or cooking is the ultimate shame. In Cuba, where women's participation in the paid workforce has grown rapidly over the last 20 years, one writer noted that although male Communist Party militants may offer to do the washing, they insist that their wives hang it out to dry so that the neighbours won't find out!

The Peasant

Peasant women in rural areas labour under many obligations; their duties include childcare, maintaining the home, and a number of specialised jobs on the farm. Often women tend the animals and a small vegetable plot, while the men look after the main food crops. Housework in peasant farms can be far more time-consuming than in the cities, since women may have to carry water over long distances, collect firewood, and make long trips to markets in nearby villages.

As commercial agriculture has encroached on the traditional peasant farms, this pattern has been disrupted. Peasant farms have been squeezed by large landowners and by subdivision between members of each new generation, so that they are rarely productive enough to maintain a family. This forces their owners to find work on the big commercial farms. Men's greater access to education and training has meant that they take the permanent jobs on new mechanised farms, and women have been relegated to temporary work at harvest time.

With food in short supply, parents favour boys to stay and eventually inherit the farm, and many young girls are packed off to the city as domestic servants. As a result, young women have outnumbered men in the exodus to the cities which has marked the last 50 years of Latin American history.

Women still supply most of the workers in a number of labour-intensive export industries. They pick coffee, tobacco or cotton, and produce new export crops such as strawberries in Mexico or peanuts in Brazil. In Colombia the women weed, fumigate, pick and pack carnations for Europe's florists, suffering frequent respiratory problems and miscarriages from the pesticides to which they are constantly exposed.

Latin America's agrarian reform processes have largely failed to benefit women, their apparent 'gender blindness' masking discrimination in favour of men. Most reforms hand out land to individuals identified as 'heads of household', by custom a man, except for widows and single mothers. Instead of being treated as producers in their own right, peasant women are seen as the equivalent of urban housewives and hence as dependents. In traditional Andean culture, farms are owned equally by husband and wife, so the new reforms marked a step backwards for women. In most cases the reforms helped permanent workers, rather than seasonal workers. When General Velasco expropriated Peru's cotton plantations in the late 1960s, women represented 40 per cent of their seasonal workforce, but held few permanent jobs. The reform gave the plantations to their permanent workers organised into co-operatives, and as a result women made up only two per cent of members on the new cotton co-operatives. In Chile and Venezuela, agrarian reform laws specifically decreed that land given out under the reform should be passed to the beneficiary's sons when he died.

Women have integrated rapidly into the workforce in new forms of agriculture, particularly goods designed for agro-export such as ornamental plants and cut flowers (Costa Rica, Guatemala, Colombia) and tropical and temperate fruit destined for North American supermarket shelves. These sectors pay better than traditional forms of agriculture such as sugar-cane harvesting, where the back-breaking labour required made them mostly – although by no means exclusively – the preserve of men.

Neoliberal Reforms

The debt crisis which began in 1982, and the ensuing process of neoliberal reform, has hit women hardest. As employers shed jobs, they have preferred to sack women, since women are not seen as breadwinners and are generally under-represented in trade unions. Public spending cuts have targeted 'female' professions in health and education, and the limited choice of jobs open to women has made it hard for them to find other employment. Poor women have increasingly turned to the informal sector and part-time work to make ends meet. By 2002, the most common jobs among Latin American women were in the largely informal service sector.

In their role as mothers, women have been hit by price rises in basic foods as subsidies are cut, making it harder to feed a family. As education and health budgets have been cut, mothers have had to find increasing sums for school notebooks or medicines. Clothes must be endlessly patched when there is no money to buy replacements. All these tasks add to the growing burden of keeping the family afloat. The stress of family life has also led to increased cases of alcohol abuse among men, leaving women to face the frequent domestic violence and family breakdown that

The Price of Structural Adjustment

'The tiny adobe house is crammed with gnarled *pailliris* (mining women) in patched shawls and battered felt hats whose calloused hands work breaking up rocks on the surface in search of scraps of tin ore. Outside, the scene is one of high-altitude poverty, all greys and browns in the thin air. The paths between the miners' huts are strewn with plastic bags and human excrement, dried black in the unforgiving *altiplano* sun. Rising beyond the squalid settlement, the barren hills and grey slagheaps of the tin mines complete the bleak panorama. The litany of poor women's woes begins, gathering momentum as it goes:

"Before, it was not too bad, but now we never have a good month. We're mainly widows or abandoned. My husband left to look for work and never came back. Now I have to look after four kids – I can't pay for their schoolbooks and clothes. I've been doing this work for seven years now and my lungs are finished. I've vomited blood for weeks at a time and still had to keep working.

In the old days, women used to stay at home because the men had work. Now, with the recession, we've had to go out to work. Many of our children have been abandoned. Their fathers have left and there's no love left in us when we get home late from work. We leave food for them, they play in the streets – there are always accidents, and no doctors. I feel like a slave in my own country – we get up at 4 a.m. and at 11 at night we are still mending and patching."

The speaker, Josefina Muruchi, breaks down in a coughing fit. Suddenly, in a mixture of Spanish and Quechua, all the other women burst into speech, unleashing a torrent of pain and suffering. In the gloom, most of the women are sobbing.

"This is *doloroso* for us. We have nothing. Nothing. Only coca [a stimulant leaf chewed to suppress hunger] to keep us going. It's the children, we want them to study, but they're so malnourished and the price of tin is so low. Our kids say 'mami, I want to help' and don't do their homework, but then they fail their exams and have to repeat the year and the teachers are always asking for money and we haven't got it and because our children are so ashamed they drop out of school. If I start vomiting blood again, what's going to happen to my children?" '

Duncan Green, *Silent Revolution: The Rise and Crisis of Market Economics in Latin America*, London: LAB, 2003

follow. As one Bolivian miner says: 'In my work I am happy. I joke with my compañeros, I work in peace. And then I come home and I see my wife and children undernourished, poorly clothed. It is then that I have a sense of the problems in my life and I get filled with rage.'

Women In Politics

Driven in part by a need to unite to confront the economic crisis of recent years, growing numbers of women have begun to participate directly in political life. In the new social movements such as Mothers' Clubs, Base

Christian Communities and neighbourhood associations, women have built a bridge between the traditionally female world of home and family, and the predominantly male sphere of political activism.

Before the social movements appeared, women were largely excluded from political life. Although a small suffrage movement of largely middle-class women had won the vote in the whole of Latin America by 1961, this did not lead to the expected upsurge in political participation.

In Argentina, Juan and Eva Perón mobilised women as their footsoldiers in the Peronist Women's Party, led by Evita. Yet despite some progressive legislation, the 'father and mother of the nation' never challenged the ideal of wifely submission displayed by Evita herself. The Peronists introduced women's suffrage in 1947 and gave children born out of marriage equal rights before the law. In 1955 Perón's decision to legalise divorce alienated the Catholic Church and helped to bring brought about his downfall at the hands of the military. It was Perón's second wife, Isabel, who became Latin America's first female president, followed by interim or acting female presidents in Bolivia, Haiti and Ecuador and latterly full terms for Violeta Barrios de Chamorro in Nicaragua (1990–97) and Mireya Moscoso Rodríguez in Panama (1999–2004). In socially conservative Chile, that the inauguration of Michelle Bachelet in 2006 marked an extraordinary break with the past. A doctor and single mother of three, Bachelet promptly announced a cabinet in whch half the ministers were women.

Elsewhere, few women have reached the leadership of political parties and trade unions. Even in cases where women are politically active at the grassroots level, for example in textile workers' unions, they thin out rapidly further up the union hierarchy.

In Brazil, the rise of the PT in the late 1990s blurred the division between social movements (where women play a stronger role) and the political party, allowing women to take a more prominent role in decision-making, with several prominent women ministers in the PT government after 2003. Elsewhere, quotas were used to ensure a minimum level of women's representation in elective posts. In Argentina, the electoral law establishes a compulsory 30 per cent quota for women candidates for electoral posts, while Brazil has a 20 per cent requirement. In Costa Rica, the Law on the Promotion of Social Equality for Women, which aims to protect women's political equality, does not include a quota system but mandates political parties to provide effective mechanisms that will encourage women to participate in elections, particularly to the governing bodies of the parties and to state bodies. Despite such measures, less than 15 per cent of parliamentarians were women by the turn of the century.

During the left-wing Popular Unity government of Salvador Allende in Chile (1970–73), women divided along class lines; middle-class women organised 'marches of the empty pots' to protest at food shortages and economic chaos, while women in the shantytowns worked in support of the Allende government. In Chile and elsewhere, many left-wing men have been suspicious of an independent women's movement, arguing that it would prove to be a right-wing defender of the status quo, but also unwilling to give up their own privileged status in the home. As Yanci, an activist in El Salvador's women's movement comments: 'In all the key moments of our history, women have always participated, but we have been anonymous. Women have made the coffee so the compañeros could think better. Women cook while the men take the important decisions!'

Unlike the traditional left, which has often ignored women in its political programmes, the right and the military regimes of the 1970s and 1980s stressed the importance of the family, paying homage to the traditional Latin American icon of the long-suffering mother. The names of right-wing pro-military organisations such as Argentina's 'Tradition, Family and Property' encapsulated the conservative Catholic message. Such an ideology recognised and applauded women only as long as they remained safely in the 'female sphere'. When women dared to trespass into public politics, the military's chivalry proved short-lived. In Argentina, 30 per cent of those 'disappeared' by the military were women. The traumatised mothers of disappeared children, meeting on their fruitless round of the different military barracks in search of news, came together to form the Mothers and Grandmothers of the Plaza de Mayo. Every Thursday under the military government, a small but indomitable band of women wearing white headscarves walked silently around the Plaza de

Table 4.1:
Date of women's suffrage in the Americas

United States	1920
Ecuador	1929
Brazil	1932
Uruguay	1932
El Salvador	1939
Guatemala	1945
Panama	1945
Argentina	1947
Venezuela	1947
Chile	1949
Costa Rica	1949
Bolivia	1952
Mexico	1953
Honduras	1955
Nicaragua	1955
Peru	1955
Colombia	1957
Paraguay	1961

Source: J. Nash and H. Safa, *Sex and Class in Latin America*, New York: Praeger Publishers, 1980

Mayo in front of the Presidential Palace in Buenos Aires, their placards carrying old, fading photographs of their children. As one mother described it, 'from washing, ironing and cooking we went out on to the streets to fight for the lives of our children.' The human rights movement they created grew to play a crucial role first in forcing the generals to hand power over to an elected government, and then in putting the military's leaders in jail for killing their children.

The Mothers of the Disappeared were able to protest because they did so *as mothers*, effectively preventing the military from using outright repression as they did against virtually all other protest movements. By using the generals' own ideology against them, the women of the Plaza de Mayo opened up the first possibilities of public resistance, which grew into the mass protest movement that helped to remove the military from power.

Military rule forced women to take to the public arena to defend their families in many other countries. In Brazil, opposition to the military took off in the late 1970s with the Cost of Living Movement, made up of women protesting at the suffering being inflicted on poor families by the military's economic policies. In Peru and Colombia, organisations of mothers and relatives of the disappeared have yet to obtain answers from a military that kills their sons and daughters with virtual impunity. In each case the crushing of traditional political parties has enabled women's organisations to expand into the political vacuum, sowing the seeds of the region's new social movements.

The grassroots women's organisations have had a difficult relationship with Latin American feminism. The military period coincided with the rise of feminism in the North, and many returning exiles in the 1980s brought with them feminist ideas from their experiences in London, Paris or New York. However, they did not find it easy to combine their new beliefs with political activism in the shantytowns, as two working-class activists from Chile recall:

'We were always very wary that we would lose our independence if we let middle-class women in. The difference is that we work with our class identity and middle-class feminism doesn't, they work only with gender. They say women's problems are common to all women. We have things in common with middle-class women but we also have other problems that middle-class women don't have, like the housing shortage, debt problems, unemployment, and we're not going to advance as women if the two things aren't closely linked.

Gender discrimination may be the same but the class situation is different. Working-class culture is more rigid – we've got more brakes. Perhaps because of the influence of religion and perhaps because we've got less choice – we haven't got the economic freedom to do what we want.'

Politics is Personal

'One gets to know people and find out about the problems of others in the neighbourhood....Yes it's a healthy thing to get out of the house to be with lots of people, each talking about their own problems. Getting to know about others' problems you forget your own. Getting out, mixing with people, with different neighbourhoods, but mainly in the struggle ... one learns, one even learns to talk a bit better.'

'I had a lot of activities in the church but at home I couldn't break away from a load of things I felt were my duty because I'm a woman, a mother. I just couldn't break away. I began to be aware of this through the women's group and I said to hell with it all because it wasn't me who should be doing them! At home, when my husband and children had a bath I would get them towels and lay out all their clothes for them to dress.... Suddenly I realised that it wasn't just me, everybody had to change. I think, or rather I thought, that I had to make the meals, clean the house, control household expenditure, pay the bills, it was up to me. Now we divide everything between us ... it's much better.... When I discovered myself as a woman, that I have the same rights as everyone else, my relationship with my children changed, everything changed, and our relationship improved 100 per cent. My relationship with my husband got better, I mean it was as if we had just met now, three years later. He wouldn't accept it at first but in time he began to see that it was a need, my need.'

Teresa Pires de Rio Caldeira, 'Women, Daily Life and Politics', in Elizabeth Jelin (ed.), *Women and Social Change in Latin America,* London: Zed Books, 1990

'Feminism of the upper class or middle class is a long way from our feminism. We've tried to work with middle-class feminists but they talk about a different world from ours. For example, they did a workshop where they told us we've got to value ourselves, stop serving the biggest steak to the men. Of course poor women like us aren't very familiar with steaks! Once we went to a feminist meeting where they told us we should watch blue films to improve our sex lives. That was very shocking to our women. We've been to their women's centres because they have the resources to offer legal advice or psychologists for battered women. It's another world, all carpeted, with pictures on the wall, everything brand new. We felt uncomfortable. The only time we'd been in houses like that was as domestic servants. We are the ones these women use as their servants.'

JO FISHER, *Out of the Shadows: Women, Resistance and Politics in South America,* London: LAB, 1993

The nature and tactics of the new social movements reflect their predominantly female origin. Stressing the need for internal democracy, social movements aim to improve local communities, usually by putting pressure on local or national governments. They fiercely defend their independence from political parties or the state – both male-dominated. Many of their demands reflect women's immediate needs: campaigns for day nurseries for working women, for better health care, street lighting, running water or electricity are often seen by the women involved as extensions of the struggles they face as wives and mothers. On occasion, the movements' strengths have also proved to be their weaknesses. Once immediate demands have been achieved – for example, the local authority has agreed to put in street lighting – the movement often disintegrates.

After the return to civilian government in Argentina, the Mothers of the Disappeared found it hard to maintain the unity and determination they showed under military rule. New governments often stole the clothes of the women's movement, passing laws to outlaw domestic violence, creating a national women's office (in Chile), or setting up women's police stations (in the case of Brazil). New laws and constitutions did not always translate into changes in real life, but the women's movement has found it hard to move from opposition to the perilous new world of co-option and engagement with professional politicians. Nevertheless, the experience of meeting other women and organising successful campaigns has transformed many women's lives and could lay the foundations of a new and democratic politics for the future.

Masculinities

In a mostly machista environment where men and their desires are valued and assigned power over those of women, women have naturally long been the focus of gender studies. But increasingly scholars, activists and individual women and men are realising that changing negative attitudes about women and their lives means changing men. Traditional ideas of masculinity, sexuality and identity are being questioned as never before. A pioneering project by the Nicaraguan popular education organisation Cantera seeks to get men to ask what it means to be a 'real man', and to question ingrained attitudes towards power, domestic abuse, and personal responsibility.

At the same time, some speak of a 'crisis of masculinity' in a region where women's activities are widening, and access to the labour market is growing. There is some evidence that men are beginning to participate a lot more in domestic labour in childcare. But if they want to become 'new men', Latin American men have their own battles to fight. In Argentina, for instance, a man who does housework is, variously, *dominado* ('dominated'), *pollerón* (someone who hangs on his wife's skirts), or a *máquina de lavar* ('washing machine').

Homosexuality in Latin America

Attitudes and legislation on homosexuality vary enormously across the continent. Latin American machismo appears to have a complex relationship to homosexuality and finds lesbianism incomprehensible.

Masculinity, Homosexuality and Prostitution in

'Fidel knows everything'

'"Fidel" is code for the entire state apparatus in Cuba, so much has the Revolution been personalized in him. This young man from Guantánamo explained to me that 'Fidel' was far more interested in stopping female prostitution than male. *Pingueros* [male prostitutes] could walk the street "openly", he said. This difference makes sense when sex work is viewed in the context of the nationalist project. Cuban women are used in the same way – and by the same men – who are invading the island economically. The state has been forced by economic exigency to admit capitalist incursion and relinquish some of its economic and ideological autonomy. *Jineteras* [female prostitutes] demonstrate this in their very bodies, and so they are an intolerable reminder of the growing power of external capital in internal affairs. This, "Fidel" cannot abide. But *pingueros*, at least representationally if not also practically, are quite the opposite: they represent the strength of the powerful Cuban phallus conquering the bodies of foreigners. No autonomy has been lost, and symbolically at least, no Cuban body has been defiled. In fact, in a *pinguero*-tourist sex act, the Cuban has invaded the tourist, "screwed" him, as it were. The renowned Cuban phallus, well known in the gay world and about which writers such as Pau-Llosa, Stavans and Arenas have commented, is perhaps the one entirely Cuban resource that Cuba has left.'

G. Derrick Hodge, 'Colonisation of the Cuban Body: The Growth of Male Sex Work in Havana', NACLA *Report on the Americas*, 2001

Countries such as Colombia and Peru have a tradition of transvestite homosexuality stretching back to pre-Columbian times, while studies from Nicaragua and Cuba suggest that heterosexual men break no taboos by having sex with other men, provided they are the dominant partner. Social stigma is reserved for those who behave in an 'unmanly' effeminate way. In this sense, homosexuality (for men) is not so much what one is as what one *does*; the importance placed on active/passive roles is also a clear reflection of how sexual relations in Latin America have long been viewed in terms of power. Even so, there is little of the kind of rabid 'queer-bashing' found in the US or Europe. Perhaps because of the lower level of discrimination, gays in Latin America do not always identify themselves exclusively in terms of their sexuality, and the gay pride movement is much weaker than in the North.

In many countries homosexuality is not specifically outlawed, but more general laws such as 'offences against morality' are used to harass gays and lesbians. Cuba under Fidel Castro has come in for severe criticism over its treatment of gay men, in particular those with HIV and AIDS. In the mid-1980s, the Cuban government was condemned for its draconian initial policy of locking up HIV-positive people in state sanitoria, sometimes against their will. Closer examination, however, revealed a complex situation: the policy of quarantining patients was the state's normal reaction to previous epidemics such as dengue and African swine fever; the quarantine policy was only possible in the first place because the Cuban health service had the capacity to implement it – in other countries in Latin America, AIDS patients receive or little or no state support. In any case, by the early 1990s, the policy had been substantially liberalised with most patients free to leave the sanitoria on home visits, and about three in four seropositives transferred to an outpatient system.

Lesbianism, like other aspects of women's sexuality, is largely considered passive and unthreatening. Many Latin American lesbians feel that the relative invisibility of lesbianism is not so much a condoning of it as active discrimination – more proof that society simply does not take it very seriously. Lesbian movements emerged out of feminist groups and ideology, but are distinct in each country. For example, in Nicaragua, the lesbian and feminist movements were both shaped by a very strong class consciousness, which was itself a product of the Sandinista revolution.

Social Movements and the Struggle for Change

The first sign of the squatters is a huge red flag flapping above a depression in the hills a few hundred yards away. Across two barbed wire fences and an arid, sandy hillside lies the cluster of huts thrown up weeks ago by forty landless families. They have called the encampment 'Hope' (*Esperança*). Already the inhabitants are making the first improvements: tiles are starting to replace plastic sheets on the roofs of the huts, whose walls are made from branches tied together with twine. To provide safety in numbers, 500 people originally occupied the site. When ten armed policemen promptly arrived to evict them, the children stood in front with stones; behind them came the women and adolescents, followed by the men armed with their primitive farming tools. The policemen backed off without a fight, allowing the squatters to get on with planting their first crops of yams and fennel.

The red flag belongs to Brazil's Movement of Landless Workers, the MST. The MST leads landless peasants and the urban poor in well-organised invasions of waste land in the cities or uncultivated farmland elsewhere. Standing amidst newly ploughed furrows thirsty for rain, one of the squatters explains: 'People came here for land. We weren't interested in riches – land created people and people must live from it. The owner says the land is his, but if he doesn't even farm it, how can that be?' As he talks, the skies open. Rain sheets across the grey fields and through the torn plastic roofs, on to the dripping but delighted farmers.

By the end of 2000 more than half a million families were living on 3,800 agrarian reform settlements. About one fifth of the families are members of the MST. Since then about another 200,000 families have been settled. The MST is still mobilising for a radical programme of agrarian reform, but just as important are its activities to mobilise support among other sectors – homeless, neighbourhood groups, Catholic church groups, hiphop groups and so on – for a 'national project' to end Brazil's enormous social inequalities. Agrarian reform isn't enough, they say. The MST has become a reference point throughout the world, particularly in South Africa, Paraguay, Uruguay, and Bolivia.

The MST is one of a number of social movements whose political activity, in this case over the explosive issue of land, takes place outside the channels of formal politics. Many of the new movements took off under military rule in the 1970s, when conventional opposition politics was suppressed. Today, in Latin America's shantytowns, women's organisations pressure local councils for food and milk for their children, and neighbourhood committees demand electricity or paved roads, while in the rural areas peasant organisations lobby for land reform or bank loans for their farms. In Peru, Colombia and Central America, human rights organisations demonstrate and protest about the 'disappearance' of their loved ones; in Brazil, radical Catholics run 'Base Christian Communities' to discuss the Bible and its message for the poor. What such a diverse range of organisations have in common is their use of direct action to improve their lives.

Trade Unions and Social Movements

Trade unions in Latin America occupy a very different place in society than in Europe or the US, since they represent that minority of workers who have stable jobs in the formal sector of the economy and are therefore relatively privileged compared to the mass of peasant farmers and the urban poor. In countries such as Mexico, Brazil and Argentina, most of the main trade unions were set up under corporatist governments during the early years of import substitution, and have never had any real degree of independence. Nevertheless, some trade unions have been at the forefront of the radical left. In Chile they were the first to take to the streets to begin the long campaign to topple General Pinochet, while in Brazil from 1978 a new independent union movement led the fight against the military dictatorship.

One side-effect of neoliberalism and the debt crisis has been the reduction of corporatist regimes' ability to keep the unions on a tight leash. Austerity measures and falling wages have driven a wedge between the union membership and their pro-government leaderships in countries such as Argentina and Mexico, fuelling efforts in these countries to establish a new unionism independent of the state.

The period since the 1970s has seen a spectacular growth in so-called new social movements. At the heart of the phenomenon lies the work of the progressive Catholic Church, which through its 'Base Christian Communities' has formed generations of activists and leaders. Shanty-town dwellers, women's groups, indigenous and environmental movements, and human rights organisations have joined radicalised trade unions and peasant associations to create a new form of grass-roots democracy which involves large numbers of people who previously had little role in the party political process.

Although the social movements form a broad category, they have certain points in common:

- They are often based on a locality rather than a workplace, unlike traditional trade unions;

- They organise around specific and immediate demands, rather than wider appeals for structural change;

- They practise a much higher degree of internal democracy and show a far greater level of women's participation than either left-wing political parties or guerrilla groups;

- They generally demand improvements from the state rather than confront vested interest groups such as landowners, the military and big business.

So called 'catalyst' groups such as radical priests, social workers, progressive non-governmental organisations (NGOs), feminist groups and political party activists often play an important role in helping to establish groups by encouraging organisation and discussion. The more traditional catalysts often found it hard to let the new groups take control:

I still thank the church for having opened my eyes. Working with the mothers' clubs, I learned how important we women are and how important it was for us to get organised. We managed to set up dozens of mothers' clubs. The women were well organised, and were taking on all sorts of activities.

Then all of a sudden the church pulled the rug out from under us. It stopped the programme and took away all our funds. Why? They said there was no more money, but we don't think that's what happened. We think they were afraid of how far we'd gone. It was the church that first started organising us women. I'd never done anything before getting involved in the mothers' clubs. The church forged the path for us, but they wanted us to follow behind. And when we started to walk ahead of them, they decided that

State workers' union protest, Bogotá, Colombia *(Latinphoto)*

maybe organising the women wasn't such a good idea after all.

Elvia Alvarado, *Don't Be Afraid Gringo*, San Francisco: Food First, 1987

The roots of the new generation of social movements lie in the period of military rule which began with the Brazilian coup of 1964. Politics as usual came to a stop in countries such as Chile, Argentina and Brazil, as the generals banned or severely curtailed the activities of political parties. Opponents of the government or those wishing to press for improvements to their lives had nowhere to channel their protest, and new single-issue campaigns grew rapidly to fill the resulting political vacuum.

Other factors coincided to fuel their growth. The period of military rule coincided with the rise of feminism in the industrialised countries and the sudden expansion of the student population within the region, which provided both activists and direction to the new movements. Military rule also coincided with the heyday of the radical church, in the wake of the Medellín bishops' conference of 1968. The harsh economic programmes unleashed by some of the military governments, notably in Chile after 1973, made necessity a mother of political invention, as women set up soup kitchens to cope with the hunger that suddenly assailed the shantytowns.

Grassroots organisations such as Brazil's Cost of Living Movement or Argentina's Mothers of the Disappeared were instrumental in forcing the military to withdraw from power, but their victories in the early 1980s sometimes carried the seeds of future defeat. As dictatorship has given way to democracy, the new social movements have faced difficult choices about how to relate to the political parties and governments that have taken back political life from the protesters. Their central problem, according to the Mexican writer Jorge Castañeda, is that:

> Without participating in electoral competitions, they run the risk of being rendered marginal, forsaking significant opportunities to advance the aspirations of their members. But by participating, they are immediately subject to the contradictions of any electoral process: whom to vote for, whom to run, what to do if elected, how to govern. There is no solution to this dilemma.

Part of the problem lies in the very nature of social movements. Local needs and their solutions, such as land distribution or greater spending on social services, often require action by the national government. Recognising this, many social movements have attempted to link up their vast array of groups into broader district and even national networks in order to lobby the government. In growing to such a size, however, they risk losing the internal democracy which distinguishes them from orthodox political parties. After decades of co-option and betrayal, social movements are understandably wary of ceding power even to elected leaders, and attempts at wider coalition building have often broken down or been hijacked by populists who promise the earth without ever being able to deliver.

In some countries, recession and neoliberal reforms made survival so difficult and time-consuming for the poor, that many had no energy left for activism. In Chile, adjustment has created an atomised society, where increased stress and individualism have damaged its traditionally strong and caring community life. 'Relationships are changing', says Betty Bizamar, a 26-year-old trade union leader. 'People use each other, spend less time with their family. All they talk about is money, things. True friendship is difficult now. You have to be a Quixote to be a union leader these days!'

In Brazil on the other hand, social movements have survived the transition to democracy rather better, building a strong, vibrant 'civil society' and forming the foundations of the region's most impressive left-wing party, the Workers' Party (PT). The PT was set up in 1979 under the military government by the social movements themselves, led by a new generation of radical trade unionists such as Brazil's current President,

Luís Inácio Lula da Silva. The trade unionists came together with rural unions, radical Catholics, left-wing intellectuals, shanty-town movements and a number of other currents to try and set up a party controlled by the membership which would avoid being absorbed into the Brazilian political establishment. In an astonishingly short time the PT became a major national force: Lula narrowly missed the presidency in the 1989 elections, and was overtaken at the last minute by Fernando Henrique Cardoso in 1994, eventually going on to win in 2002. At less exalted levels, the PT has won mayoral elections in several major cities, including São Paulo, and in 1994 won a good number of seats in both houses of Congress. Although the PT has suffered debilitating splits and arguments through its attempt to reconcile its diverse membership with internal openness and democracy, its successes and rapid rise to political maturity have given many social movements hope that they can build a national party that will remain true to its origins.

In Mexico, the Party of the Democratic Revolution (PRD) is a similar ramshackle coalition of fringe parties and social movements. The PRD was formally set up by Cuauhtémoc Cárdenas after he missed coming to power in 1988 thanks to the most blatant of frauds by the ruling Institutional Revolutionary Party (PRI), which shut down the computers half way through the count. Since then, however, the PRD has struggled. In the 1994 election, it was easily defeated by the PRI, and in 2000 came third behind both the PRI and the victorious pro-business party, the PAN. Hopes for the 2006 election have been raised by the failure of the PAN government, led by Vicente Fox, and the appeal of the PRD's new leader, the charismatic mayor of Mexico City, Andrés Manuel López Obrador.

The Andean region has seen an explosion of progressive grassroots activism in parallel, though not always in partnership, with the burgeoning indigenous movements of the early 21st century. Ecuador suffered a series of constitutional crises as mass protests forced out three of the six presidents who served between 1997 and 2005, and Peruvian governments continue to rely on the wavering support of indigenous groups. It is in Bolivia, however, that new social movements have had the most impact. The rise of Evo Morales and the Movement towards Socialism at a political level, culminating in Morales' election to the Presidency in 2005, has developed in tandem with the organisation and radicalisation of the *campesinos* throughout the country. Their main point of contention was the proposed privatisation and sale – to the US via arch-rival Chile – of the nation's natural gas reserve. A series of roadblocks and running protests have crippled the energy infrastructure and prevented the construction of a pipeline towards Chile.

Morales tapped into the discontent and, after a narrow loss in 2002, became President in 2005 in an unprecedented first-round victory. Like Lula, his success has been built on the organisational power of a coalition

The Water Wars

'Oscar Olivera is a leader of the *Federación Departamental de Fabriles* (factory workers), but also he was the leader of the *Coordinadora del Agua* (Water Committee), and more recently of the of the *Coordinadora del Gas* (Gas Committee). His office is up two flights of rickety stairs, just around the corner from the main square in Cochabamba. It has a fine view over the leafy plaza, and this is traditionally the place where demonstrations in the city happen. He recounts the story of the "water wars":

"During 1999 and 2000 there was an accumulation of public outrage. People felt wholly alienated from the way in which decisions were being made by just a small group of people. The water issue brought us together, because water has been scarce here for 50 years. The political class here is short-sighted and corrupt. The increase in water tariffs would have absorbed about one fifth of the income of many people in the city. For the *campesinos* it represented the appropriation of a resource which they had always used. The *regantes* (farmers of irrigated land) were the prime movers. They had their own forms of organisation and for them water belonged to the community; it could not just be privately owned or managed. The mobilisation over water brought together city and country, man and woman, informal worker and formal. It was something completely new. It made people aware of the nature of the economic model. What people want is social justice, respect and health.

With the water war, people recovered their voice. The issue of natural resources is fundamental in bringing people together. They took the decisions, since there was no caudillo out in front. It was a big victory. Water was not privatized in the end, and Bechtel (the foreign multinational company slated to buy the supply) was kicked out. More importantly, people became aware that it was possible to get bad policies changed. If there had been no victory in the water war, there would never have been a gas war. But we have to be like water itself: transparent and always moving forward." '

John Crabtree, *Patterns of Protest: Politics and Social Movements in Bolivia*, London: LAB, 2005

of social movements; like Lula he may also find himself the target of anger and frustration if popular demands for wealth distribution and the halting of privatisation are not met.

Anatomy of a Protest: The Cochabamba Water Wars

Today, Bolivia stands at the vanguard of political change based on the power of social movements. On several occasions in the early 21st century, broad coalitions of farmers, indigenous peoples, and workers brought the country to a standstill, demanding better access to resources, and protesting against the sell-off of precious natural assets, mainly water, oil and gas. Bolivia is also South America's poorest country – the only other

Latin American countries where poverty rates are higher are Haiti and Nicaragua.

The use (or abuse) of water has long been a conflictive issue in the politics of the Cochabamba valley, a verdant, fertile plane poised between the arid highlands and the lowlands. The problem of water shortage in the valley, and the difficulties of managing an equitable distribution between different users, helps to explain the violent response to the Banzer government's scheme in 1999 to privatize Cochabamba's water supply. Existing users found themselves facing huge increases. Over the years, local organisations evolved around the need to defend what are considered ancestral rights – known in Bolivia as *usos y costumbres* (uses and customs). In what came to be known as the 'water war', farmers joined forces with urban residents and coca growers to mount a lengthy, bitter and sometimes violent campaign to force the government to retreat from its plan to sell off Bolivia's water to foreign multinationals.

Justice and Truth

As the 20th century came to a close, retired life for the former military dictators of Latin America looked decidedly less rosy than it once had. General Augusto Pinochet, who had presided over widespread torture, incarceration, murder and disappearance in Chile, was arrested in London while undergoing an operation in 1998. He was released, but later rearrested in Chile after a court in 2004 ruled him fit to stand trial. After years of immunity from prosecution Pinochet and the Argentines General Harguindeguy and the naval officer Adolfo Scilingo have been brought to the dock for the first time, with more to follow. The tireless efforts of human rights groups were beginning to pay off.

Truth commissions had initially reported on the atrocities in Argentina and Uruguay as early as 1985, during the transition to democracy, but it was not until the late 1990s that high-profile arrests were made. The first wave of post-transition legal commissions was focused more on the pursuit of truth than of justice. In the 1990s, Latin American governments tried to forget the twin traumas of military oppression and economic crisis and instead promoted reconciliation and national unity.

Guatemala's truth commission was particularly thorough and set new standards for investigation. Details of illegal killings throughout the long civil war shocked many observers, but were able to provide a starting point for some degree of national healing and aided the democratisation process. As traumatic as it was to revisit these incidents, including the mass murder in 1982 of 143 villagers at Rio Negro, it was deemed necessary, as it had been in South Africa, to record – and, in theory, to learn from – the nation's collective trauma.

Peru also attempted a process of reconciliation through truth in the aftermath of Shining Path's long uprising. The report found that while the guerrillas had been responsible for around half of the 69,000 deaths during the long insurgency, the military or government-sponsored militias had killed or 'disappeared' an almost equal number of people. Laws put into place by Alberto Fujimori and backed by another ex-president, Alan Garcia, have ensured that – so far – the conclusions of the truth commission cannot be used as prosecuting evidence.

However, as the 1990s came to a close, there were increasingly powerful calls for justice and an end to the culture of impunity which had protected the retired military leaders. In part, this desire for prosecutions was related to the political shift towards the left throughout the region. Both Lula in Brazil and Nestor Kirchner in Argentina had suffered personally at the hands of the military juntas and this may have inspired them to tackle impunity with more vigour. Days after his election, Kirchner purged the Argentinian military of officers with links to the juntas and cleared the way for prosecutions to take place, while under Ricardo Lagos's government in Chile the Supreme Court finally lifted General Pinochet's immunity and declared him fit to stand trial.

It is difficult to predict just how many military leaders will be punished for the crimes they committed against their own citizens before advancing age and natural mortality allows them to cheat judgement; nevertheless, the families of those killed or disappeared by the juntas are closer to justice now than ever before.

The Struggle to Regain a Lost Identity

After the demise of the military governments, amnesty laws and pardons allowed those responsible for the disappearance of some 30,000 people in Argentina to walk the streets freely. But in the late 1990s, a protest movement emerged in the shape of the Daughters and Sons for Identity and Justice against Forgetting and Silence (HIJOS). This organisation of children of the disappeared, exiles and political activists demanded that amnesty laws be repealed. They took to the street, performing 'escraches' – from escrachar, an Argentine slang word for 'uncover' – to root out and publicly denounce human rights violators. The protestors would gather outside the homes of known torturers in an attempt publicly to expose and humiliate them.

Another related struggle is that of the children kidnapped from their parents, often in captivity, and given to 'adoptive' military families. In some cases, children were unknowingly brought up by their parents' torturers and murderers, who kept their true identity secret. In recent years groups such as the Grandmothers of the Plaza de Mayo have led the fight to have these children's kidnappers prosecuted, as immunity for such crimes was not bestowed by the original Amnesty laws.

Jimena Vicario

'Jimena was born in Rosario, in May 1976. From when she was little she knew that she was adopted. Susana, her adoptive mother, was unmarried and worked as a haematologist at the Pedro de Elizalde Hospital in Buenos Aires.

"I remember the moment when I asked how she had adopted me. I was three years old. I remember that she told me that you could put your name down on a list in the court and when babies appeared the court would call the first person on the list and they got the baby."

Jimena's parents were called Juan Carlos Vicario and Estela Maris Galichio. Juan Carlos was kidnapped in Rosario on 5 February 1977. On that same day Estela Maris was with Jimena in Buenos Aires applying for their passports. Both were kidnapped while carrying out the application in the Central Department of the Federal Police. Jimena was nine months old.

In 1984 two elderly women knocked at the door of Jimena's house. Both were members of the Abuelas [Grandmothers] de Plaza de Mayo. They'd received a report and were following it up. Susana wasn't in at the time.

"I had already noticed that over the previous few months lawyers started turning up every day. I remember that Susana was on duty at the hospital and one night she called me to ask me to tell her the number of a lawyer from her address book, which she'd left at home. She had an older brother who was in charge of things since their father died. I saw that the brother was coming round a lot, they used to shut themselves away in her room to talk and I realised that something was up.

One evening she sat me down in my room and said. 'The thing is this, you know you're adopted, and that there is a woman who says she's your grandmother. You're going to go to court with a judge, they're going to call you to do a blood test ...'

I asked who the family was, so she showed me a photo that had been published in the national daily *Clarín*, along with an interview with my grandmother, a photo of me when I was a baby and a photo of my parents. The photos in the newspaper were very dark and I said no, that can't be me." '

Andres Jaroslavsky, *The Future of Memory: Children of the Dictatorship in Argentina Speak*, London: LAB, 2004.

That the story of these kidnapped children has taken so long to emerge – and to be dealt with by the Argentine authorities, and by society as a whole – is testament to the pervasive legacy of silence that terror bestows, but it is also a sign of a new era in which the law is being used to redress impunity. A more difficult task is restoring identity to these children, whose reactions to the news that not only are they adopted, but that their 'parents' might be their biological parents' murderers, are ambivalent and complex.

Latin America today bears little resemblance to the simple divisions portrayed by the warriors of either the Cold War or the class war of previous decades. Identity is fragmented, shifting and multiple. Individuals define themselves along the axes of ethnicity, gender, politics, age and consumer preference. These dimensions of identity are interwoven with notions of human rights as a central part of citizenship. All this has grown up despite the stark economic Darwinism of the last two decades, as neoliberalism has incubated new, complex and challenging social and political movements and ideas that could yet provide the basis for a post-neoliberal order.

Culture and Religion 5

CONTENTS

Writing on the Wall: Culture, Identity and Politics

Every evening the suburbs and shantytowns of Latin America grind to a halt as anyone with a television settles down in front of the latest *telenovela*, or soap opera. TV-less neighbours drop by for the show and an animated discussion about the latest twist in an often bewildering plot. Afterwards, telenovela addicts can go online for an extra fix of gossip and opinion on one of the hundreds of dedicated websites that cater to Latin America's 56 million internet users. And addicts they are: when the last episode of *Cradle of Wolves* was shown, a lurid account of a ruthless heroine with an eye-patch who committed a series of gruesome murders, Mexico's underground drivers refused to go to work and the public transport system closed down.

In Europe and North America, Latin America is better known for its literature and music than for its soaps. Salsa and merengue are favourites on European dance floors, like the tango and bossanova before them. Latin American literature has become so popular that, in the words of critic and translator Nick Caistor, it 'has become the equivalent of the Amazon rainforest, providing oxygen for the stale literary lungs of the developed world.' Latin American novelists such as Mexico's Carlos Fuentes, Argentina's Jorge Luis Borges, Chile's Isabel Allende, Peru's Mario Vargas Llosa, or Colombia's Nobel prize-winning author, Gabriel García Márquez, have become international celebrities, periodically joined by rediscovered greats such as Pablo Neruda. In the US, Allende and García Márquez received the ultimate literary accolade (at least in sales terms) of being selected for the Oprah Winfrey Book Club. Yet at home the audience for one episode of the top Mexican or Brazilian soaps exceeds the entire continent's readership of classics such as *One Hundred Years of Solitude*, which has sold twenty million copies worldwide and is considered by Fuentes to be the greatest novel in Spanish since *Don Quixote*.

In his work, García Márquez draws heavily on the traditional 'popular culture' of his native Colombia, filling his books with the tales of travelling singers and story-tellers, remembered from his childhood. He has turned his hand to other genres, from journalism to film to writing soaps, and challenges those intellectuals and critics who have in the past derided telenovelas as cheap, tacky melodrama churned out by Latin America's media giants. Such critics frequently hark back to a 'pure' popular culture in the countryside, free of the taint of capitalism and technology, yet such views risk reducing the idea of 'popular culture' to a quaint but increasingly irrelevant folklore destined for the museum. Popular culture would paradoxically cease to be the culture of the people, with its constantly evolving mix of traditional and modern styles.

Ever since the conquest, Latin America's dispossessed peoples – indigenous villagers, descendants of African slaves, and poor mestizos – have developed varied and unique cultural forms by constantly absorbing new influences into a bedrock of tradition. The indigenous people of the Andes and Central America kept alive pre-conquest textiles and pottery, while adopting Spanish stringed instruments and combining them with their own panoply of flutes and drums. Traumatic events such as the conquest and murder of the Inca emperors are today recalled through the cultural memory of street theatre and dance, yet traditional styles are still evolving. In Guatemala, widows of men killed or disappeared by the military during their counter-insurgency campaigns in the early 1980s now include stylised images of helicopters in their traditional weaving patterns, where they join images of Spaniards on horseback from the time of the conquest. In Brazil the Kayapó people expertly wield imported video cameras to record their traditional dances and rituals for future generations. The Kayapó explain that they find their own ceremonies more interesting than Brazilian national TV. The cameras also come out at meetings with the Brazilian authorities, to be played back to the bureaucrats should they try to renege on a promise.

The survival of ancient cultural traditions was frequently achieved in defiance of the colonial authorities' attempts to impose European ways. The greatest battleground for the defence of tradition was religion. Traditional indigenous religion and culture are inseparable; music, costumes and dance are part of an annual round of rituals and feast-days linked to the seasons and the agricultural cycles of sowing and harvest. To the Catholic Church, charged with a mission to convert the heathen, the pantheon of indigenous deities had to be crushed, the temples overthrown and practices such as ancestor worship stamped out. In order to appease the authorities, indigenous communities adopted Catholic forms, but subverted their content. The Christian saints took on the characters and powers of the different indigenous gods, and All Souls Day, known in Spanish as the 'day of the dead', became an opportunity for ancestor worship. Every year on 2 November, Mexican families still go to the cemeteries to picnic with their dead. Throughout the continent the cycle of fiestas, carnivals and saints' days play a central role in community life:

> In all of these ceremonies the Mexican opens out. They all give him a chance to reveal himself and to converse with God, country, friends or relations. During these days the silent Mexican whistles, shouts, sings, shoots off fireworks, discharges his pistol into the air. He discharges his soul. This is the night when friends who have not exchanged more than the prescribed courtesies for months get drunk together, trade confidences, weep over the same troubles, discover that they are brothers, and sometimes, to prove it, kill each other.
>
> OCTAVIO PAZ, *The Labyrinth of Solitude*, London and Chicago: University of Chicago Press, 1950

In Mexico, visions of the Virgin Mary began to occur soon after the conquest, the most famous being the Virgin of Guadalupe, who appeared to a poor villager at Tepeyac, north of Mexico City, the site of a traditional indigenous shrine to Tonantzin, the Aztec earth goddess. A flow of miracles forced the disapproving Church authorities to recognise the event, and the Virgin of Guadalupe's shrine became the most important holy place in the Americas. She also became a symbol of emergent Mexican identity, representing both earth goddess and dark-skinned Virgin Mary, who had chosen to appear to an indigenous person rather than to a member of the white elite. In Bolivia, paintings by mestizo artists of the colonial period transformed the Virgin into Pachamama, the Andean earth goddess. Sometimes the subversion of Catholicism was even more deliberate. The Mexican muralists of the 1920s were particularly influenced by contemporary accounts of a religious dance around the statue of the Virgin in a Puebla village, during which the statue toppled over to reveal a small stone carving depicting the goddess of water, hidden beneath the Virgin's skirts for centuries, and surreptitiously worshipped throughout that time.

In the Bolivian mines, Catholic and pre-Columbian beliefs are fused in the figure of the *tío* (uncle). The tío is the god of the underworld whose domain includes the tin mines where, for five centuries, many of Bolivia's indigenous people have toiled in unhealthy and dangerous conditions. Since the Christian God resides in heaven, the tío has become equated with the Christian devil, but without the qualities of evil normally ascribed to him. In the mines, the tío must be placated and asked for help to avert the all-too-frequent rockfalls and explosions. His statue glares out from niches cut into the walls of the mines, but the miners seem on affectionate terms with him, handing him cigarettes or coca to chew. At carnival time they offer him the blood and heart of a llama. As they prepare to cut the llama's throat, the miners, their cheeks bulging with coca, cry out 'for the health and prosperity of our section', 'may there be no more accidents'. Blood collected in a chipped china plate is then smeared on the walls of the mine to bring good luck for another year.

Above ground, the carnival brass bands and 'devil dance' of young men dressed in the elaborate, horned and multicoloured masks of the tío, have moved down from the pitheads to the town centre and become a tourist attraction. These days it is the shopkeepers and middle classes who dance in the masks, which have become too elaborate and expensive for a miner to buy. In the dance the Archangel Gabriel, a pink-skinned, blue-eyed European representation of good, fights the devils in ritual combat. The god of the mines, like the miners he protects, comes off worst in this clash of cultures.

In traditional indigenous beliefs, sacred properties were not confined to a god, but filled everyday objects, which could themselves be worshipped or asked to bring good luck. Everything from a hill, to a tree or a carving could be seen as holy. To the Catholic Church, these practices were idolatrous, and public worship of objects (other than saints) was stamped out, but many of the beliefs were passed down through the family, principally from mother to daughter. Along the way, they were fragmented and transformed into what became known as 'folk magic', involving faith-healing and other 'magical' practices. Today, throughout Latin America, such beliefs as *mal de ojo* (evil eye) and the sale of love potions are commonplace amongst indigenous people and mestizos alike. Even such eminently rationalist, western figures as 'the Liberator', Símon Bolívar, have been turned into quasi-religious icons. Stores throughout Venezuela sell 'Liberator' aphrodisiacs and his name is invoked in faith-healing.

This interweaving of the sacred with everyday life is one reason why writers such as García Márquez insist that their style, often labelled 'magical realism', is merely an accurate portrayal of the life and stories of their native world. In Latin America everyday 'magic' and 'reality' are so interwoven as to be inseparable. García Márquez has particular trouble separating life from art: in 1996, hours after he had sent off the final proofs of his latest book, *News of a Kidnapping,* real-life kidnappers abducted the brother of ex-president César Gaviria. Their main demand? That García Márquez take over as president to 'save the fatherland'.

In Brazil, the African slaves on the sugar plantations of the Northeast managed to retain their cultural identity through music and dance. Plantation owners even encouraged erotic dances to keep up morale amongst their slaves. Today on Rio's beaches young black men can still be seen performing capoeira, a traditional slave dance combining both expressive performance and ritualised martial arts. In recent years, as the Brazilian community in Europe has begun to assert itself, capoeira has spread in popularity to non-Brazilians as a leisure activity. As increasing numbers of blacks left the sugar plantations and moved to the shantytowns and tenements of the cities, African religions resurfaced in

Blessing Cars in Bolivia

'Bless this vehicle. May the driver drive in a Christian way. May the motor not use too much petrol.' So goes the much-repeated blessing by the old Irish priest as he totters along a queue of new cars, jeeps and trucks decked out in garlands of yellow and red flowers.

At Copacabana, on the shores of Lake Titicaca, the highest lake in the world, the cars have come from all over the country to be blessed at the shrine of the country's favourite Virgin.

The priest sprinkles holy water on the driver, the upholstery and the engine and moves on. After the blessing the owners shower petals over their new (and now sanctified) cars. Next comes the beer, shaken vigorously then squirted over wheels, upholstery and down expectant throats. Off go the firecrackers, as the smells of gunpowder and beer blend in the clear Andean air.

On the outskirts of the town another ceremony is taking place half-way up a small rocky outcrop topped by another shrine to the virgin. Here, overlooking the silver-blue expanse of the lake, Bolivia's indigenous traditions take over from Catholicism.

A family arrives with a toy pick-up swathed in bright paper streamers. An elderly indigenous priest blesses them and their cherished vehicle, mumbling in a mixture of the Spanish Mass and the native Aymara language.

Little bells ring. There is a fizz and a splat as the priest sprays beer to the four points of the compass. A palpable sense of calm and spirituality ensues. If the blessing wins divine approval, the family will get their dream car and bring it to the church below to be blessed.

The services mix prayers to Pachamama, the indigenous earth mother, with invocations to God and the Virgin Mary. Pachamama and God; petrol consumption and incense. In Bolivia there is no dividing line between 'traditional' and 'modern'.

the shape of Candomblé. Candomblé is based on the personal relationship between an individual and a pantheon of African deities, each with a different personality and tastes. As in the Andean religions, music, dance and worship are inseparable. The gods appear through the possession of chosen 'sons and daughters' and receive ritual offerings, songs and dance.

African and Portuguese cultures combined to produce samba and carnival, a joyous three day euphoria of dance, music, sex and beer which has become synonymous with Brazil:

In the official parade grounds – the Sambadrome – I thought the silence eerie until I realised it was in fact a solid wall of sound, a percussive din that did not sound like music and advanced gradually towards the spectators on an elaborate loudspeaker system set up on either side of the central 'avenue', or parade space. At the head of the noise was a gigantic waggling lion's head that floated down the avenue and overtook us, giving way to dazzling hordes in red and gold. A marmalade-thick river of people swept past; outlandish dancers in feathers and capes, ball gowns and G-strings, hundreds of drummers, thousands of leaping princes singing at the top of their lungs. Drowning in red and gold, I struggled to focus. In the ocean of feathers and banners faces emerged: brown, white, pink, tan, olive. Young men bopping in sweat-drenched suits; old women in cascades of flounces whirling ecstatically; middle-aged men and women with paunches and eyeglasses bouncing happily in their head-dresses and bikinis.

ALMA GUILLERMOPRIETO, *Samba*, London: Jonathan Cape, 1990

Carnival's origins lay in festivals brought from Portugal, messy affairs in which the populace pelted each other with flour and water and indulged in gargantuan feats of eating and drinking. Over the years dance and music acquired increasing importance, and local carnival associations grew up to organise floats for processions through the streets of Rio. The centre of carnival culture moved from the rich European suburbs to the poor black favelas, provoking one well-to-do reader of the *Jornal de Notícias* in Bahia to write in 1901:

the authorities should prohibit those [African drum] sessions and *candomblés* that in such quantity are overflowing on our streets these days, producing such great cacophonous noise, as well as those masquerades dressed in [typical black costumes] singing their traditional samba, because all of that is incompatible with our current civilised state.

The associations metamorphosed into the samba schools, enormous permanent organisations based in Rio's favelas which each year take on the task of building the increasingly monumental floats, and organising thousands of drummers and costumed dancers into their various 'wings'. The vast expense of carnival and the elaborate costumes have so far not forced the samba schools out of the favelas, but there has been a slow erosion of the poor communities' involvement in carnival as a whole. Outside designers and artists are now hired to create the floats, costumes are farmed out rather than made by the women of the favela, and each school's procession is now fronted by TV stars, usually white.

Two Cultures Clash

In Latin America culture and politics have been inextricably linked since Pizarro's conquistadores ransacked the temples of Cusco and melted down the Inca empire's finest wrought gold and silver into ingots to be sent home

Magical Realism

The real as magical – electricity comes to Macondo

'Dazzled by so many and marvellous inventions, the people of Macondo did not know where their amazement began. They stayed up all night looking at the pale electric bulbs fed by the plant that Aureliano Triste had brought back when the train made its second trip, and it took time and effort for them to grow accustomed to its obsessive toom-toom. They became indignant over the living images that the prosperous merchant Bruno Crespi projected in the theatre with the lion-head ticket windows, for a character who had died and was buried in one film and for whose misfortune tears of affliction had been shed would reappear alive and transformed into an Arab in the next one.... When someone from the town had the opportunity to test the crude reality of the telephone installed in the railroad station, even the most incredulous were upset. It was as if God had decided to put to the test every capacity for surprise which was keeping the inhabitants of Macondo in a permanent alternation between excitement and disappointment, doubt and revelation, to such an extreme that no one knew for certain where the limits of reality lay.'

The magical as real – Macondo is stricken by a plague of insomnia

'With an inked brush [José Arcadio Buendía] marked everything with its name: *table, chair, clock, door, wall, bed, pan.* He went to the corral and marked the animals and plants: *cow, goat, pig, hen, cassava, caladium, banana.* Little by little, studying the infinite possibilities of a loss of memory, he realised that the day might come when things would be recognised by their inscriptions but that no one would remember their use. Then he was more explicit. The sign that he hung on the neck of the cow was an exemplary proof of the way in which the inhabitants of Macondo were prepared to fight against loss of memory: *This is the cow. She must be milked every morning so that she will produce milk, and the milk must be boiled in order to be mixed with coffee to make coffee and milk.* Thus they went on living in a reality that was slipping away, momentarily captured by words, but which would escape irremediably when they forgot the values of the written letters. At the beginning of the road into the swamp they put up a sign that said MACONDO and another larger one on the main street that said GOD EXISTS.'

Gabriel García Márquez, *One Hundred Years of Solitude* (trans. Gregory Rabassa), London: Jonathan Cape, 1970

to Spain. After the conquest the Spanish authorities initially banned fiction, fearing it would excite the minds of the locals and fan subversion. During the colonial period the social and economic divide between the white ruling elite and the dark-skinned masses was mirrored in the gulf between their two cultures. In their art academies and concert halls Latin America's elites pursued a purely European aesthetic and made regular visits to its cultural capitals of Paris or Rome. Werner Herzog's 1982 film, *Fitzcarraldo*, recounts one particularly bizarre example of the forced implantation of European culture: – a rubber baron's folly in the shape of a 2,000-seat opera house in

Manaus, in the heart of the Amazon jungle. After it opened in 1897, opera companies from Milan, Paris and Madrid sailed up the Amazon to sing at the theatre, which boasted curtains from Alsace, stone from Portugal, Venetian crystal and English wrought ironwork. When the rubber boom came to an end, the theatre closed down until its restoration in 1990, when Plácido Domingo sang in *Carmen* to a full house. Meanwhile, away from the paved streets of the city centres, a rich and separate popular culture was actively combining ingredients of indigenous, African and European culture into a uniquely Latin American cocktail.

Many 19th-century writers, notably Argentina's essayist and president

---

Latin America's Melting Pot

Little Tamales from Cambray
To make 4,200,000 small tamales
by Claribel Alegría

Two pounds of mestizo cornmeal
a half-pound loin of Spanish immigrant
all finely chopped and cooked
with a packet of ready-blessed raisins
two tablespoons of Malinche's milk
one cup of troubled water
then fry the conquistador's helmets
with three Jesuit onions
one small sack of multinational gold
two dragon's teeth
add one presidential carrot
two tablespoons of pimps
the fat from Panchimalco Indians
two Ministry tomatoes
half a cup of televised sugar
two drops of volcanic lava
seven pito leaves
(don't get me wrong, it's a soporific)
set it all to boil
over a slow fire
for five hundred years
and you'll discover its unique aroma

From Amanda Hopkinson (ed.), *Lovers and Comrades: Women's Resistance Poetry from Central America*, London: Women's Press, 1989

Note: 4,200,000 is the population of El Salvador, of which tamales are the national dish. Malinche was the name of the indigenous mistress of Cortés, who betrayed the Aztec emperor Cuauhtémoc to the Spaniards.

Domingo Faustino Sarmiento, portrayed popular culture as a form of barbarism which must be fought through the introduction of civilised (i.e. European) values, described by one author as 'the civil war between the swallow-tailed coat and the poncho.' Yet popular culture also offered middle-class writers and artists an apparent solution to a conundrum that has dogged the continent's intelligentsia since the conquest: the riddle of Latin America's identity. As Simón Bolívar lamented, 'We are not Europeans, we are not Indians, but a hybrid species between the aborigines and the Spaniards.' After independence, and particularly as modern nation states began to form towards the end of the 19th century, the search for a national and continental identity played an essential role in the formation of a common sense of nationhood. The influence of European romanticism made writers and artists look for such an identity in Latin America's own version of the 'noble savage', an authentic innocent untainted by tawdry modernity. In Argentina the romantic figure of the gaucho, the self-reliant cowboy of the pampas, spawned a series of novels and poems in the dying years of the century, glorifying rural life at a time of massive migration to the cities. Although a caricature, *gauchismo* offered a sense of belonging to a distinctive culture, playing much the same role as the glorification of the cowboy and the 'winning of the west' in the US.

The search for a Latin American identity and debate over politics and art took on greater urgency in the political and cultural ferment that followed the Mexican revolution of 1910–17. The revolutionary Mexican government set about forging a new national consciousness. Under the patronage of a dynamic education minister, José Vasconcelos, a group of Mexican artists began to cover the walls and ceilings of public buildings with murals depicting scenes from Mexican history and allegorical portraits of the revolution. In preferring walls to canvas, the muralists sought to make art the property of the people, not a commodity for sale to the highest bidder. The movement came to be dominated by the 'big three', Diego Rivera, José Clemente Orozco and David Alfaro Siqueiros. Between them, they developed what has been called the greatest public revolutionary art of the century, a maelstrom of unforgettable images of indigenous villagers, conquistadores, heroic workers and bloated capitalists. Rivera, in particular, drew heavily on pre-Columbian designs and the popular artists of his time, notably the skull images of José Guadalupe Posada, who had earned fame prior to the revolution for his satirical cartoons.

Although perhaps unintended by the artists, the murals helped the state to establish enduring myths of a new Mexico that had thrown out the rich white capitalists and now belonged to the poor mestizos and the indigenous peoples. The muralists' combination of revolutionary zeal with an unquestioning faith in technological progress both excited and enraged the US art establishment. In California in 1933, Rivera's patron, John D.

Rockefeller, ordered his 'Man at the Crossroads' destroyed because Rivera refused to remove the figure of Lenin from an allegory of progress in the modern age.

The work of the Mexican muralists has inspired political street art throughout Latin America ever since. In Nicaragua following the Sandinista revolution of 1979, the walls of the cities were quickly adorned with revolutionary iconography. Figures like Che Guevara, Sandino, Allende and Zapata joined Bolívar and others on the roll call of Latin America's secular saints. When the Sandinistas fell from power in 1990, one of their opponents' first actions was to whitewash the walls of Managua; in 2005 Ecuador's capital, Quito, became the scene of a graffiti battleground between the various factions vying for power in the wake of the flight of President Lucio Guitérrez.

The Mexican experience was the first example of a phenomenon repeated throughout the continent in the following years. Populist governments took power in major nations such as Mexico, Brazil and Argentina, combining limited social reform with a drive to turn them into industrial powers. By promoting a sense of patriotic identity with its own myths and symbols, populist leaders such as Brazil's Getúlio Vargas and Argentina's Juan Domingo Perón could build the national unity needed to implement their model of development and ensure the legitimacy of the state. In Brazil, Vargas seized on samba, carnival and football and used state money to turn them into national icons. Vargas built the Maracanã stadium, the biggest football ground in the world, and transformed carnival into a major international event. Both samba and football were ideal for the purpose, being poor people's pastimes which the state could use to weld people together at both local and national level.

The political importance of literature and art also showed in the great political weight acquired by the intellectual, a figure of far greater status in Latin America than in Britain or the US. In the 19th century, poet José Martí fought for Cuban independence, while Sarmiento played a key role as president in forging modern Argentina. Rómulo Gallegos, author of Venezuela's classic novel, *Doña Barbara*, was also that country's president. In this century, two accomplished historians, Joaquín Balaguer and Juan Bosch, spent several decades vying for the presidency of the Dominican Republic, while writers and poets such as Chile's Pablo Neruda, Mexico's Carlos Fuentes and Octavio Paz and Guatemala's Miguel Angel Asturias have served their countries as ambassadors. In 1987 Peru's Mario Vargas Llosa unwisely decided to abandon the pen for the campaign trail and run for president against Alberto Fujimori in 1990 before returning, chastened, to literary life. Even musicians got in on the act when top salsa singer Ruben Blades unsuccessfully ran for Panamanian president in 1994.

Mexican political scientist Jorge Castañeda believes that intellectuals fill serious gaps in Latin American political life, acting as a conduit for ideas from abroad, and speaking on behalf of groups in society: 'Intellectuals are nearly always substituting for someone or something.... They fight for labour rights in lieu of unions and denounce human rights abuses in the place of judges or the courts. They decry injustice, oppression and electoral fraud on behalf of weak or nonexistent political parties, and write pamphlets revealing and condemning corruption, substituting for a fettered, often marginal press.'

Electronic Ambassadors

The rapid pace of urbanisation since the turn of the century has had a seismic impact on popular culture. Towns and cities act as the entry point for foreign influences, while the most remote rural areas remain repositories of traditional culture. As the rural poor flocked to the shantytowns around the major cities, they brought with them traditional customs, which blended with the new influences. In Peru this melting pot has produced what is known as chicha culture, named after a potent local brew. Chicha music has combined the traditional wailing lament of the Andean *huaynu* with tropical music and electric guitars to become the sound of Lima's shantytowns.

Salsa, probably Latin America's most successful musical export in recent years, is itself a mongrel mixture of Cuban dance styles such as son, *rumba* and *chachacha*. In the late 1960s, Fania Records, a Latin record label in New York, had the inspired idea of repackaging this baffling range of musical styles as 'salsa', and the music took off , becoming a central part of the Latino identity movement.

The introduction of new electronic media has transformed popular culture in the present century. Film, radio, TV and increasingly, the internet, have become the main channels of public communication in society, thereby acquiring a central role in creating and passing on cultural values. The mass media have also become a battleground in the struggle to define Latin America's identity. Increased dependence on Western technology has given huge influence to foreign film and TV exporters, with the film industry in particular dominated by Hollywood. Other media, such as radio and TV, have shown greater success in becoming largely Latin American in character, playing an important role in forging national identities.

It is difficult to overestimate the importance of the US as a purveyor of mass culture. The record shops of Latin American cities blare out the latest musical genres, both from the US and, increasingly, home-grown versions. Middle-class youth covet the latest Levis or trainers just as much as their North American or European counterparts. Dubbed or subtitled US films of the *Speed* and *Terminator* school form the staple diet of scruffy cinemas throughout the continent. Especially since the Cuban revolution of 1959,

Teenagers in Mexico's Chapultepec Park. *(Latinphoto)*

many artists and writers have come to see North American influence in the media as another facet of US political and economic domination of the continent. They argue that its domination allows the US to instil its values into Latin Americans, acting as a subliminal ambassador which can reach into the poorest home with a dazzling image of the giant to the north. Latin America's intellectuals have stressed the political importance of creating and sustaining a separate Latin American culture in the mass media, as a means of finding a political alternative to US domination.

Historically, the high cost and advanced technology required in film-making has meant that Latin America's cinema has lived in the shadow of films from the US and other industrialised nations, but at different moments it has managed to produce high-quality films which have challenged the Hollywood monopoly. Until the 1960s most Latin American cinema consisted of low-budget musicals, comedies and melodramas whose characters and themes were summed up by the critic John King as 'good women who bear the stigma of fate, weak men caught in the trap of a man-eater, rooms and brothels reeking with smoke and moral turpitude, eyes bloodshot with alcohol and grief, innocence, violent death.'

Yet Latin American cinema has also been intimately involved in politics since the days when the Mexican revolutionary, Pancho Villa, signed an exclusive contract with the US Mutual Film Corporation, granting it exclusive rights to film his battles. For US$25,000 he agreed to fight in daylight whenever possible, to rerun scenes of battle if the cameras had missed the real thing, and to reschedule firing-squad executions from 4 a.m. until after dawn.

The Cuban revolution marked a watershed for the continent's film-makers, as Havana quickly became the centre of a politically committed 'New Cinema', dedicated to portraying Latin America's conflicts, especially with the US, through a brand of social-realist cinema and documentary. The 1960s and early 1970s saw young radical film-makers using a low-budget, hand-held-camera style to film life, warts and all, in favelas and villages across the region, producing classics such as *Blood of the Condor* (Jorge Sanjinés, Bolivia) and *Battle for Chile* (Patricio Guzmán, Chile). Havana became the host of an annual Latin American Film Festival and invited film-makers from every corner of the Third World to come and study at its international film school.

The New Cinema dominated the 1960s, but soon afterwards the optimism began to wear thin as military dictatorships in the Southern Cone drove film directors into exile and the Cuban government started to show growing intolerance towards dissident writers and directors. Cuba illustrates a problem that has beset the Latin American cinema since its inception. In the absence of private capital, it has frequently had to rely on state support, leaving it open to manipulation and censorship, or simply asphyxiation by a state bureaucracy that cares little for artistic innovation.

In the 1980s and 1990s, government austerity programmes cut state funding and led to a slump in film production in many countries. Since the final years of the 20th century, however, Latin American cinema has experienced a dramatic rebirth. In Argentina, the economic crisis of 2001 coincided with the beginning of a flowering in home-grown cinema, with the vast success at home and abroad of crowd-pleasing films such as *Nueve Reinas* and *El Hijo de la Novia* and art-house films such as *Mundo Grúa* and *La Ciénuga*. In Mexico some joint ventures of private and public capital scored initial successes with films such as *Danzón* and *Like Water for Chocolate*. More recently, *Amores Perros* and *Y Tu Mama También* provided back-to-back hits for Mexican heart-throb Gael García Bernal, before he went on to collaborate with the feted Brazilian director Walter Salles in the film adaptation of Che Guevara's *Motorcycle Diaries*. *Y Tu Mama También*'s director, Alfonso Cuarón, struck gold when he was asked to direct the third Harry Potter movie. Cuba, on the other hand, remains cash-strapped and now produces few films – the success of the 1990s being *Strawberry and Chocolate*, a mild critique of gay issues directed by Tomás Gutiérrez. The film that perhaps more than any other summed up the new global appeal of contemporary Latin American cinema was *Cidade de Deus* (City of God) by Fernando Meirelles and Katia Lund. European and North American

Walter Salles on Contemporary Brazilian Cinema

I come from a country and also a continent whose identity is in the making. We're a very young culture, and I think that things are not yet crystallised. So the films that are made in our latitudes, I think, carry that sense of urgency. It's as if the people that you meet on the street and the stories that they bring can influence you directly. Imagine trying to do that in Los Angeles – it's impossible because there's no one in the streets! So little by little, I think my generation became very porous to that. But I think it's not all that different from what the Italian neo-realists did 50 years ago, by taking the camera out of the studio and taking it closer to the faces in the street.'

From an interview with Geoff Andrew at the National Film Theatre, London, 2004

audiences are at last prepared to watch challenging subtitled films, a sea change which has helped many budding directors to obtain investment. The problem for new film-makers lies in distribution, where Hollywood has a stranglehold throughout Latin America. It is a sad truth that many young directors score success at foreign film festivals while awaiting a release for their films at home.

Latin America's film audiences are nevertheless dwarfed by those for its TV networks. Heavily patronised by the state, which recognised its political potential, Latin American TV has grown rapidly. Latin Americans watch an average of just under five hours of television each day, and this figure is rising. There are more than 100 million TV sets in the region, reaching more than 90 per cent of the population, and their favourite viewing is the telenovelas that dominate prime time. Brazil and Mexico have even become TV exporters, breaking into the US market to build a large following for their soaps among the growing Hispanic population. Harder to understand is Russia's fascination with Latin soaps. In 1992 Televisa's *Los Ricos También Lloran* (The Rich Also Weep) broke all viewing records, while Boris Yeltsin's successful bid for re-election in 1996 was partly put down to his brainwave in engineering a special scheduling of TV Globo's *Tropicaliente* to dissuade Russians from leaving town on polling day. At the turn of the century, popular titles included *Maria la del Barrio* (Maria From the 'hood), *Corazón Salvaje* (Savage Heart) and *Abrázame mas Fuerte!* (Hug me Harder!)

From the mid-1960s, when the first national telenovela was filmed, Latin America's soaps have built on the melodramatic tradition in popular theatre and film, developing rapidly into a major cultural commodity dominated by Brazil and Mexico and their giant media conglomerates, TV Globo and Televisa, which rank fourth and fifth in the world league table of media giants. They have become increasingly global, notably in the US where they produce much of the content for the growing US Hispanic cable channels.

No other company consistently produces as many popular Spanish-language novelas as the Mexican giant Televisa, which is known as *la fábrica de los sueños* (the dream factory). Its soaps are often variations on a fairly standard formula: a struggle between good and evil; an obligatory love story; a baroque plot which only addicts could disentangle; and an emphasis on individual emotion and melodrama. Compared to European or US soaps, Latin American telenovelas are more likely to use historical settings and are time-bound, using an intense nightly burst of 100–200 episodes to tell a full story from beginning to climax to end.

In recent years, more social and political content has found its way into the telenovelas. In *Dos Mujeres y un Camino* (Two Women and One Road), a popular Mexican telenovela, the star played an assimilated Latino who returns from the United States to live in Mexico. Characters poke fun at him because of his limited command of Spanish. In Colombia, *Adrian Está de Visita* (Adrian is Visiting), released in 2002, broke new ground by casting a black leading man with a white woman as his love interest. This is nothing short of revolutionary in a telenovela industry accustomed to featuring only white actors in leading roles.

An analysis of telenovela plots in Brazil showed that the affair usually takes place between lovers from different classes. In a country as profoundly unequal as Brazil, where social mobility is minimal, the soaps raise important issues, but unlike real life, they provide a happy ending as love triumphs over class barriers. In recent years, telenovelas have taken on a number of political issues such as landlessness and the environment in *O Rei do Gado*, in Brazil, or the highly topical question of government corruption in Mexico's *Nada Personal* or Venezuela's *Por Estas Calles*. TV Globo's *Mujeres apasionadas* (Passionate Women) dealt with alcoholism and gender equality. Unfortunately, the ratings for such programmes have not always lived up to expectations, as script writers have struggled to reconcile the conflicting demands for escapism and social comment. One exception was *Yo Soy Betty la Fea* (I am ugly Betty), a Colombian series that challenged telenovela orthodoxy by casting its lead as a distinctly unglamorous woman struggling to stay honest in Colombia's fashion business. The series doubled the ratings of rival shows and triggered national debates in the press.

The founding of Telesur in 2005 marked a new step for Latin American TV. Paralleling the Arab *Al Jazeera* (not least in being underwritten by oil money, in this case from the Venezuelan government), Telesur will be a pan-continental news channel broadcasting from a Latin American perspective: perhaps it can be thought of as *Al Bolívar*. Aram Aharonian, the Uruguayan journalist who will be the general director of the channel, says it will be 'the first counter-hegemonic telecommunications project known in South America.' President Chávez hopes Telesur will become a strong competitor to CNN and Univisión, broadcasting over one channel throughout South America via satellite from its headquarters in Caracas.

Latin America Online

As elsewhere, the digital and internet revolution is transforming the way Latin Americans use the media. By mid 2005, 56 million Latin Americans (10 per cent of the population) were online, and numbers were rising much faster than in the more saturated markets of the US and Europe. TV billionaires such as Mexico's Carlos Slim and Venezuela's Gustavo Cisneros are investing billions in moving into multi-media and web-based activities, as well as slugging it out over control of the lucrative cable and satellite TV markets (one in ten of the region's homes already pays for cable TV, rising to as many as four in ten in Argentina). The battle shows both the risks and potential benefits of the new electronic age. While the big players may dominate the main stations, the proliferation and fragmentation of communications channels create spaces for other voices which in the past had no way of making themselves heard. New media increasingly make use of audience participation (one US Spanish-language channel now allows the audience to vote online on its preferred ending to the latest telenovela), while the proliferation of weblogs and dedicated sites allows new generations of Latin Americans to find a voice and a virtual community of like-minded people.

The political impact of such changes has barely begun to be felt. Until the *New York Times* published Herbert Mathews' Sierra Maestra interview with Fidel Castro in 1957, the revolutionary movement in Cuba was virtually unknown to the rest of the world. In 1994, the Zapatistas' charismatic Subcomandante Marcos was issuing lyrical communiqués on the internet within hours of their uprising. Anyone with a laptop and a modem could follow the struggle in the depths of the Lacandón jungle (http://www.fzln.org.mx/index.php), and there was nothing the Mexican government could do about it. While the site has its fair share of communiqués and 'denuncias', Marcos' laconic postings are a long way from the traditional Puritanism of the Latin American revolutionary leader. In an idle moment in 2005, he wrote to the Inter-Milan football team to challenge them to a game against the Zapatistas. 'Given the affection we have for you, we're not planning to submerge you in goals,' the letter promised. 'As we wait for your reply, we'll continue with our rigorous training regime.' Inter-Milan, one of Italy's biggest and most famous clubs, have built links with the Zapatistas by funding sports, water and health projects in their part of Chiapas. Inter's captain, Javier Zanetti, said he was willing to consider the challenge.

Football might help with writer's block. In 2004, Marcos joined the tradition of novelist/politician crossovers when he wrote to Pablo Ignacio Taibo II, a successful writer of detective stories set in Mexico City, proposing that they team up to write a detective story in alternating chapters. The writer accepted co-authorship with a hunted guerrilla leader because 'it had the enormous attraction of insanity'.

The impact of the internet on the popular movement extends far beyond the Lacandón jungle, of course. Neighbourhood assemblies in Argentina, following the financial crash of December 2001, organized through email and websites. Email has drastically cheapened communication costs for pressure groups and social movements across the region. At a global level, the internet provided the basis for the organisation of three World Social Forums, in Porto Alegre, Brazil, gathering thousands of international participants from every part of the globe.

Other activists, however, warn against over-hyping the political potential of the Internet. Access remains dominated by the middle class, and the digital divide could easily become another driver of inequality. One activist in Peru talks about the new underclass of the *'desenchufados'* – the 'unplugged ones'.

Intellectuals and the Left

The cultural impact of the Cuban revolution spread far beyond the cinema. In a continent preoccupied with its identity, Cuba became a symbol of resistance to US domination and the search for a new Latin America, where culture was at the service of the people. In the early years of the revolution, the Cuban National Ballet performed classical and folk dance in factories during the lunch breaks, mobile cinema vans took film to isolated villages for the first time, and Havana became an international centre for writers, poets, film-makers and musicians. According to García Márquez, 'the definition of a Latin American "intellectual of the left" became the unconditional defence of Cuba.'

In the 1960s everything was new: 'New Song' in Chile blended traditional Andean music with folk ballads and revolutionary lyrics, 'New Cinema' recorded real life rather than cinematic fantasies, and the 'New Novel' established a worldwide readership for writers like García Márquez, Fuentes, Cuba's Alejo Carpentier and the Argentine Julio Cortázar. While the 1960s phenomenon in Europe peaked in 1968, Latin America's cultural boom reached its zenith a year earlier. In 1967 the Guatemalan author Miguel Angel Asturias became the first Latin American novelist to receive the Nobel prize, Gabriel García Márquez published *One Hundred Years of Solitude*, and Che Guevara was killed in Bolivia. With Che died the optimism of a generation who had grown to believe in imminent revolution. In Cuba the beginning of the 1970s saw the government curtailing cultural freedom and arresting the dissident poet Heberto Padilla, leading many prominent figures such as Mario Vargas Llosa to part company with the revolution after fiercely criticising Fidel Castro.

Gloom settled over much of Latin America in the 1970s. Coups in Chile and Uruguay (1973), and Argentina (1976), coupled with the growing intolerance in Havana, led to repression and exile for many intellectuals, and a climate of hostility, fear and censorship for those that remained. The clampdown's best-known victim was Victor Jara, Chile's top exponent of 'New Song'. Jara was murdered, along with thousands of others, in Santiago's infamous football stadium shortly after the coup. In an act of extraordinary malice, the soldiers crushed the guitarist's fingers before killing him. In exile, other musicians such as the Chilean group Inti Illimani, toured the world giving concerts aimed at raising awareness and money for the solidarity movement. Safeguarded by exile and international fame, established writers responded with novels of dictatorship: Paraguay's Augusto Roa Bastos published *I The Supreme*, while García Márquez produced *Autumn of the Patriarch*.

The Nicaraguan revolution of 1979 brought a chink of light to an otherwise sombre panorama. In that country, poetry workshops sprang up in such unlikely places as the secret police and army barracks; a national literacy crusade brought the printed word for the first time to hundreds of thousands of peasants; an internationally acclaimed writer, Sergio Ramírez, became vice-president; state-sponsored musicians, dancers and circus performers sought to recover national traditions, and revolutionary murals adorned the walls of even the smallest village. In Ramírez' words: 'Once we lifted the yankee stone which weighed Nicaragua down, everything that was fundamental and authentic had to surface again: dances, songs, popular art and the country's true history.'

In the Southern Cone, the 1980s brought the military's slow retreat from power. In Argentina, war over the Falklands/Malvinas forced the military to treat youth as the saviours of the country rather than potential delinquents. Radio stations were ordered to stop broadcasting music in English, giving 'national rock' access to the mainstream media for the first time. The military invited rock stars to take part in pro-war concerts, but instead an anti-war movement sprang up, whose anthem became León Gieco's song, 'Sólo le pido a Dios':

> I only ask God
> not to make me indifferent to war
> It is a great monster that tramples on
> the poor innocence of the people

Following defeat in the Falklands, the end of the dictatorship led to a new cultural flowering, for example in Argentine cinema. But the widespread joy at the departure of the generals was tempered by the impact of the recession and the identity crisis of the left, leaving progressive musicians without the sense of grand purpose that marked the revolutionary 1960s or the struggles against dictatorship in the 1970s.

Life After Magical Realism

Latin America's literary establishment remains dominated by the grand old men of the 1960s boom, but new novelists and poets have also emerged. One of the most important developments has been the rise of a generation of women writers, after centuries in which recognised authors were almost exclusively male. Writers such as Chile's Isabel Allende, Brazil's Clarice Lispector and Mexico's Elena Poniatowska and Laura Esquivel are gaining growing readerships both within Latin America and abroad. Allende's *House of the Spirits* became the first genuine bestseller by a woman in Latin American history, and since the 1980s she has cemented her reputation as one of the most commercially successful Latin American authors.

Elena Poniatowska has developed a style of documentary narrative to provide a 'people's eye view' of key moments in modern Mexican history, such as the social impact of the earthquake of 1985, and the 1968 Tlatelolco massacre of student protesters by the government. She has pioneered a form of writing in which middle-class women journalists and anthropologists work with working-class and peasant women to produce memorable life stories such as *Let Me Speak*, by Domitila Barrios de Chungara and Moema Viezzer, and *I, Rigoberta Menchú*, by Rigoberta Menchú and Elisabeth Burgos-Debray. In recent years Central America has also produced some renowned woman poets, notably Claribel Alegría (El Salvador) and Gioconda Belli (Nicaragua).

Interest in new Latin American writers has grown along with the booming interest in US-based Latino writers such as Cristina García (Dreaming in Cuban), Julia Álvarez (*In the time of the Butterflies*), Oscar Hijuelos (*Mambo Kings Play Songs of Love*) and Francisco Goldman (*The Long Night of the White Chickens* and *The Ordinary Seaman*), who have created a hybrid US/Latino genre.

Through novels such as *Betrayed by Rita Hayworth* and *Kiss of the Spider Woman*, Argentina's Manuel Puig has challenged the radical orthodoxy of the 1960s, with its scorn for Hollywood and cheap mass entertainment. Puig argues that writing off the cultural preferences of a large percentage of the population is an elitist mistake by intellectuals from the traditional left. Instead, they should be embracing mass culture. His characters belie the idea that Latin Americans are passive recipients of whatever the media throw at them; they are quite capable of indulging themselves with Hollywood fantasies while keeping a clear sense of their own identities. Puig also deals with issues of gender and sexuality in a way that has moved some women critics to describe him as the best creator of female characters in Latin American fiction.

In recent years, magical realism has started to seem stale to new generations of writers, who have instead portrayed the grimy drug- and violence-filled reality of Latin America's shantytowns and city centres, rather than the sleepy rural world of García Marquez's Macondo. Chilean author Alberto Fuguet ironically brands the new genre 'McOndo', yet another Latin American syncretic combination of old and new, external and internal influences.

Although the euphoria of the 1960s was lost in decades of militarism and economic crisis, its cultural impact lives on in the continued quest for a truly Latin American identity. While Latin America continues to import its political and economic models from outside, often with disastrous results, the arts, especially music and literature, have always been more successful in finding words and rhythms that are authentically Latin American. If the region is to find its own way out of the recession and confusion of the late 20th century, its rich variety of cultural forms is bound to play a central role. García Márquez as always, is in the vanguard, writing *The General in his Labyrinth* about Simón Bolívar in 1990. 'For me, what is fundamental is the ideology of Bolívar: the unity of Latin America,' he says, 'That is the only cause I'd die for.'

In his best-selling album *Buscando América* (Searching for America), Panama's salsa maestro Ruben Blades sums up the pressing challenges that lie ahead:

> I'm searching for America and I fear I won't find her
> ... I'm calling America but she doesn't reply
> those who fear truth have hidden her
> ... while there is no justice there can be no peace
> ... if the dream of one is the dream of all let's break the chains and begin
>   to walk
> ... I'm calling you, America, our future awaits us
> before we all die, help me to find her.

Latin America and Sport

Historically, football has played a political role in Latin America, particularly under the military dictatorships in Brazil and Argentina. The 1964 military coup came at a time when Brazilian football was at its height, the national team having won two successive world cups and turned their stars – many of them black – into national heroes. But the generals could not resist the temptation to gain political capital from this opium of the people. A military official was appointed as the head of the Brazilian Confederation of Sports; he sought to impose greater discipline and teamwork on the individualist style of Brazilian football. The national team promptly went into decline until the players' anarchic genius was unfettered once more. The 1978 world cup took place in Argentina in the midst of a wave of human rights violations and disappearances two years

Football is Latin America's most popular game – and cultural export. *(Latinphoto)*

Football, Corruption and Politics

In the 1978 world cup no expense was spared to present the best image of Argentina to the world. Despite inflation running at 165 per cent, three new stadia were built, at Mendoza, Córdoba and Mar del Plata. Television, telephone and telex facilities had to be completely overhauled. A US public relations company, Burson-Marsteller, was given a million-dollar contract to buff up Argentina's tarnished image. The finance minister, Juan Alemann, put the cost of the project at US$700 million, much more than the subsequent cost of the 1982 cup in Spain. He called it "the most visible and indefensible case of non-priority spending in Argentina today". Mindful of Perón's example, the generals decided that it was worth it, but only if the national team were successful.

The generals had put their faith in a talented young manager, César Luis Menotti. They also took out a little insurance. Eight years later the Sunday Times published what it said were details of how Argentina bribed Peru on the eve of a crucial match. Argentina needed to beat Peru by at least four goals to overtake Brazil and so reach the final. The Argentinians knew the precise scale of the task in front of them, because Brazil's match against Poland had conveniently been scheduled for earlier in the day. Peru had looked a decent side but on the night in Rosario they were torn apart 6–0. Some Peruvian players were dropped, others played out of position. Peru's Argentinian-born goalkeeper was a flimsy barrier. The newspaper's anonymous sources said that Argentina's central bank released US$50 million in credits to Peru and that Argentina shipped 35,000 tons of grain, and possibly weapons as well.'

Chris Taylor, *The Beautiful Game*, London: LAB, 1998

after the military coup. The military junta used the national team's victory to seek both national and international legitimacy.

Latin America has always exported its commodities to rich consumers in the North, and sporting talent is no exception. European football teams import new generations of highly talented Latin American players, while many North American baseball teams depend on Latino talent for success. Despite local fanaticism for spectator sports, the finest talents are often prised away by the lure of fame and riches in the North.

US marines involved in the spate of gunboat diplomacy of the late 19th and early 20th century left baseball behind them as one of their more positive legacies. European visitors to revolutionary regimes in Nicaragua and Cuba were suitably startled to find baseball the national game (similarly the Dominican Republic), with huge pride attached to players from all three countries to have made it in US teams. In New York there is no rivalry as fierce as that between the Amazin' Mets and the Yankee 'Evil Empire', and this multi-million dollar contest is underpinned by Latin American talent. Disparaging commentators have criticised the Mets for using Spanish as their everyday clubhouse language, while the Yankees have sought to expand their marketing operation throughout the Western hemisphere. Pedro Martínez, Carlos Beltran and José Reyes against Alex Rodriguez, Jorge Posada and Mariano Rivera? This is not simply an inter-borough rivalry – it is a truly inter-continental contest. US and Canadian players now head south to the Dominican Republic, Mexico, Puerto Rico or Venezuela for the Winter League season – this is a way of keeping fit, but more importantly it is a way of raising the profile of Major League Baseball in those countries from which the next generation of superstars will be drawn.

Thy Kingdom Come: The Church

In the main square in front of Guatemala's national palace, a paunchy preacher in a shiny new bomber jacket is haranguing the crowd. Grinning as he shouts into a fat blue microphone, he talks of drought, disease and salvation, exhorting everyone to praise the Lord. An 'Alleluiah' rises from the largely female audience. The preacher is an Evangelical Protestant, and he is standing outside the capital city's Roman Catholic cathedral. Inside, everything is cool and white after the dust and heat of the square. The smell of candle-wax fills the air as a queue of indigenous worshippers of all ages wait to pray to and kiss the wounds of a dark-skinned statue of Christ, his legs worn shiny from the stroking of thousands of hands. Catholicism has the cathedral, but the Evangelical preacher has the crowds. The crusading zeal of the Evangelicals is winning millions of new converts every year, threatening the last bastion of global Catholicism. Even so, by 2004 more than half of the world's Catholics lived in Latin America.

In Guatemala, as in most of Latin America, old belief systems are breaking down, producing a kind of religious supermarket where worshippers shop around between Catholicism and the different Evangelical churches. But there are other, more exotic offerings on the shelves: in the church of a lakeside town in the indigenous highlands, the townsfolk, both Protestant and Catholic, also worship Maximón, an enigmatic Mayan combination of St Peter and Judas, with a penchant for cigars and liquor. In Brazil, African spiritist religions such as Candomblé and Umbanda, which arrived with the slaves, are also doing battle for the souls of the poor.

Christopher Columbus had a triple purpose when he set sail for what he imagined would be Asia in 1492. In the words of Bernal Díaz del Castillo, a comrade of Hernan Cortés in the conquest of Mexico, Columbus and the conquistadores who followed went 'to serve God and His Majesty and also to get riches.' In the year that Columbus 'discovered' America, the Spanish, led by Ferdinand and Isabella, finally drove the last Muslim king out of Granada, bringing to an end the 500-year war to expel the Moors from Spanish soil. That same year, a royal decree expelled all Jews from Spain. With Spain united, the Vatican looked to the Americas as the next great crusade. Two years after Columbus landed, the Pope decreed in the Treaty of Tordesillas that Spain and Portugal could divide the New World between them, with a mission to convert the heathen.

Despite well-intentioned efforts by the Crown and the Church to restrain the worst excesses of the colonists, evangelisation took second place to the mass extermination of the indigenous people through disease and slavery. When Columbus despatched 500 indigenous slaves back to Spain, he commented in his diary, 'Let us in the name of the Holy Trinity go on sending all the slaves that can be sold'. Under the *encomienda* system, Spanish officers were granted large numbers of indigenous labourers in return for bringing them to Christ. It is not clear how many were successfully converted before dying in the mines or on the *haciendas*.

From the start, there were dissident friars who expressed their revulsion at the treatment of the indigenous people. Just 19 years after Columbus first landed, a Dominican named Antonio de Montesinos, on the island of Hispaniola (today the Dominican Republic) outraged his Christmas congregation with his questions: 'by what right do you keep these Indians in such a cruel and horrible servitude? … you kill them with your desire to extract and acquire gold every day.… Are these not men? Have they not rational souls? Are you not bound to love them as you love yourselves?' Five centuries on, many Church workers are still asking the same questions of Latin America's elites.

The sermon changed the life of one young landowner in Montesinos' congregation, a man by the name of Bartolomé de las Casas. Shortly afterwards, Las Casas gave up 'his Indians' and travelled to Spain to begin a lifetime's crusade to persuade the Spanish Crown to end the extermination of the continent's native peoples. First as a Dominican friar, then as a bishop, Las Casas became the indigenous inhabitants' foremost defender, and his book *A Short Account of the Destruction of the Indies* gives a graphic portrayal of their suffering under the conquistadores. In one famous debate in 1550, the 76-year-old bishop took on the leading Spanish scholar of his day, Juan Ginés de Sepúlveda, to argue that the enslavement of the indigenous communities was theologically unacceptable, and that indigenous civilisation was in many ways superior to that of the Europeans.

Not only the Dominicans, but also the Franciscans and the Jesuits brought with them a more enlightened version of Christianity. In the early 17th century the Jesuits set up vast *reducciones* (missions) covering much of Paraguay, where Guaraní communities could live and work safe from the depredations of Portuguese slavers. In these sanctuaries, the Guaraní developed their skills in working metal, stone and wood to levels of artistry matching anything in Europe. In the end, however, the burgeoning Brazilian state drove out the Jesuits and the Guaraní were enslaved.

From its earliest days in Latin America, the Roman Catholic Church supported the colonial authorities in return for being made the official religion and receiving the tithe – a levy on all wealth generated in the Indies. In consequence, an increasingly complacent and materialist priesthood lost touch with the poor. In 1748, one report to the Spanish king commented:

> it seems relevant to mention here what a priest from the province of Quito told us, during his visitation of this parish, in which – between feasts and memorial services for the dead – he received each year over 200 sheep, 6,000 poultry, 4,000 Indian pigs and 50,000 eggs. Nor is his parish one of the more lucrative ones.

The independence wars of the early 19th century threatened this cosy relationship and split the Church between pro- and anti-Spanish factions. Usually the upper echelons of the Church supported the empires, while local priests like Miguel Hidalgo and José María Morelos in Mexico went as far as taking up arms in the independence cause. Both were captured and executed. Despite these schisms, independence leaders subsequently swore allegiance to Rome, and soon came to a series of agreements with the Vatican which maintained Catholicism as the state religion.

Later in the century, the Church paid the price for backing the most backward sections of the elite, usually via the Conservative parties, when

Liberal reformers severed the Church–state relationship in Ecuador, Brazil, Cuba, Honduras, Nicaragua, Panama, Chile and Mexico. Liberal governments limited Church control over education and confiscated its property. The countries where the Church was disestablished later became the most fertile ground for the growth of the radical Catholic Church and the Evangelical Protestants. Anti-clericalism reached its height in post-revolutionary Mexico, where the tensions between Church and state following the Mexican revolution of 1910–17 led the Church to suspend public worship for three years from 1926. Ninety priests were executed during the ensuing Cristero rebellion of Church militants, whose name came from their battle cry '*Viva Cristo Rey*' ('Long live Christ the King'). A wartime speech by one Mexican general, J.B. Vargas, encapsulated the virulence of anti-clerical feeling:

> It is enough to have some idea of the terrible history of the Inquisition for one to realise that priests and cassocks reek of prostitution and crime. Confession is an industry invented to seduce maidens, to win over Catholic ladies and transform fathers and husbands into chaste replicas of Saint Joseph.... The Pope is a crafty foreigner who accumulates wealth in collaboration with the exploiting Friars who swindle the foolish people for the benefit of a country quite other than their own.... Nowadays, if Jesus Christ were to come down, the first thing he would do would be to hang them like rabid dogs.

The rebellion ended when the government backed down and allowed limited autonomy for the Church, though with greatly reduced influence.

While Catholicism remained essentially European at the top, cultural cross-fertilisation was occurring at a local level. From the earliest days of the conquest, many traditional indigenous beliefs and practices were incorporated into a 'folk Catholicism', where Catholic saints rubbed shoulders with Andean gods in the niches and on the altars. In Bolivia's historic mining town of Potosí, the wild baroque carvings of the San Francisco Church look distinctly pagan. Bare-breasted goddesses are interwoven with the ubiquitous symbols of sun and moon, while at the very top of the building, an Inca warrior looks out sternly over the city. A minute, red-cheeked indigenous boy explains, 'we built this for ourselves when we Indians weren't allowed in the Cathedral.' Folk Catholicism has come in for particular criticism by the Evangelicals, who see it as even more pagan than the pure Roman version. 'We take the cross up to see our crops grow,' says an indigenous peasant woman in Peru's Sacred Valley, 'that's our belief. We worship the Catholic religion. Mother Earth (pachamama) as well. Only the Catholics still believe in Mother Earth and the Cross. The other religions, the Evangelicals, don't worship these any more.'

The Modern Church

The social turmoil of the 1930s, with broader suffrage, the beginnings of urbanisation and the rise of mass politics in the cities, brought home the growing irrelevance of the Church's traditional allies, the Conservative parties and land-owning elites. The Vatican began to wake up to the disastrous condition of its Latin American operation. Grown fat and lazy through its links to the rich, the Church had only the shallowest roots among the poor majority with which to confront a new era of change and mass involvement in politics. Paradoxically, in a continent where the overwhelming majority declared themselves Catholic, few went to church and the ratio of priests to parishioners was far lower than elsewhere in the Vatican's empire.

The Church embarked on a crusade, loosely termed Catholic Action, to organise its lay members and extend its influence within groups such as students, peasants, women, workers and the middle classes. The new emphasis was on social issues, and the movement grew with the emergence of Christian Democrat parties after the Second World War. Church leaders saw such organisations as a bulwark against the expansion of communism, and religious organisations in the US contributed funds and personnel as the Cold War gathered momentum in the 1950s. Yet, although the Church acquired renewed political influence, it failed to increase significantly the numbers of active worshippers and reduce its social isolation. In the 1960s only 20 per cent of baptised Catholics regularly attended mass, compared with 80 per cent in Poland or Ireland; there was only one priest for every 5,700 believers compared to a ratio of 1:830 in the US. In addition, the first signs of the imminent explosion of Protestant Evangelicalsm were beginning to alarm the bishops.

As the 1960s wore on, events threatened to overtake the Vatican. The Cuban revolution in 1959 and the failure of Christian Democrat governments to deliver reforms led to the radicalisation of many grassroots Church workers and activists. Some student sections even split off from the Christian Democrat parties to become the nuclei of guerrilla organisations. In Colombia, a radical young priest, Camilo Torres, took up arms to fight with the National Liberation Army (ELN), declaring, 'the Catholic who is not a revolutionary is living in mortal sin.' Torres died in a shoot-out with the army in 1966.

The course of events in Latin America gave an added urgency to the Second Vatican Council, a massive shake-up ordered by Pope John XXIII to drag the worldwide Catholic Church into the modern era. In four years of meetings with 2,500 bishops from across the globe, the Council charted a new direction. It changed its vertical chain of command for a looser structure based on consultation with local churches. It redirected its attention to life in the contemporary world, especially emphasising issues

The Lord of the Miracles procession in Lima, Peru. *(South American Pictures)*

like human rights, justice, freedom and peace. The Church had a duty to pass moral judgements on the state when it contravened basic human rights.

Vatican II, as it became known, had a seismic effect on the Latin American Church, leading in 1968 to the meeting of Latin American bishops in Medellín, Colombia. Medellín took the Latin American Church far beyond Vatican II. In new teaching that embraced the newly emerging Latin American 'Liberation Theology', it identified unjust social structures as sinful and called for radical change. Despite its fundamental focus on peace, it came close to justifying popular insurrection as a response to 'institutionalised violence':

> One cannot help seeing that in many parts of Latin America there is a situation of institutionalised violence, because the actual structures violate fundamental rights and this situation demands global changes of a bold, urgent and deeply new kind. We should not be surprised that 'the temptation for violence' arises in Latin America.

The bishops then went on to establish a new organisational model to implement these revolutionary new ideas. They suggested the setting up of Base Christian Communities (CEBs), grassroots groups of working-class or peasant Catholics who would study and reflect on the Bible and use it as a basis for action. This pastoral expression of Liberation Theology was called the 'preferential option for the poor'.

Medellín was a political and theological explosion. The Church abandoned nearly five centuries of largely cosy cohabitation with Latin America's elites in favour of an active commitment to the poor and oppressed. The picture varied enormously between countries; in Chile the Catholic Church became a centre of opposition to the Pinochet dictatorship, and through its *Vicaría de la Solidaridad* played a vital role in documenting and publicising the armed forces' violation of human rights. Radicals also gained substantial influence in Brazil and Central America, whereas the Colombian and Argentine Churches remained true to their conservative past.

The CEBs became a crucible for a process known as *conscientización* (consciousness raising) whereby the poor became conscious of injustice and organised to change their lives. As one Salvadorean peasant leader recalls, many went on to lead social movements or even guerrilla organisations:

'What made me first join the farmworkers' union was when I compared the conditions we were living in with those that I saw in the Scriptures; the situation of the Israelites for example … where Moses had to struggle to take them out of Egypt to the Promised Land … then I compared it with the situation of slavery in which we were living. Our struggle is the same: Moses and his people had to cross the desert, as we are crossing one right now, and for me, I find that we are crossing a desert full of a thousand hardships, of hunger, misery and exploitation.'

From JENNY PEARCE, *Promised Land*, London: LAB, 1986

CEBs treated the Bible as a manual for action. The story of Jesus throwing out the money-lenders acquired enormous political impact when brought up to date through a CEB Bible study group. The groups also had a

---

The God of the Poor

From the *Misa Campesina* (Peasant Mass) by Nicaraguan singer Carlos Mejía Godoy

You are the God of the poor,
a human and a simple God.
The God who sweats in the street,
the God of the withered face.
That's why I speak to you,
just like my people speak,
because you are the worker God,
the labouring Christ.

democratising effect, since the shortage of priests meant that many groups were led by local lay catechists, both men and women, many of whom went on to become popular leaders in their own right. One of them was Rigoberta Menchú, a Guatemalan indigenous woman who became a peasant leader and went on to win the Nobel Peace Prize in 1992. In her autobiography, I, *Rigoberta Menchú*, she describes the impact of becoming a catechist:

> When I first became a catechist, I thought that there was a God and that we had to serve him. I thought that God was up there and that he had a kingdom for the poor. But we realised that it is not God's will that we should live in suffering, that God did not give us that destiny, but that men on earth have imposed this suffering, poverty, misery and discrimination on us.

CEBs took firmest root in Brazil, where they were instrumental in starting the protest movement which helped to drive the military government from power in 1985. They also formed an essential part of the social movements which went on to challenge for power through the Workers' Party (PT). They played a vital role in Nicaragua, where the radical Church supported the insurrection that overthrew the Somoza dictatorship. In El Salvador, the CEBs were at the forefront of the upsurge in the protest movement which ended in a bloodbath in the early 1980s and a prolonged civil war.

Yet the Church paid a high price for its 'option for the poor'. Within the Church hierarchy, conservative bishops began to backtrack on the Medellín commitments almost as soon as the conference was over. With the advent, in 1978, of Pope John Paul II, an uncompromisingly anti-communist Polish prelate, the backtracking in Rome was quickly transformed into a full-blooded hue and cry against the perils of liberation theology. It led to the marginalisation, investigation and silencing of its leading clerical figures; it brought two formal Vatican documents fiercely critical of liberation theology and its exponents, both under the signature of Joseph Ratzinger, today Pope Benedict XVI. There was additionally the disowning of the so-called 'popular church', and the expulsion from their religious orders of three progressive priests who had taken ministerial posts in Nicaragua's revolutionary Sandinista government. The Vatican counter-attack was intense and resonated well with US policy in Latin America under President Ronald Reagan.

The progressive Church also became a target for military repression. 'Be a patriot, kill a priest', ran one death-squad slogan in El Salvador in the late 1970s. Dozens of clerics were killed, the most celebrated being Archbishop Oscar Romero, shot while saying mass in the capital, San Salvador, in 1980, and six Jesuit leaders, together with their housekeeper and her daughter, all gunned down in 1989. An even greater slaughter awaited the lay preachers, who died in their hundreds. As a result, the

---

Base Communities in Brazil: a critical perspective

'Deep down, pastoral agents thought that base communities would be the spearhead of a social revolution, a social transformation, a new society. So working in base communities was a way of preparing for the new Latin American society. At that time the base communities were seen as the spearhead of the opposition. They were the alternative. People said that basic change might take time, even into the next century, but base communities were the alternative. But the lay people who entered the base communities had no intention of engaging in social revolution or changing the church.... They didn't have such vast ambitions. What they wanted was greater independence, a community life with more independence from priests. And that's still what they want, but the priests aren't interested. Lay people do not need complicated courses, they need a "strong initial spiritual push", a very strong message. The pentecostals do that and so do the charismatics. But if you begin with very intellectual meetings, things are going to be slow. What is required is entering into the people's psychology. It has to be a conversion moment, like the early Baptists and the Methodists.'

Phillip Berryman, *Religion in the Megacity: Catholic and Protestant Portraits from Latin America*, Maryknoll, NY: Orbis Books, 1996

Salvadorean CEB movement was devastated.

By the mid-1980s, doubts were starting to surface among radical Catholics about the effectiveness of the CEBs. Field research revealed that most CEB members were not the poorest but often had steady jobs, and that many were much less socially active than had been imagined. Other studies suggested that the numbers had been greatly exaggerated: instead of the two million active CEB members routinely claimed for Brazil in the mid-1980s, 250,000 seems a more realistic estimate. In Latin America as a whole, CEBs only existed in a maximum of ten per cent of parishes, and even there such communities were small islands in a sea of Catholics whom the church scarcely touched.

The research also showed that, far from representing a lasting handover of power from the Church hierarchy to the laity, successful CEBs were heavily dependent on the good will of sympathetic bishops, the active involvement of priests and nuns at local level, and funding from a range of foreign (usually European) agencies.

Partly, the CEBs were a victim of their own success in forging generations of leaders for the new grassroots social movements. As those movements took off, many of the most dynamic CEB leaders went with them. In Brazil, large numbers of the best CEB activists devoted themselves to building up the Workers' Party; in Nicaragua, the Sandinista revolution had a similar effect on a hitherto dynamic CEB movement.

In the 25 years of John Paul's papacy, the Latin American church leadership was transformed, gradually and systematically, from a socially committed and pastorally audacious episcopacy into a rather cautious conservative body hugely dependent once more on the word from Rome. The mechanism was the Vatican's most potent weapon – the power to appoint bishops. Every single bishop is appointed by the Vatican from a short list provided by the local Papal Nuncio, the Vatican's ambassador. Anyone openly sympathetic to a liberation theology view of the world and the Church was simply barred from consideration.

That said, once the Cold War was over in the 1990s, the Catholic hierarchy was freed from anti-Communist preoccupations, enabling it to take on many demands formerly put forward by the progressive Church, particularly in response to the social impact of neoliberal reforms. The idolatry of the market and the unacceptable face of globalised capitalism became a regular part of Rome's discourse and were echoed and amplified in Latin America. 'Neo-liberal capitalism carries injustice and inequality in

Archbishop Romero of El Salvador

The progressive Church's most famous martyr, Oscar Arnulfo Romero, was an essentially conservative man who was radicalised by his contact with El Salvador's poor and the worsening violence of the army and its associated death squads. As Archbishop of San Salvador, Romero publicly attacked both the economic system and human rights abuses in weekly sermons which were picked up on dilapidated radios in peasant huts and shantytowns throughout the country.

On the economy
'The cause of all our ills is the oligarchy – that handful of families who care nothing for the hunger of the people but need that hunger in order to have cheap, abundant labour to raise and export their crops.'

On violence
'Profound religion leads to political commitment, and in a country such as ours where injustice reigns, conflict is inevitable.... Christians have no fear of combat; they know how to fight but they prefer to speak the language of peace. Nevertheless, when a dictatorship violates human rights and attacks the common good of the nation, when it becomes unbearable and closes all channels of dialogue, of understanding, of rationality: when this happens, the Church speaks of the legitimate right of insurrectional violence.'

On 23 March 1980 he signed his death warrant by appealing directly to the soldiers carrying out attacks:

'In the name of God, and in the name of this suffering people whose laments rise to heaven every day more tumultuous, I beg you, I ask you, I order you in the name of God: Stop the repression.'

The next day he was killed with a single shot while saying mass at a local hospital chapel.

its genetic code', proclaimed Honduran Cardinal Oscar Rodríguez. In 1995, Latin America's bishops concluded, 'We cannot remain indifferent to the extreme poverty, growing unemployment, uncontainable violence and corruption and impunity that sink millions of families in anguish and pain.' But by then the grassroots movements, which might have given teeth to such statements, were in decline.

When John Paul II died early in 2005, the ensuing speculation about his successor was in great part focused on Latin American figures who were *'papabile'*. Brazilian, Honduran, Mexican, Argentinian and Chilean cardinals of very different hues in their theology and pastoral practice were certainly in the frame. It looked for a brief moment as if the Latin American Church might actually inherit the kingdom. But it was not to be – at least not for the time being.

Benedict XVI, the new pontiff from Germany, the former head of the Vatican's doctrinal watchdog agency, has had only limited contact with Latin America, much of it in adversarial combat with its progressive thinkers. It seems likely, however, that his energies will be focused on Europe and the best that Latin American Catholics can expect is a period of 'benign neglect' from Rome.

A New Reformation

One of the principal causes of the disillusionment with the CEBs was the meteoric rise of the Pentecostal Protestant Churches over the same period. 'Evangelicals', as they are commonly called in Latin America, are born-again Christians committed to converting others to their own brand of Christianity. Evangelical services typically involve rhythmic clapping, chanting and swaying, leading to a cathartic mass euphoria. The Pentecostals believe that true Christians are taken over by the Holy Spirit during religious gatherings, culminating in speaking in tongues and faith healing. The name comes from a biblical reference to the 'Day of the Pentecost' when Jesus' disciples were visited by the Holy Spirit and received the 'gift of tongues' to enable them to preach and evangelise in other languages.

The tide of Pentecostalism has rapidly swamped the traditional Protestant Churches of Latin America, such as the Lutherans and Presbyterians. These are small groups generally set up by immigrants from northern Europe, and have largely middle-class congregations. In 1936, Pentecostals represented just two per cent of Central American Protestants; by the turn of the century they exceeded 90 per cent.

With the exception of the Assemblies of God, which have at least eight million worshippers in Brazil alone, the Evangelical movement in Latin America is divided up into innumerable separate churches, disparagingly labelled 'sects' by their opponents. Often these are the personal vehicle of

Brazil's Universal Church of the Kingdom of God

Latin America's fastest-growing Evangelical Church was established in 1978 by Bishop Edir Macedo, a former lottery-ticket vendor. It now owns a weekly newspaper with a circulation of 700,000, a TV network and dozens of radio stations. Its churches operate in 35 countries worldwide. The Universal Church's annual income is estimated at US$750 million, on a par with Volkswagen Brazil.

The Church runs two-hour services which focus on different issues each day: family problems, health and sickness, prosperity, the presence of the Holy Spirit, and the expulsion of demons. Macedo claims to have cured AIDS and brought people fortune. He has certainly made himself rich – he is a brilliant fund-raiser. Tithes are seen as proof of belief. In one of his many books for the faithful, he cites famous people who have paid tithes and become millionaires, such as 'Senhor Colgate, Senhor Ford and Senhor Caterpilar [sic]' ...

a single pastor. When a congregation grows, it will often splinter into new churches. Although this reduces the coherence and influence of the movement as a whole, it means that Evangelical Churches remain rooted in their communities. Pastors display a zeal rarely encountered in their Catholic counterparts. In the middle of a war zone in Nicaragua in the 1980s, Evangelical pastors could be found three days from the nearest road, walking between peasant huts in search of converts. The Catholic Church was nowhere to be seen.

The social message of the Evangelicals is one of individualism, hard work and sobriety. Evangelical pastors are fiercely hostile to collective organisations such as trade unions. Critics, especially radical Catholics, have accused them of encouraging political passivity that only benefits the powerful and denies the poor the ability to organise to improve their lot. Evangelicals respond that their focus on immediate steps such as giving up drink and working hard actually has more immediate impact than the search for long-term social change. The proof is that Evangelical Churches are far more popular than the Catholics among the poorest communities. As one famously barbed quote from a Brazilian Baptist pastor put it, 'The Catholic Church opted for the poor, but the poor opted for the Evangelicals.'

In any case, Evangelicals believe that true salvation lies in an individual's relationship to God; as one Costa Rican group sings, 'I've got nothing in this world, but a mansion in the next.' Carlos Chávez, a 46-year-old Evangelical of the Elim Church in San Salvador, explains: 'The Lord changes the Evangelical's life. He makes him more patient, more passive, more humble, more loving, more centred in what he does.' Carlos showed a typically Evangelical view of El Salvador's bloody civil war:

The war is the fulfilment of the prophecies – the Lord told his disciples there would be wars, plagues, famines and earthquakes, and these would be signs of his coming. As Evangelicals, the war doesn't torment us, it brings us joy, because it's a sign that Jesus is coming soon. We don't intervene in the conflict. What we do is pray to God that things should change. Today God's people don't struggle with arms, but with prayer.

This essentially conservative message contrasts with the more progressive doctrines gradually being adopted by many of the traditional Protestant Churches. Grouped together in the Latin American Council of Churches (CLAI), these older groups have built ecumenical links with the more progressive Catholic Church, although not endorsing the full content of Liberation Theology. The CLAI has attempted to turn Protestant attention to issues such as the drug war and the debt crisis, but remains a small voice with very limited influence.

Protestant preachers and TV broadcasts tap into the anxieties of life in modern Latin America – health, jobs, crime and family breakdown. Many authors connect the rise of Protestantism to urbanisation. Peasant migration to the cities severs an individual's links to the community, resulting in isolation and confusion. In such circumstances, evangelism can offer both a supportive community and a strong sense of purpose and identity. The emphasis on sobriety is particularly attractive to many women whose partners have alcohol problems.

The most recent and fastest-growing Pentecostals have also left behind the more austere side of Protestantism, absorbing the practices of popular religion that were often abandoned by embarrassed Catholic priests in the aftermath of Medellín. In Brazil particularly, the use of faith healing, magic, holy water, song, dance and possession shows the Pentecostals' readiness to adopt the trappings of the Afro-Brazilian religions, even as they vilify them as devil worship. To the outsider, Bishop Macedo's exorcist priests bear a remarkable resemblance to their counterparts in Candomblé. African religions and Evangelicals are often in conflict, yet increasingly share similar methods. In Honduras, Evangelicals have made inroads among the black garifuna community (descendants of the original Carib people), urging them to abandon their traditional religion. But the converts find the Evangelical services familiar. 'I used to dance for the world, now I can do it for the Lord', explains one teenager.

In countries with large black communities, African spiritist religions are on the rise, despite the efforts of the Evangelicals. Edilson is a *pai de santo*, or Candomblé priest, in Brazil's black capital of Salvador, centre of the former slave trade. He operates from his house in a well-established favela, with two rooms devoted to Candomblé, the fascinating hybrid of African and Catholic influences. In the first room, Christ and the saints hang alongside Candomblé's African gods, or *orixás*, faceless figures of beaten copper. A set of conga drums and a large urn of holy water also stand by ready for ceremonies which combine drumming, drinking and possession by any one of the pantheon of orixás. In the second room, known as the 'room of the slave', Edilson intones a prayer in the African Yoruba language before entering to sprinkle cane spirit, or *cachaça*, over the altar and light a candle. 'People come to purify themselves when they're sick or have spiritual problems', he explains. 'The Evangelicals are always speaking against us', he adds, 'but the Catholics are more ready to coexist – many people here have two religions.'

Figures on the Protestant explosion should always be treated with caution. The Protestant Churches often exaggerate them, while the Catholic Church suffers an equal tendency to minimise them. However, many sources accept that since the 1960s the number of Protestants in Latin America has risen 12-fold to 60 million. Although 60 million people

Table 5.1:
Religious Demographics in Latin America

Country	% Catholic	% Protestant or other
Argentina	92	2
Bolivia	95	5
Brazil	80	20
Chile	89	11
Colombia	90	10
Costa Rica	76	24
Cuba	n/a	n/a
Dominican Republic	95	5
Ecuador	95	5
El Salvador	83	17
Guatemala	75	25
Honduras	97	3
Mexico	89	11
Nicaragua	85	15
Panama	85	15
Peru	90	10
Paraguay	90	10
Uruguay	66	3*
Venezuela	96	4
Latin America	86	14

Source: CIA World Factbook, 2004
*Uruguay's survey included an option for non-believers, which was selected by 31% and gives an indication of just how nominal the Catholic identity may be for many Latin Americans.

represents only about 14 per cent of the total population, and most of the rest describe themselves as Roman Catholics, virtually all Protestants are active churchgoers, whereas the rate among Catholics may be as low as 15 per cent. In terms of active participation, Protestants may already outnumber Catholics in several countries.

A further source of confusion over the figures is the growing fluidity of people's religious affiliations. One recent study in Costa Rica showed that there were almost as many ex-Evangelicals as current ones. Two thirds of those leaving returned to the Catholic Church. Others happily shopped around, worshipping at both Catholic and Protestant Churches during the course of a week, as well as moving regularly between different Pentecostal denominations.

Evangelicals in Politics

Although the growth of the Evangelical Churches has fed on social chaos, suffering and the divisions within the Catholic Church, other influences have attracted severe criticism from progressives of both Catholic and Protestant backgrounds. The Latin American Evangelical movement is financed and heavily influenced by right-wing Evangelical groups in the US, which have sent thousands of missionaries, run aid projects which also serve as recruitment drives, and trained new generations of local pastors to spread the word. 'Televangelical' preachers like Jimmy Swaggart and Pat Robertson are household names in many Latin American nations, where the resources of the multi-million-dollar Bible Belt TV and radio chains buy hours of airtime. A new breed of US-based Spanish-speaking 'super preachers', such as Argentina's Luis Palau and Spanish Harlem's Luis Cortés, has now joined their ranks.

Suspicions that US televangelists' agenda in Latin America might not be purely spiritual were heightened in 2005, when Pat Robertson suggested on his TV channel that the United States should assassinate Venezuelan President Hugo Chávez. Although some radical Catholics claim the Evangelical movement is entirely funded and controlled by Washington, many local sects have few ties to the US, and the astonishing speed of their expansion shows that they meet a real spiritual and social need in the region.

The Pentecostal Church itself has so far shown little interest in politics, with some isolated exceptions to both left and right. Guatemala has provided both Latin America's first Pentecostal dictator, General Ríos Montt (1982–83), and President, Jorge Serrano (although he was forced into exile after trying to seize power in 1993). Even there, however, the fragmented and apolitical nature of the Pentecostals means that the Catholic Church remains a much more powerful political force.

In many ways, the Evangelical Churches are a more genuine 'church of the poor' than their Catholic rival, and they could undergo the same kind of radical political conversion as occurred within the Roman Catholic Church in the 1960s. There are a few signs of isolated changes of this kind. In Chiapas, where Protestants have suffered violence and expulsion from indigenous communities at the hands of local bosses of the ruling PRI, Evangelicals came out in support of the Zapatista uprising, while there are some high-ranking Evangelicals in Brazil's Workers' Party, such as Benedita da Silva, the country's first black woman senator, who went on to become Minister for Social Welfare in the early years of the Lula government.

In the religious melting pot of today's Latin America, systems of belief and ritual are ever more fluid and intertwined. The disparate influences of Africa, Europe and indigenous traditions that have so shaped the region's culture are seen equally at work in the religious sphere, producing a range of hybrid religions which are uniquely Latin American.

In this uncertain world, the Catholic Church must fight a war on at least two fronts. First it must contend with growing secularisation, as increasing numbers of Latin Americans, particularly in the middle class, abandon religion altogether.

Secondly, if it does not find a way to revive its withered grassroots and reconnect with the lives of ordinary Latin Americans, it will continue to lose ground to Protestant Evangelicals.

Conclusion

Latin America is in ferment. The signs of modernity and change are everywhere: the internet, TV and public transport have transformed the lifestyles and aspirations of all but the most isolated communities; the sharp hustling world of the city has replaced the slow seasonal cycle of rural life. Politically, the region's depressing round of dictatorship and democracy has been replaced by an unprecedented degree of political stability and civilian government. A Catholic continent is going through a breakneck process of conversion to Pentecostal Protestantism.

But scratch the surface, and ample evidence will be found of continuity beneath the froth of change. Old evils persist, as Latin America's system of economic apartheid, an unbridgeable gap between rich and poor, has been widened even further in recent years. A battery of external influences – including the IMF, Northern governments and international capital markets – has frogmarched the region down the road to unregulated 'savage capitalism', an implausible remedy for the continent's social and economic ills. The region's authoritarian traditions are evident in the style of 'exclusionary democracy' that has characterised the region's return to elected government.

Other continuities provide grounds for optimism. Latin America's extraordinary ability to absorb and transform outside influences remains undimmed. Ever since the conquest, foreign invasions, be they cultural, political or religious, have been steadily 'Latin Americanised' into distinctive syntheses of traditional and modern.

Brazilians joke that their country 'is the land of the future, and always will be'. The same might be true of all Latin America, whose political and economic systems squander the region's vast wealth and human potential. Those systems must change if Latin America is to struggle free from five centuries of want and waste. With governments and the right held hostage by market economics' seemingly invincible power, the left appears to be the only hope for change. In the aftermath of the end (outside Colombia) of the guerrilla wars, and the collapse of Communism, a new generation of centre-left political parties and leaders now governs in South America (again with the exception of Colombia). Hedged in by market forces, however, they have so far struggled to find a stable path to growth with equity.

One source of such a new direction stems from what Latin Americans call 'social effervescence', the proliferating grassroots community groups who struggle for immediate improvements to their lives. The range of new players is impressive – women's organisations, shanty-town movements, peasant groups, indigenous federations, trade unions, environmental movements. This burgeoning political pluralism with its promise of empowerment offers grounds for hope that Latin America's centuries of inequality and injustice may yet be overcome.

Chronologies

Section 1: The Curse of Wealth: Economics

1493	Columbus introduces sugar-cane in Hispaniola
1545	Silver discovered in Cerro Rico, Potosí
1690s	Brazilian gold rush begins in Minas Gerais
1808–26	Latin American independence: Britain takes over from Spain as the major trading partner and foreign power
1922	Venezuela strikes oil
1929	Wall Street Crash and ensuing depression in the US and Europe pushes Latin America into industrialisation
1930s	Great Depression – collapse of commodity prices
1938	Nationalisation of Mexican oil industry
1958	Brazil becomes Latin America's leading industrial power
1973–74	First oil price rise leads to wave of loans to Latin America. Foreign debt soars.
Early 80s	Beginning of cocaine boom
1982	Mexico defaults on interest payments on its foreign debt, swiftly followed by most other Latin American governments. Start of Debt Crisis and two decades of neoliberal reforms, including renewed emphasis on commodity exports
1982–91	Latin America pays a net US$219 billion in debt repayments to the North – US$500 for every Latin American
late 1980s	Neoliberal reforms gather pace throughout Latin America
1989	Announcement of austerity package in Venezuela provokes riots in which at least 276 people die
1994	Start of the North American Free Trade Agreement (NAFTA), between Mexico, the US and Canada enables Mexican economy to become effectively cheap labour addition to US, reducing its dependence on commodity exports. Mexican currency crisis and subsequent economic recession raises fresh doubts over neoliberal model

1995	Start of Mercosur, or Southern Cone Common Market, comprising Argentina, Brazil, Uruguay and Paraguay
2001–2	Crisis engulfs Argentine economy
2001–3	One third of Mexico's maquiladora assembly plants relocate to China
2002	44% of Latin Americans (221m people) living in poverty
2003	Annual wholesale value of US cocaine market reaches $35bn. Latin America is sole supplier. Only oil is worth more
2005	Global commodity price boom due to Chinese demand boosts Latin American growth

Section 2: Ballots and Bullets: The State, the Military and Politics

1808–26	Wars of independence free Spanish America from colonial rule
1889	Brazil abolishes the monarchy and becomes a Republic
1910–17	Mexican revolution
1926	Augusto César Sandino returns to Nicaragua to begin a guerrilla war against occupying US forces
1928	Caudillo General Plutarco Calles establishes the National Revolutionary Party (later the PRI) in power in Mexico; the PRI goes on to establish an effective one-party state
1930s	Urbanisation and industrialisation produce new political parties, led by populists
1939–45	Second World War establishes US as dominant military power in Latin America
1946	Juan Domingo Perón elected president of Argentina
1948	Costa Rica abolishes army
1949	Brazilian Higher War School founded, becoming central to spread of Cold-War national security doctrine
1958	The two main parties in both Venezuela and Colombia agree to share power in order to end decades of instability and military rule
1959	Cuban revolution marks first successful guerrilla campaign and leads to wave of foquista guerrilla insurgencies throughout Latin America. This is seen by military as proof of international communist conspiracy
1964	Military seize power in Brazil and rule for 25 years. The coup marks beginning of wave of military takeovers
1967	Death of Che Guevara in Bolivia
1968	Medellín conference of Latin American bishops galvanises the left by creating Base Christian Communities across the region

1970	Peru's Shining Path movement founded in remote Andean province. In Chile, Salvador Allende becomes the world's first elected marxist president
1973	Allende murdered during the military coup which brings General Pinochet to power
1976	Argentina's military seize power
end 1976	At least two-thirds of people on mainland Latin America live under dictatorial rule
1979	Sandinista-led insurrection in Nicaragua becomes second guerrilla victory in the Americas. Founding of Brazilian Workers' Party (PT), based on the support of the 'new social movements'
1980	Founding of Farabundo Martí National Liberation Front (FMLN) in El Salvador
1980s	Civil wars in El Salvador and Guatemala marked by unprecedented human rights abuses by military. US backs Contras in proxy war against Sandinista government
1982	Argentina loses Falklands/Malvinas war, military government fallsand democracy returns; senior officers subsequently imprisoned on human rights charges
1989	Chile's Christian Democrats lead coalition that wins elections to end Pinochet presidency. General Stroessner ousted in Paraguay. US invasion of Panama. Fall of Berlin Wall marks end of Cold War; difficult times ahead for military in Latin America, and identity crisis on left
1990	Sandinistas voted from power in presidential elections
1990	Chile's General Pinochet becomes the last of the military dictators to leave office
1992	Peace agreement in El Salvador following military stalemate between army and guerrillas. Military removed from politics
1994	Zapatista uprising in Chiapas, Mexico. US troops intervene to oust military government in Haiti
1998	Hugo Chávez elected president in Venezuela
2000	PRI loses in Mexican elections after 71 years in power
2002	Lula and the Workers Party (PT) win Brazilian presidential elections, beginning centre-left realignment across the region
2005	Every Latin American country except Cuba and Haiti ruled by elected leader
2005	Colombia only country in South America with an avowedly pro-US, right-wing president

Section 3: Land, the City and Environment

1519–35	Spanish Conquest: colonisers introduce new animals and crops and take back to Europe novelties such as tomatoes, maize, tobacco and potatoes; Spanish hand out land and forced labour to their officers through the encomienda system
1538	First slaves brought from Africa to work Latin America's sugar plantations
1881	Communal land-ownership by indigenous peasants banned in El Salvador, enabling coffee plantations to expand onto indigenous lands
1899	United Fruit establishes a monopoly over Central American banana production
1917	Beginning of Mexican land reform – the greatest in Latin American history
1920	First shantytowns recorded in Rio de Janeiro
1930s	Industrialisation leads to explosion of shantytowns and environmental deterioration in cities. Start of industrialisation leads to mass migration to the cities
1950	41.2% of Latin Americans live in towns
1950s on	Expansion of commercial agriculture throughout Latin America
1952	Bolivian revolution redistributes land and ends the near-feudal status of indigenous 'serfs'
1959	Cuban revolution: state farms take over sugar production
1960	500 people invade land in Lima to found the Cuevas settlement
1961	Washington launches Alliance for Progress, which supports land reform programmes throughout Latin America
1964	Military coup in Brazil: new government promotes agro-exports and the colonisation of the Amazon basin
1966	Brazil's military government unveils 'Operation Amazonia' to colonise and industrially develop the rainforest
1970	Population of Cuevas settlement in Lima reaches 12,000
1978	Argentine military government bulldozes shantytowns in clean-up campaign before World Cup
1979	Nicaraguan revolution: half of the country's farming land is included in a land reform
1980	64.7% of Latin Americans live in towns. Brazilian government decrees tax incentives for enterprises taking part in the Grande Carajas development programme
1980s	500,000 gold prospectors pour into the Amazon, bringing disease and destruction to the Yanomami people

1982 on   Under pressure from debt crisis, governments try to increase
agro-exports, in many cases by giving more power to large
landowners. Debt crisis and ensuing neoliberal reforms lead
to massive rise in informal sector

1984   Brazil's Landless Workers Movement (MST) founded. Opening
of giant Itaipú dam between Brazil, Argentina and Paraguay

1985   US Congress forces World Bank to temporarily suspend road-
building loans due to their environmental impact and include
environmental criteria in its project assessments. Mexico City
earthquake, thousands made homeless

1988   Chico Mendes, leader of Amazon rubber-tappers, assassinated
by landowners

1990   Chilean government declares first ever 'environmental state of
emergency' in Santiago

1992   World Summit on the Environment and Development held in
Rio de Janeiro

1994   Zapatista uprising in Chiapas, Mexico prompted by
government's attempts to privatise communal land-holdings

1998   90% of all soybeans grown in Argentina are genetically
modified (GM)

2002   77% of Latin Americans live in towns

2004   Total remittances from 25m Latin Americans living abroad
come to $46bn, more than foreign investment and aid
combined

2005   Less than a quarter of Latin Americans live in the countryside,
more than half of them below the poverty line. 16% of the
Amazon rainforest now destroyed, and a further 3.5% (25,000
sq km) being lost every year

Section 4: Identity and Rights

c. 30,000 BC   First people reach the Americas across the Bering Straits from
Asia

1492   Columbus arrives in the Americas, to be met by the friendly
Arawak people

1519   Cortés invades Mexico with 600 men

1535   Pizarro completes conquest of Inca empire

mid 16th C   Arawak population of the Caribbean extinct within 50 years
of Columbus' arrival

1781   Tupác Amaru lays seige to Cusco, the former Inca capital, in
indigenous rebellion. Amaru captured and executed

1930s on   Mechanisation of agriculture and growth of cities encourages
young women to migrate from the countryside to the towns

1960s	Officials of Brazil's government agency for indigenous people use poison, machine guns and disease to 'clear' land for large landowners
1961	Paraguay becomes last Latin American country to give women the vote
1971	US Peace Corps expelled from Bolivia, accused of sterilising indigenous women without their knowledge
1975–85	UN Decade for Women encourages some improved legislation on gender issues
1975	Cuban government passes law making childcare and housework equal responsibility of men and women
Late 1970s	Women in Brazil's Cost of Living Movement lead opposition to military rule
1976–83	Argentina's Mothers of the Disappeared lead opposition to military rule, inspiring similar movements in Central America and the Andes
1979	Nicaraguan revolution: women head health ministry and police and government bans use of women's bodies in advertising
1982 on	Debt Crisis and neoliberal reforms make life harder for women
1982–83	In Guatemala, 400 indigenous villages destroyed, 40,000 killed in counter-insurgency operations
1990	Violeta Chamorro wins Nicaraguan presidential elections
1992	Indigenous groups throughout the Americas condemn the official celebrations of the quincentenary of Columbus' arrival in the Americas. Rigoberta Menchú wins Nobel Peace Prize
1993	Proportion of female-headed households now stands at one in five across Latin America
1994	Indigenous rebels from Mayan groups lead Zapatista uprising in Chiapas, Mexico. In Ecuador, indigenous organisations cut off cities in protest at economic structural adjustment measures
1995	New quota rules in Argentina ensure that one in four Congresspeople is a woman – one of the highest proportions in the world
2000	Alejandro Toledo elected president of Peru, after stressing his indigenous origins during the campaign to oust Alberto Fujimori
2003	Average Latin American woman has 2.5 children, down from 6 in the 1950s
2006	Evo Morales inaugurated as Bolivian president – the first indigenous head of state in South America

Section 5: Culture and Religion

1494	In the Treaty of Tordesillas the Vatican divides up the New World between Spain and Portugal
1826 on	Independence leaders sign concordats with the Vatican, maintaining Catholicism as the state religion
1896	First moving picture shown in Buenos Aires
1910–17	Mexican revolution begins attempt to construct a new mestizo consciousness, especially through the work of muralists such as Diego Rivera
1923	Brazilian government sets up country's first radio station, which soon bows to popular demand for broadcasts of samba music
1926–29	Mexican Church suspends public worship to protest at state harassment. Ninety priests executed during the 'Cristero rebellion'
1959	Cuban revolution promotes attempt to build a radical and distinctive Latin American cultural movement
1960s on	Born-again Protestant churches begin to expand rapidly throughout Latin America
1962–65	Second Vatican Council commits the Church to work for human rights, justice and freedom
mid 1960s	First telenovelas broadcast in Brazil and Mexico
1967	Gabriel García Márquez publishes One Hundred Years of Solitude, which sells more than twenty million copies worldwide
1968	Latin American bishops, meeting in Medellín, Colombia, adopt a 'preferential option for the poor'
1971	Cuban government arrests the dissident poet, Heberto Padilla
1973	Singer Víctor Jara killed by the army following military coup in Chile
1978	John Paul II becomes Pope and leads conservative offensive within Church against 'liberation theology'
1979	Nicaraguan revolution provides state support for poets and artists
1980	Assassination of radical Archbishop Oscar Romero of San Salvador
1982	General Efraín Ríos Montt seizes power in Guatemala, becoming the region's first evangelical dictator. García Márquez wins Nobel Prize for literature
1989	In El Salvador, Army assassinates six Jesuit priests, their housekeeper and her daughter, leading to the withdrawal of

	US support for the military and the end of the civil war
1990	Peruvian novelist Mario Vargas Llosa loses presidential elections to Alberto Fujimori
1991	Guatemala's Jorge Serrano becomes the region's first elected evangelical president
1992	Columbus quincentenary prompts continent-wide soul searching. Televisa's soap 'The Rich Also Weep' takes Russia by storm
1994	Zapatista rebels in Chiapas use the Internet to bypass government censorship
1996	90% of Latin Americans have access to a TV set
2005	Pope John Paul II dies, to be replaced by even more conservative Pope Benedict XVI. No let-up in sight for Latin American progressive Church. Estimated number of Protestants rises to 60 million, from 5 million in 1970. 56 million Latin Americans (10% of the population) have access to internet

Further Reading

Section 1: The Curse of Wealth: Economics

Eduardo Galeano, *Open Veins of Latin America*, London: Latin America Bureau, 2000.

Duncan Green, *Silent Revolution: the Rise and Crisis of Market Economics in Latin America*, (second edition) London: Latin America Bureau, 2003.

Jon Hellin and Sophie Higman, *Feeding the Market: South American Farmers, Trade and Globalization*. London: ITDG publishing, 2003.

Gabriel García Marquez, *One Hundred Years of Solitude*, London: Jonathan Cape, 1970.

Miguel Leon-Portillo, *The Broken Spears : The Aztec Account of the Conquest of Mexico*, Boston: Beacon Press; 1992.

Nick Rowling, *Commodities: How the World Was Taken to Market*, London: Free Association Books, 1987.

Rosemary Thorp, *Economic History of Latin America in the Twentieth Century: Progress, Exclusion and Poverty*, Philadelphia: John Hopkins University Press, 1998.

Timothy A Wise, Hilda Salazar and Laura Carlsen, *Confronting Globalization: Economic Integration and Popular Resistance in Mexico*, Bloomfield, CT: Kumarian Press, 2003.

Section 2: Ballots and Bullets: The State, the Military and Politics

John Lee Anderson, *Che Guevara: A Revolutionary Life*, New York: Grove Press, 1997.

Edward L Cleary, *The Struggle for Human Rights in Latin America*, New York: Praeger, 1997.

John Crabtree, *Patterns of Protest: Politics and Social Movements in Bolivia*, London: Latin America Bureau, 2005.

Andrés Jaroslavsky, *The Future of Memory: Children of the Dictatorship in Argentina Speak*, London: Latin America Bureau, 2004.

Elizabeth Jelin, *State Repression and the Struggles for Memory*, London: Latin America Bureau, 2003.

Subcomandante Marcos, *Our Word is Our Weapon*, London: Serpent's Tail, 2001.

Hugh O'Shaughnessy, *Pinochet: the Politics of Torture*, London: Latin America Bureau, 1999.

Thomas E Skidmore and Peter H Smith, *Modern Latin America*, Oxford: Oxford University Press, 2000.

Section 3: Land, the City and Environment

Sue Branford and Jan Rocha, *Cutting the Wire: The Story of the Brazilian Landless Workers' Movement*, London: Latin America Bureau, 2002.

Binka le Breton, *Trapped: Modern-Day Slavery in the Brazilian Amazon*, London: Latin America Bureau, 2003.

Alan Gilbert, *The Latin American City*, London: Latin America Bureau, 1998.

Duncan Green, *Hidden Lives: Voices of Children in Latin America and the Caribbean*, London: Latin America Bureau, 1997.

Susana Hecht and Alexander Cockburn, *The Fate of the Forest: Developers, Destroyers and Defenders of the Amazon*, London: Penguin, 1990.

Chico Mendes, *Fight for the Forest: Chico Mendes in His Own Words*, London: Latin America Bureau, 1992.

JJ Thomas, *Surviving in the City: the Urban Informal Sector in Latin America*, London: Pluto Press, 1995.

Bill Weinberg, *War on the Land: Ecology and Politics in Central America*, London: Zed Books, 1991.

Section 4: Identity and Rights

Sylvia Chant with Nikki Craske, *Gender in Latin America*, London: Latin America Bureau, 2002.

Edward L Cleary, *The Struggle for Human Rights in Latin America*, New York: Praeger, 1997.

John Crabtree, *Patterns of Protest: Politics and Social Movements in Bolivia*, London: Latin America Bureau, 2005.

Eduardo Galeano, *Open Veins of Latin America*, London: Latin America Bureau, 2000.

Ian Lumsden, *Machos, Maricones and Gays in Cuba: Cuba and Homosexuality*, London: Latin America Bureau, 1996.

Rigoberta Menchú and Elisabeth Burgos Debray (ed), *I, Rigoberta Menchú*, London: Verso, 1984.

Patrick Neate and Damian Platt: *Culture is our Weapon: AfroReggae in the Favelas of Rio*, London: Latin America Bureau, 2006.

Lynne Stephen, *Women and Social Movements in Latin America*, London: Latin America Bureau, 1997.

Peter Wade, *Race and Ethnicity in Latin America*, London: Pluto Press, 1997.

Philip Wearne, *Return of the Indian*, London: Latin America Bureau, 1996.

Section 5: Culture and Religion

Philip Berryman, *Religion in the Megacity: Catholic and Protestant Portraits from Latin America*, London: Latin America Bureau, 1996.

Alma Guillermoprieto, *Samba*, London: Bloomsbury, 1990.

Alma Guillermoprieto, *The Heart that Bleeds: Latin America Now*, New York: Knopf, 1994.

Alberto Elena and Marina Díaz López, eds., *The Cinema of Latin America*, London: Wallflower Press, 2003.

John King, *The Cambridge Companion to Modern Latin American Culture*, Cambridge: Cambridge University Press, 2004.

Hernando Calvo Ospina, *Salsa: Havana Heat, Bronx Beat*, London: Latin America Bureau, 1995.

Octavio Paz, *The Labyrinth of Solitude*, London and Chicago: University of Chicago Press, 1950.

William Rowe and Vivian Schelling, *Memory and Modernity: Popular Culture in Latin America*, London: Verso, 1991.

Maya Roy, *Cuban Music*, London: Latin America Bureau, 2003.

Philip Swanson, *Landmarks in Modern Latin American Fiction*, London: Routledge, 1990.

Chris Taylor, *The Beautiful Game*, London: Latin America Bureau, 1998.

Index